TINY TIM

AND

MR. PLYM

Life As We Knew It

TINY TIM

===== **AND** =====

MR. PLYM

Life As We Knew It

Vivien Kooper & Stephen M.Plym

EDEE ROSE PUBLISHING
Long Beach, California

Edee Rose Publishing
4645 E. Anaheim Street, Long Beach, CA 90804
Phone: (562) 961-0077   Fax: (562) 248-0222
Email: info@Tiny-Tim.net   Web site: http://www.Tiny-Tim.net

Cover & Interior Design:
Sue Chidester Sealy, Golden Monarch Graphics,
goldenmonarch@aol.com

Book Consultant:
Flo Selfman, Selfman & Others PR/Marketing,
floself@aol.com

FIRST EDITION
Printed in the United States of America

Publisher's Cataloging-in-Publication
(Provided by Quality Books)

Kooper, Vivien.
   Tiny Tim and Mr. Plym : life as we knew it
Vivien Kooper and Stephen M. Plym. -- 1st ed
   p. cm
   ISBN 0-9746887-1-1

   1. Tiny Tim, d. 1996.   2. Plym, Stephen M.
3. Singers--United States--Biography.   I.Plym,
Stephen M.   II. Title

ML420.T553K66 2004   782.42164'092
                                        QB133-1747

Any uncredited photographs and materials from collection of Stephen M. Plym

Dedication

This book is dedicated to my beautiful and loving wife,
Dawn De'An Plym. I love you forever and a day!

--Stephen

Contents

Publicity Photo 1992

Tiny Tim and Dick Martin

Foreword

I will never forget the day I met Tiny Tim.

It was January 1968. Tim had appeared in some small clubs in the east, but was totally unknown. This was <u>long</u> before Miss Vicki, Johnny Carson, and Tiny's appearance on *The Tonight Show.*

We were in the midst of preparing for our first taping of *Rowan & Martin's Laugh-In.* The show had not yet gone on the air, but word was out that this might be a big hit. The intensity of the public reaction to the preview special, with its new format, was also taking its toll. We had to live up to the "hype." We were working 24/7 and had not yet settled into a groove, so we were under intense scrutiny by the network. NBC was still "not sure" and questioned everything we did.

We were deep into an intense writer's meeting when Digby Wolfe, who had enormous creative input into the show, interrupted the meeting and asked if he could introduce me to someone. I said, "Not right now, we're in the middle of an emergency." Hell, that whole first show was an emergency. Digby said, "I'm sorry. I must insist." He walked into the office with Richard Perry, who was a well-known record producer and executive at Warner Bros. Records. They introduced me to Tiny Tim and a new adventure was underway. Tim was dressed head to toe in wrinkled plaid polyester. He had a shopping bag, out of which he took a paper bag, out of which he took a beat up ukulele. He immediately began to play his ukulele and sing in a falsetto voice, while blowing kisses to everyone in the room.

I don't remember ever having been more blown away, stunned, and hysterical. I wasn't sure that it was not cruel to laugh at Tiny Tim, but I could not help myself. Within a few seconds, we realized that Tim was enjoying this as much as we were.

After his second number, we committed to putting him on our first show, taping two days later with or without network approval. This booking was definitely "without" network approval. Remember now. This was our first show. New format. No stars, just funny people and we were going on opposite *Gunsmoke* and *Lucy*, AND one of our guest stars was to be TINY TIM, a virtually unknown vocalist and ukulele virtuoso singing songs out of the twenties.

Dick had not met Tim, nor did he have any idea of what was happening. We were taping the opening of the premiere show. Dan and Dick were talking and Dan introduced this week's new discovery, "For the first time anywhere. Here is Tiny Tim." Dick stood and watched as Tim blew kisses, pulled that old ukulele out of that beat-up shopping bag, and in a high falsetto voice, sang *Tiptoe Through the Tulips*. No one had ever seen anything like this before. Dick did not know what to do. He just stood there in shock.

The only uncertainty at that time was the network. They were not convinced that we could actually put anyone who was that bizarre on primetime television as a guest star on our first show. The idea was totally outrageous and so was Tiny.

Out of desperation, we explained to NBC that this was a big star in disguise. Tim went on the air. The network was still not sure and admonished me for having told them that he was a big star. I showed them the reviews and said, "If that isn't a big star, I don't know who is." As they say, the rest is history.

Tim's guest shot generated so much critical acclaim that we even got an "I told you so" from the network, which is always the ultimate network compliment.

The appearance of Tiny Tim and the overwhelming reaction to his appearance was one of the moments that helped to define the outrageous nature of *Laugh-In* and also helped to build an audience. Yes, we helped give Tiny Tim his big break, but we must remember he helped us a lot, too.

As Tim and I became good friends, I realized how much more there was to this truly unique individual. He was kind and gentle and very nice to everyone. His knowledge of music was vast and bridged all forms and types of music. He knew the composers and performers. He also usually knew all of the lyrics, which he would perform for you on a moment's notice, accompanying himself on the ukulele. In addition, he had memorized the names of every baseball player, including batting averages and win/loss records.

I remember one time when Tim came to the studio to make another appearance on *Laugh-In*. By then, the cast had really grown to love him and the country loved him too. As a welcoming gesture, the cast put a lot of flowers in his dressing room. Tim came out of the dressing room. He was almost in tears. He hurried onstage to tell me how upset he was that we had killed so many flowers to decorate his room. Tim didn't want anything to die. It was then that we fully realized what a caring person he was.

After the *Laugh-In* success, Tim was booked by Johnny Carson and he continued on his successful career. Tiny was even subsequently married on *The Tonight Show*. It was really very sweet when Tim and Miss Vicki exchanged vows. Miss Vicki was surprised and pleased to discover how amorous Tim was. Some people thought he was gay. Far from it. Tim was "horny." He always called his bride Miss Vicki, but the rest of the relationship was quite intensely romantic.

Tim and I corresponded back and forth for many years. Almost 25 years after we met, we had a *Laugh-In* reunion. Naturally, we invited all of the past cast members including Tiny Tim. He came to the Loew's Hotel in Santa Monica and joined most all of the original cast members as well as some of the most frequent guest stars.

All the cast and many of the guest stars sat onstage and we had a press conference with the media and fans asking questions, which each of the cast members would answer. In the middle of this, Tiny Tim stood up and gave a thorough, comprehensive, and intelligent analysis of the phenomenon that had become known as *Laugh-In*. Tim was our biggest fan, and we were his. It was nice to hear him say that we meant as much to his success as he meant to ours.

Tiny Tim was truly an eccentric. He was also a very gentle gentleman. In Europe and England the eccentric is celebrated and revered. The phenomenon of Tiny Tim reminded everyone of the American obsession of hiding our eccentrics. Well, we did not hide Tiny. The audience loved him. We loved him. He cared. He cried and he laughed. He was extremely articulate and very well educated on a number of issues. He had a wonderful sense of humor and realized that his own persona and lifestyle were, indeed, somewhat bizarre, but he enjoyed it and he enjoyed the fact that we enjoyed it.

Because of his eccentricities, many times people overlooked what was, indeed, a rather impressive talent. One of the first people to recognize this was Mo Ostin, head of Reprise and Warner Bros. Records. Mo realized that it would be difficult to merchandise Tiny Tim as a normal recording artist, but he was one of his early fans, as was Richard Perry, who also realized that Tiny Tim was a major talent.

Stars come and go. Tim will be with us forever. I am just glad that *Laugh-In* helped make Tim's star shine.

To quote the original Tiny Tim, "God bless us every one," and I am quite certain that God has done just that. I hope God has learned to like the sounds of Tim's ukulele mixed with the angels' harps. What a jam session that must be.

--George Schlatter
Beverly Hills, California

Publicity Photo 1992

Mr. Plym and Tiny Tim

Preface

It is my hope that, as we part the stage curtains, peek behind, and eavesdrop at Tiny Tim's dressing room door, I can set the record straight. It's a damn shame that anyone as original, eccentric, and amazing as Tiny Tim should go down in history as nothing but a freak or a clown. Now don't get me wrong — he was definitely a clown. But like every clown, when you wipe off the greasepaint, the story you find behind the big nose, the funny shoes, and the wild hair is more of a trip than all the jokes and gags. And it puts tears in your eyes even as it's making you laugh.

During the years I was Tiny's personal manager, we shared a lot of the ups, downs and hairpin turns that made up his incredible life. He was the most fascinating, loving, charming, honorable, hard-to-figure, multi-talented, dysfunctional and misunderstood cat I've ever met.

Wait a minute! Did I say "personal manager?" Let me add babysitter, taxicab service, personal priest and confessor, personal banker whom he knew he could always hit up for a loan, and the one shrink he could actually afford — 'cause I didn't charge him anything. All things considered, it's fair to say I knew him as well as you can know another human being.

Tiny told me over and over again how he hoped that after he made his passage to the great garden in the sky, I'd write a book about him. "God knows, you certainly never made any money on me during my lifetime," he would joke. "I certainly hope you do so after I am gone!" And then he would always add, "Just make sure if you do tell my story, that you don't pull any punches. Tell it all."

Okay, Tiny. This is for you, pal. I miss you very much.

--Mister Plym

Introduction

Tulip: *noun.* Any of several bulbous plants...
widely cultivated for their showy, various colored flowers.

What you are about to read is really two stories in one.

First, this is the story of a once-in-a-lifetime friendship, the rarest kind of friendship, the kind that changes lives, brings redemption, and offers deliverance from the longest, darkest nights of the soul. The bond that was born in 1971 between Tiny Tim and his close friend, confidante and eventual manager, Stephen Plym, lasted twenty-five years, all the way up until Tiny's death in 1996. Through divorces for them both, high points and downslides in both of their careers, and Tiny's constant battle with personal demons, public ridicule and humiliation, there was always Tiny Tim and "Mister Plym."

Plym's story of his life with Tiny, as he might tell it sitting on a barstool, does not pretend to be a full account of Tiny Tim's life and times. Considering human nature and the frailty of memory, it may not necessarily even be absolutely accurate or complete. What you will find inside are those most hidden secrets we share only when we care to — or under the influence of really strong liquor, or sodium pentathol.

Secondly, this is a memoir about the fascinating Herbert

Butros Khaury, better known as Tiny Tim. His overblown persona obscured the person, so up until now, his was the story of a man who was famous simply for being famous. Who was the man who could turn every head in a restaurant, or turn the lobby noise of the Plaza Hotel in New York into a hushed silence? Who was the curiosity that had even the most celebrated stars chasing him through Caesars Palace in Las Vegas, just for an autograph?

In every life, facts are established — when and where we are born, whom we marry, the identities of our parents and children, the date we pass away. This book is not a collection of bare bones and data, but rather a story only Plym can tell, of who Tiny Tim was *really*, behind the falsetto voice and the ukulele, beyond the pet tricks, painting a picture of Tiny's life from the inside looking around, rather than from the outside looking in. Tiny shared with Mister Plym many things he never told another soul, with the admonition to tell the whole truth when the time came. That time is now, and in these pages, Stephen Plym lets you ride along in secret on the adventures the two of them shared.

♦ ♦ ♦

For many, Tiny Tim will be remembered as a media phenomenon. He was, after all, one of the first entertainers to get his face plastered over every one of those newfangled inventions that they called television sets. His marriage to Miss Vicki on Johnny Carson's *Tonight Show* broke viewership records. Maybe you were one of the millions who watched. More effective than having his face on a cereal box, his image on the box with the rabbit ears earned him a permanent place in our folklore. His name recognition was also due to the fact that when he did appear, he was out of this world. Literally.

Strange as Tiny Tim was, you meet someone like him every day, everywhere you go. You see someone like him hiding from the boss behind the cubicle at work, and trying to work up his nerve to ask a girl for a date on campus. You might see a guy like Tiny, hands clasped together, praying in a wooden pew in church and then at the counter in the drugstore, embarrassed to ask for condoms, adult diapers, or hemorrhoid creme.

This is perhaps the strangest aspect of his story — that while he was unquestionably one of our more bizarre celebrities, the human condition is always more or less the same. Like many of us, he had trouble balancing his religious beliefs with his sexual appetites. Like many of us, he wanted desperately to be loved and appreciated but was acutely aware of his flaws and limitations. He needed success but wasn't sure what to do with it once it was his.

Plym has heard it said that Tiny Tim's contribution to pop culture was really insignificant, because he never laid new ground or pioneered new territory, but could there have been Kiss, David Bowie, Alice Cooper, the Village People or Boy George without there first being Tiny Tim? By redefining what it meant to be a performer, and stretching the boundaries of what it meant to sing and entertain, he set the stage for many who were to follow.

By unapologetically standing outside the norm, Tiny gave everyone permission to be human, to be flawed, to be an outsider and an original. He had the courage to get up on stage and sing with his whole heart and soul the songs of those troubadours and minstrels he deeply admired — even when he knew that he would be laughed at and criticized. In so doing, he gave us permission to be ourselves.

In his very refusal to disguise his humanity and vulnerability, by letting his hair down when everyone else's was cut short, Tiny Tim taught us what it means to be fallible — and how much fun it can be.

Above and beyond everything else, Herbert "Tiny Tim" Khaury was a living, breathing example of the importance of not taking oneself too seriously. When the world did laugh at him, he always laughed along, too, enjoying the joke as much as the next guy. Maybe more....

--Vivien Kooper

Where the Road Begins

Tiny fact: Tiny Tim always wore a tie.
Morning, noon, and night.
Mister Plym never saw him without a tie. Ever.
He even wore one to bed.

"If people complain about the good ol' U.S.A.," Tiny loved to say, "they should pack up their cares and woes and check out of here. Our great country was not built on complainers ... it was built on doers!"

So he did it. He thrust out his chin, lifted up his head, and walked into the recruiting offices of the U.S. Army, proud to be a citizen of our great nation.

Walking in, he ran smack into a wall of heavily starched men, close-shaven and buzzed flat on top with tattoos on their arms and muscles popping beneath their shirt sleeves.

Yikes! They didn't look too friendly. From their side, they saw him coming, dropped their jaws, and waited for the punchline. Someone must have put the poor slob up to it. He couldn't be for real. He stood before them, gangly, soft, and pasty looking, his wavy hair hanging wildly below his slumped and rounded shoulders. What in the hell was he doing there?

"When I walked into the recruiting office, there were many other boys there to join up," Tiny recalled, "as well as several army men. By the time I walked ten feet, a strange hush came over the entire room. Everybody stopped what they were doing and simply stared at me. Someone barked, 'Hey, you! Just what the hell are you supposed to be? Is there a circus in town or what???' A circus?! How rude."

Poor Tiny, loner that he was, he didn't spend enough time around people to see himself as they saw him. It was probably just as well. Looking down at himself that day, he didn't see a misfit or a freak. He had to have had an inkling by then that he was a bit unusual, but from his perspective, all he knew for sure was that he was ready, willing, and able. Or, ready and willing, anyway. Uncle Sam had asked for its young men. He was young, wasn't he? No argument there. He was a man, wasn't he? Well... the guys there that day weren't so sure.

"Look buddy," he heard them saying, "we're busy here! Out ya go!" The man stood up from his desk, stiffened his finger like a missile, and pointed to the door.

"I was completely mystified and frankly a little bit hurt," Tiny remembered. "I said, 'But isn't this where you sign up to join the great United States Army? I am Herbert Khaury, sir, and I am volunteering for duty. I want to go to Korea and serve my country. Just tell me what to do and where to go.'"

They wanted to tell him where to go, all right.

◆ ◆ ◆

Let me back up. Our story begins in 1950, in a town no one's ever heard of in the heartland of America, where Mr. and Mrs.

Plym of Moline, Illinois — or Mom and Dad, as I like to call them — were introducing me to my new crib, and looking forward to the time when I might start sleeping through the night. These days I'm only up half the night, I cry a lot less, and, unless I'm having a really bad day, I hardly ever drink straight from a bottle. Anyway, that's a story for another day. As I was saying, while my sleep-deprived parents were oohing and aahing over my birth, the world outside found itself in its own stupor — The Korean War.

Yep, before I could even talk, the kid who would someday become known as Tiny Tim was about to make a decision that could have ruined everything. Of course, Tiny was as famous for his boneheaded decisions as he was for… well, being Tiny Tim. Anyway, if Tiny's plan had worked, we might never have met, he might never have gone on to become Tiny Tim, I would never have been his manager, and you would not be reading this book right now. Thank God, Lady Luck outsmarted Tiny and made sure he didn't become a military man.

Becoming a soldier was the one big roadblock that could have sent him on such a major detour that he never would have made it into show biz. Believe me, no one is more thrilled than I am that he didn't pull off his plan to enlist — no one, that is, except maybe the United States Army and that bunch of recruiters down at the Brooklyn Recruiting Office.

Now, your average declaration of war usually scares the hell out of people or pisses them off, and most people you talk to will agree that it's not good news. So you can just imagine how baffled Mr. and Mrs. Khaury were to find their son, Herbert, in seventh Heaven. The news of the Korean War had made him feel happier and more alive than he'd been in years. He was downright giddy. As his parents were scratching their heads and asking themselves why their son spent so much time in his room, little Herbert was ready to give his all for Uncle Sam and dreaming up how he was going to get himself into the war.

♦ ♦ ♦

I'll get back to Tiny and the war efforts in a minute, but first I've got to stop right here and fill you in on the little bit I do know about his teenage years. Otherwise, you won't understand why Tiny Tim, of all people, was so damned determined to enlist.

I have to say that Tiny and I did not talk a lot about his childhood or adolescence, but what he did share with me was pretty painful.

"I was not exactly a social butterfly, Mr. Plym. For some reason, the other fellows and I did not quite seem to understand each other."

Didn't seem to understand each other. Right. Try as he may, there was simply no disguise in the world that would turn him into one of the crowd. Maybe one of the reasons that Tiny and his school buddies didn't exactly fit together like a baseball and glove was the fact that even though Tiny was the world's foremost baseball fan, he was a disaster with both a baseball and a glove. As I found out years later when he talked me into letting him play ball, he was about as un-athletic as a person could be. As a teenager, every guy suffers with some kind of awkwardness, but Tiny's was a terminal case.

Most boys got to watch the fascinating science fiction movie that was their bodies morphing from little boys into young guys.

You know, that amazing thing that happens when you wake up one day with this puffed-up chest and a jaw that wasn't there the day before; when you go to pick something up and realize you've got actual muscles; and when you go to bed at night and wake up in the morning with your hormones surging through you and taking your mind off the things you used to find so fascinating — like bugs, or your bicycle. Speaking of bicycles, for Tiny, adolescence was more like someone had attached a bicycle pump to his backside and blown and blown until he was simply a bigger version of his soft, pudgy baby self.

Most teenage guys spend a lot of time posed in front of the mirror, with their hair slicked back, practicing their swagger. Tiny spent a lot of time alone. I mean a lot.

The funny thing was that while Tiny did envy the popularity of the cool boys in his neighborhood, he did not envy their style at all. His idea of an idol was someone who called people Mister and Missus, said "yes, Ma'am" and "no, Ma'am" and "please" and "thank you" — to Tiny Tim, class was the mark of a real man.

As far as Tiny was concerned, you could keep James Dean. He wanted to be like Fred Astaire.

In short, Tiny was genteel — like an English gentleman. Only he wasn't an Englishman, and here in America, especially when you're a teenager, genteel isn't going to get you much more than a bloody nose. Bloody in the American sense, I mean, not the English. All-American Tiny Tim — with that pinky-in-the-air, one-eyebrow-raised way about him, and his insistence upon calling people Mister and Miss — didn't go over real well with the street-tough, rough and tumble boys in Brooklyn.

Tiny was a lover, not a fighter, and like all good predators, the tough boys could smell Tiny coming from a mile away. You can imagine the rest. Neither Tiny nor the neighborhood boys could see it then, but the very same qualities of Tiny's that had him always on the wrong side of a good ass whipping were going to come in very handy later on in life.

So here we have… what would they call him? Herbie? I can't see him ever wanting to be called Herbie. Anyway, he was feeling completely alienated from his crowd. No wonder his life, up to that point, revolved mostly around his love affair with his radio. I can just see him, ear pressed against the radio, as the sports announcers passionately called the plays for the Brooklyn Dodgers games, or closing his eyes and listening to Bing Crosby and Frank Sinatra. His true best friends were his fantasies — or delusions, depending on your point of view — of one day becoming a singer just like them. Here was something he could relate to.

At least on the radio, if not in real life, someone was playing his song.

◆ ◆ ◆

Tiny Tidbit: Many years later, Tiny found himself signed to Reprise Records, Frank Sinatra's label. Standing in the glow of his idol, he gushed, "You're wonderful, absolutely wonderful. How marvelous it must be to have the girls in their bobby socks going crazy over you!" Tiny told me that, taking the compliments in stride, The Chairman of the Board put his hand on Tiny's shoulder, fixed him with his clear blue eyes, and said, "Tiny, Baby, those were the fuckin' days."

◆ ◆ ◆

I know, I know, you're asking, how did the story end down at the recruiting office? I'm getting there... so here you had on the one hand Tiny, an inhabitant of another galaxy, who knew damned well he wasn't ever going to grow up to be a heartthrob. Then, on the other hand, you had the fact that he absolutely, positively, no two ways about it, wanted to be wanted and adored. What do you end up with? One disappointed kid. And a (seemingly) unsolvable riddle: Where was he going to find the adoration, acceptance, and popularity he craved when he knew that there was no potion, magic trick, hallucination or voodoo strong enough to turn him into the kind of guy that usually got that kind of attention?

Just when things were looking bleak, he heard the nation's pronouncement of war. Ahh, you guessed it. Perhaps there was an answer to the riddle, after all.

For many people, including me — a story I'll get to in a minute — the call to enlist was fingernails on a chalkboard. For Herbert, the lonely urbanite, the thought of becoming an American soldier was the answer to the riddle, an answer to his prayers, and just what the doctor ordered for a shy, awkward kid with few friends and fewer girlfriends. He was thrilled. He'd be like Montgomery Clift, Humphrey Bogart, or Cary Grant in the movies. At last he would fit in, he thought, and be accepted as normal. Ha!

Oh, to be noticed, to be needed and loved! I can just see him now, clapping his hands together, and prancing around his room in his stocking feet.

◆ ◆ ◆

"…When I said, 'I am ready to fight for the good ol' U.S. of A.,' the entire room erupted with wild laughter and jeers," Tiny continued. "To say they were mocking and disapproving would be an understatement."

Taking him by the arm, the recruiter corralled him into a small room. Slamming the door behind him, the man threw himself into a chair, craned his neck, lunged over his desk, and spat at him, "Son, do you like girls?"

"I couldn't understand what he was getting at. What an odd question! What was he going to do? Fix me up on a date? Was this a match-making service or the United States Army?"

Tiny was oblivious. Try as he may, the recruiter couldn't seem to talk the strange kid from Brooklyn out of joining up, so he had to pull out the big guns. After a long pause, a twisted smile came over the recruiter's face. "Fine, son. You want to enlist? Then take off your clothes. Let's see if you can pass the physical."

"All the blood drained out of my head," recalled Tiny. "I was horrified. I had never had a physical, and I was sure the very fact that this was not the place to have an erection in front of everybody would cause me to have one. I was sure Tiny Jr. would stand up straight and salute. 'Do not betray me, please,' I was pleading with my body. 'Please do not betray me. What will people think?'"

Square stiff jaws, heads mowed like new lawns, necks thick like tree stumps, the group of hard-boiled men watched him, thinkin' "freaky kid" as he stood in his most casual "undress" uniform trying to cover his artillery with his hands.

"We're not going to stand here with this fucking fag," spat two tough boys, getting out of the line.

Fag??? Ooh. That wasn't polite. This was a theme, or as they say in music, a motif, that would repeat itself over and over in his life. The great joke. You will never, ever find anyone who loved chicks more than Tiny Tim and yet, for obvious reasons, people usually thought he played on the other team.

"Then the doctor came up...," Tiny remembered. "He came up from behind me and inserted a finger. Naturally, I let out a moan. Who could blame me? It hurt!"

The narrow-minded doctor, however, already had the creeps from Tiny and misunderstood the moaning. "Ahem, that's it then," said the doctor, who quickly stood up even taller than usual, flexed his biceps a little to reassure himself that his own manliness was still intact, and shoved Tiny out of the room.

"At last the humiliation was over, I thought. Soon, I will have the honor to don a crisp olive-green uniform and toss a weapon over my shoulder..."

Can't you just see him posing for Our American Servicemen snapshots?

So they seemed a little bit less than thrilled with him at the recruiting office. So what? He wasn't going to let a little thing like that deter him. As soon as they realized how truly patriotic he was, they would change their tune. Right? Their insults were just inconveniences to Tiny, no more than snowballs hurled at his head. Leaving the recruiting office that day, he actually believed he had withstood the persecution and passed the test.

U.S. Army, here I come!

"Yes, it is quite true. I am joining the United States Army," he excitedly told friends and family. "For Uncle Sam, I am ready to do the unthinkable. I will even cut my hair. No sacrifice will be too great if they will let me serve my country."

I can see him turning first to his left side and then to his right, looking in the mirror and wondering how he'd look with a short military haircut.

Then he waited and watched for the postman at the window like a serviceman awaits a letter from his girl back home — a letter that never arrives. Strange, but the acceptance letter seemed to have been lost in the mail. There must have been a perfectly reasonable explanation. You know, rain, snow, sleet, icy roads, the dark of night — all those things that are not supposed to stop the United States mail but sometimes do.

Not putting two and two together, he went back for more punishment. Returning to the recruiting office to find out when he might be shipped off to the front, he sat again face to face with the recruiter.

"Reporting for duty, sir," he said bravely. "What do I do and when do I leave?"

"Herbie, when they actually bomb New York City, we'll call ya!" said the recruiter. The whole room laughed until the walls shook. That sound would someday become like music to Tiny Tim's ears.

I know that particular rejection broke his heart, but life had its own blueprint for Tiny, and a damned fine sense of humor. Tiny would get a chance to serve his country, all right. His country desperately needed a laugh and he'd give it to them. Not as a soldier — but as the clown entertaining the troops.

◆ ◆ ◆

Destiny saved Tiny Tim from the army. So, that's one down. Life kept trying to derail me, and I, on the other hand, had to save myself. Or I was never going to have my career in music. Just as with Tiny, fate stepped in.

Fifteen years after Tiny's army fiasco, my own road started to unfold — not as a roaring highway, but in small side streets, each one leading to the next. When I was ten years old, my parents left the small-town mentality of Moline, Illinois, for the equally narrow-minded Southern Iowa of the 1960s. Not your average "Gee, I wonder what I'll be when I grow up, hmmm, maybe a fireman" kind of kid, I was possessed.

While Tiny was trying to join the army, I was trying desperately not to. By the time I was fifteen years old, I was already a man with a plan. A man on a mission. It was music and me all the way, and I wasn't interested in dating any other careers to see if I liked them better. I was in it with both feet, committed to my dreams, married to music, ready to go the distance 'til death do us part.

Even at that age, years before we ever met, what Tiny and I had in common was a rabid love of music. On my end, 1965 had blown in like an electrical storm and I was on fire. I wasted no time in putting a band together. Destiny was waiting, and we were taking the music express to the end of the line. I wasn't going to let anything stop us. Not the farmers who chased us away like we were crows threatening their crops. "Fuckin' long-haired hippie freaks." Not the well-groomed kids who stuck gum in our hair and laughed at us, and definitely not the United States Military.

I looked in the mirror at the sprouted hair on my chin, the dark wavy locks spilling over my collar. Then I took my temperature and decided that, thank God, I had not caught Vietnam fever. It was, however, trying to catch up with me. One way or another, I would find a way out of the draft. No way in hell was I going to fight in the war. I couldn't have known it then, but a very unusual guy living in Brooklyn was counting on me as part of his future, and I felt the pull of something — something powerful.

Luckily, a football game gone wrong sealed my fate. Hobbling around with a broken knee was a small price to pay. High numbers in the draft lottery and three deferments — including one for my knee — let me breathe a sigh of relief. Short of a catastrophic national disaster, I was safe. Sound familiar? "When they bomb your hometown, we'll call ya."

I was on my way.

◆ ◆ ◆

Like Tiny, I was a God-loving guy, even then. And like Tiny, I didn't think that meant I had to give up my life for a life of conformity and fundamentalism. The future was calling my name. Everyone else was calling me names too, but what the hell. Small price to pay for living your dream.

Much like Tiny, I secretly nursed the wounds of being made fun of for being different. In the quiet of my own thoughts I would sometimes ask God, "Why, just because we're different, why do people have to be mean to us?"

Like an apparition, a priest appeared in my life. "Don't worry, Son. God loves you just the way you are." I wanted to believe it and so I did. Thank God. Had I really believed God was following me like a fire-breathing dragon waiting to strike me dead, I probably couldn't have lived the adventure that was about to become my life.

◆ ◆ ◆

So Tiny tried to join the Army and they wouldn't have him, and I tried not to and the Army tried to snag me anyway, but it all turned out the way it was supposed to and we were both free. Free to meet the future and each other, though we had no way of knowing it then. Anyway, having successfully ducked the long hand of the Vietnam draft, and immersed myself in the role of lead singer for my band, my sights were set.

Sticking out like sore thumbs in the crops of traditional kids, our band hopped around the Midwest, wearing our long hair and our psychedelic clothes like a badge of honor. From Iowa to Missouri, Nebraska, and my old haunts back in Illinois, we took our band into the clubs, smuggling liquor and girls backstage. What could be better? Little did I know.

Then came the college years, or in my case, the college months. College was the last little hurdle, the big cane trying to pull me off the stage, the bend in the road that could have kept me from music. And from Tiny Tim. I combed my hair back, twisted it at the nape of my neck, and tried to stuff it along with my identity into the back of my collar so I could enter the world of academia.

It was no use. Life was carrying me along like a slow, rambling river set on its own course and, though I tried to hold onto college like a boulder in the middle of a river, the current was too hypnotic. So I let go.

An official college dropout, I was liberated. Not surprisingly, the other band members had also suffered allergic reactions to school and were free to reunite, but I was being called in another direction.

Disbanded, but not discouraged, I became, as I rounded the bend of my twenties, Stephen Plym, entertainment agent. Now all I needed was my first big star.

The Meeting

"Art is a line at the box office."
--Tiny Tim

As I pulled into the parking lot in Waterloo, Iowa, on my big night, it was only a small venue in a small town, but that's not what I saw. I envisioned a mob of reporters trying to get my attention and me standing by the backstage door, holding Tiny Tim up by his feet, like the catch of the day. In my mind, the headline read: "Man Catches Really Big Fish. Makes Front Page News. Life is Changed Forever."

I didn't have a clue as I opened the car door for my wife, my business partner, and even good ol' Mom and Dad, that the kind of headlines Tiny and I were going to generate would read more like: "Man Catches *Strangest* Fish Ever Seen. Makes Front Page News. Life is Changed Forever." All I knew was that I felt pretty damned proud of myself. I had booked an actual star!

Sure, I had seen *Rowan & Martin's Laugh-In* and *The Tonight Show* wedding. I was hip to the fact that Tiny was one of your more bizarre fish — er, celebrities. I hadn't just fallen off the turnip truck. The turnip truck had tried to run me down a couple of times, but that's neither here nor there. For my purposes, he would do just fine. He was a recognizable name, and that's all I needed.

♦ ♦ ♦

When I had decided to hang out my shingle as an agent, I was acting on the kind of pure blind faith reserved for the young. Mine was the unshakable belief that there was a blank page in the history books that only I could fill and that Mom and Pop Culture were waiting for me to make waves. I had thrown in my line on the naive belief that somewhere in the sea of life was a whopper with my name on it. Up until that night, only little fish were biting and I knew if something didn't change soon, I was going to starve to death. Or, worse yet, be forced to wear loafers and a tie and a get a real j-o-b.

Nervous excitement was putting a spring in my step and the night seemed to vibrate with possibilities. The younger me had spent so many nights in clubs just like that one in front of the microphone conjuring up the spirits of the world's greatest rock and roll voices. Now, I was about to be on the other side of the stagelights.

I knew that night that the arrow had found its mark. I had hit the bulls-eye. I was king of my universe at twenty-one years of age. Okay, so I wasn't Mister Pop Star but I was the next best thing… the guy who finds and presents Mister Pop Star. As I stepped inside the nightclub, time stood still. It was official. Waiting for me in the dressing room was a genuine celebrity, and yours truly was responsible for getting him there. Never again could anyone say to me, "Oh, yeah, sure, you're an entertainment agent, but have you ever booked anyone we've actually *heard* of?"

♦ ♦ ♦

My first thought when, at last, I met the curious Tiny Tim in his dressing room was, boy, he's much smaller on television. In person, the guy was big — six foot two or three inches tall. I wondered why they called him Tiny. Wasn't TV supposed to add ten pounds? Who ever heard of TV making you look shorter? My mind started to wander. Wow, if TV could make you look that much smaller, maybe Billy Barty was really normal sized. And Shirley Temple — that means she could have been a full-grown woman when she made all those movies....

As I would discover over the years, Tiny Tim had a way of defying even the most basic laws. Like the law of averages or Murphy's Law. Like nice guys finish last. Or, my own personal law that says guys in Mickey Mouse suits with long stringy hair, soft, pudgy bodies, and hook noses shouldn't be able to walk through a room full of beautiful women and pick them one by one, like a bunch of daisies. If none of those laws applied to him, why should little things like gravity or physics?

◆ ◆ ◆

As Tiny Tim offered me his hand, I jumped slightly, feeling as if — to stick with the fishing metaphor for just one more second — a cold, wet fish had slid down the lining of his jacket sleeve and into my hand. "Hello, Mr. Plym. Hello, Miss Betty," he said to me and then to my mom. He was so formal that I had to bite my lip to keep from cracking up. Was this guy for real? Who talked like that? My vocabulary was much more colorful, shall we say, if slightly less proper. Had I been the one on television, they would have had to assign someone to follow me around with a roll of duct tape to cover my mouth just to censor all my expletives. Hey, this was show business, after all. It was par for the course.

Meeting his eyes, I didn't see a man who was jaded or cynical like so many celebrities. He had an air of "Can you believe it? All of these lovely people coming to see little old me!" His voice said country club but his so-brown-they-were-black eyes were saying something much more mischievous.

He was grinning openly like a child — like he had a secret and he might let me in on it, and also like he could read my mind. It was a silly, infectious smile and he was kind of giving me the willies. His smile said he knew everything about me and he liked me anyway, like a kid might like you. In that way that, short of throwing a dirt clod at him, there was nothing I could do or say that would wipe off the smile or change his mind about me.

He was like some eccentric film star on the one hand, but the entourage said rock star — large men in dark clothes with big biceps. Everywhere I looked there were these little bottles of this and tubes of that, lotions and potions and mysterious creams. Like an old granny. It was like watching Greta Garbo as he flipped his long, wavy, shoe-polish-black hair out of his eyes and looked around, shy, and nervous.

"Wow, so this is Tiny Tim!" I said to myself, trying not to fall over backwards from the overwhelming scent as he opened his cologne bottle, shook it over his head, and let it rain over him. His dark eyes hid under two caterpillar eyebrows and peered over a nose that curved like a banana stuck to the middle of his face. Years later, I decided that God had let him choose his own face — the funniest nose, the silliest eyebrows, the widest grin. Just to make everyone laugh, and to catch them off guard, as if a really good-looking face might have been too intimidating. It was like a Mr. Potato Head face — that child's game where you construct a potato's face out of other fruits and vegetables.

When I wasn't looking, he applied his stage makeup and he nearly gave me a heart attack. Quick! Someone hand the man a towel — and if you've got a mirror, that would be good, too, I thought. He looked like he'd had too much too drink and fallen face first into a bowl of white flour. I, myself, had mastered that particular trick many times but never with a bowl of flour.

What in the world is he thinking? I wondered. The only person I could remember seeing in "white face" was Al Jolson singing "Mammy," in those now infamous, now politically incorrect movie posters.

◆ ◆ ◆

When he took the stage and the lights dimmed, there was a buzz that sounded like a room full of drunken, hysterical crickets and cicadas were trying to keep quiet. It wasn't the usual ready-to-rock-and-roll kind of vibe.

It wasn't long before his chalky makeup did the — speaking of children's games — Slip'n'Slide right into his long, unruly hair. The hot stage lights will do that. Melt the top layer right off of you.

He was like a giant rag doll on stage, dressed in mismatched tennis shoes and huge sunglasses, his costume a bizarre collection of colors and patterns. Had a lion tamer appeared out of nowhere and acrobats started swinging from the rafters overhead, I wouldn't have been surprised. I had never seen anything like him.

My mind took me back to my living room rug where I had sat, just inches from the TV, two years earlier. Like everyone I knew and millions of people I would never meet, I had watched him get married on television. The year had been 1969, the show was the *Tonight Show* with Johnny Carson, and the wife, of course, was

Miss Vicki. And like everyone else, I had balked and thought, this guy's a joke. What does that woman see in him?

What I would discover later was that he had tried to press the pause button on that television spectacle — his was the wedding that nearly wasn't. "I almost backed out of the wedding," he told me years down the line. "I was terrified and not sure if I could go through with it. Then, I thought to myself, well, I do love her in my own way and, considering the tremendous national publicity..." I found out it was probably the best judgment call he ever made — for his career, anyway.

That night at the club, Tiny Tim was in the room with us, so when we all started to get the giggles, we weren't doing it safely on the other side of a television screen.

Who in the hell was this strange creature who was blowing kisses to us from the stage? I couldn't help it. I was muttering the words, "Weirdo, creep..." even though at the same time, I was proud of my first big booking. A name talent, I kept telling myself. I was a budding entertainment agent with his first bona fide star on stage, right? Right?

♦ ♦ ♦

For all that Tiny was a visual kaleidoscope, Miss Vicki, who was sitting at our table, was the picture of stillness. She was so quiet I wanted to take a stick and carefully poke her with it to see if she'd move, like I used to do with the lizards in the backyard when I was a kid.

Did she want a drink? I thought I picked up on the trace of a smile. Was she sure I couldn't get her something? No response. Finally, I got up and got her what I was drinking and set it in front of her. Nothing. If I didn't know better, I would have thought she was a deaf mute. Maybe she was doing some kind of meditation, contemplating the deep, complex existential questions like what in the hell are we doing here? Maybe she was speechless, thinking to herself, oh my God, what have I done? I am married to this extraterrestrial? Who knows. She wasn't about to let me in on it, whatever she was thinking.

As for the six-foot, two-or-three-inch cat called Tiny, he filled up the whole stage. None of that lonesome highway man with a mournful guitar for him. He was like a whole band wrapped up into one guy, with the stage tipped on its side, a thousand tops spinning, and hundreds of lights flashing. Or that's how it felt, anyway.

An evening of absurdity, grandiosity, and song. Get yer tickets here! I was at the circus or a carnival, mesmerized, thinking, how in the hell does he do that?

I wasn't the only one who was blown away. People didn't know what to do so most of them were laughing and the mania jumped from table to table, tickling us like a flea, until we were all hysterical, completely mystified by the curious person on stage.

"Oh, Henry, doesn't he know his shirt and pants clash terribly? He's so…" "Yeah, Gladys, he must be one of those Homo sapiens." "No, dear, that's homosexual. *Homosexual.*"

If they only knew.

He was the kind of magician who lets you see the way he does the trick. He pulls out the hat, pulls the rabbit out by his ears, and then lets the audience pass the hat around. Then, while you're busy trying to find the secret compartments, his boutonniere squirts water in your face. Looking at Tiny was like the whole audience looking in a mirror and seeing a side of themselves they would never display in public — their most vulnerable selves — and it made them squirm.

The one thing we all had in common in that small venue in Waterloo, Iowa, on that night in 1971 was the sense that we had never seen anything quite like Tiny Tim.

◆ ◆ ◆

After the shock of him wore off, I started to really listen to his voice. I couldn't tell you whether he was singing *Great Balls of Fire*, an Elvis Presley song, or one of the many tribute medleys he did, but the fact was that he could sing! He could really sing. And I had brought him there.

Tiny Tim did three sets that night, at one point in the show lying down on his back and kicking his legs in the air as he sang. For some reason, I thought of Groucho Marx, taking huge strides across the floor, twitching his bushy eyebrows and tapping the end of his cigar. Or Ethel Merman, belting out the tunes. And even James Cagney. For, like them, he was a caricature of himself, so much larger than life. And, like them, he was one of a kind. I thought to myself, *that's* what filled the house that night.

What you got with Tiny Tim was a hell of a show and a hell of a voice — warm, rich, deep, and filled with vibrato and emotion. After a rousing string of songs, sung passionately and without self-consciousness, he closed with his hit single, *Tiptoe Through the Tulips*.

I wasn't the only one hypnotized by him. By the time he was done, sure everyone was still laughing, but they were also cheering and hooting and hollering. As he closed out the night, his eyes were twinkling and he met our gaze, knowing full well we had been making fun of him. Striking the full height of the falsetto he saved for his signature song, he looked out into the audience, winked, and grinned.

Ahh, I thought. Now I get it. When I had watched him on TV, when I had watched him that night in the club, I, and everyone along with me, had watched him like someone — not me of course — might watch a beautiful naked woman undress in the apartment building across the way. We watched him from a distance.

But we'd all gotten it wrong. Seeing Tiny Tim perform was not a spectator sport, it was an interactive experience. It was turning on the television and having the guy on the screen smiling and winking back to you. We may have been his audience, but it was Tiny Tim who had the best seat in the house. And it was Tiny Tim who had the last laugh. For just as we were watching him, he was watching us. And what a show he got.

As I would discover over the next twenty-five years, Tiny Tim was really a living tribute to some of our greatest performers. He loved vaudeville and it was stuck to him like gum on his shoe. He carried that tradition of exaggerated theatricality, comedy, and music into the pop music arena.

I'd find out later that, on top of being an incredible showman, he was always a gentleman, even when some bastard like me was snickering and ridiculing him. That never changed.

I eventually did — change, that is. Sure, I still laughed, but as the years went on, I was laughing with him, not at him.

♦ ♦ ♦

Between breathy sighs of "You're wonderful!" and "Thank you, thank you!" he said his good-byes, throwing kisses. Then he removed his tie, signed it and presented it as a gift to my mother. It was the first of many ties my mother, "Miss Betty," would receive from Tiny Tim.

It was also the beginning of a twenty-five-year friendship. Destiny had plans for me as she smiled down on us that night, and a sense of humor more outrageous than anything I could have dreamed. For it was then decided that my life and the life and career of this strange performer would become forever linked. Little did I know, as I closed the door to the club that night, exactly how many doors I would open and close for him, and he for me.

Twenty years later, I was to become his personal manager.

'Til Death Do Us Part, Take One:
The Wedding To Miss Vicki

Tiny fact: Tiny Tim proudly wore his long hair messed up,
and during the twenty-five years Mr. Plym knew him,
he never once picked up a comb.

Tiny Tim's wedding to Miss Vicki was the only time I have ever attended a wedding without first receiving a printed invitation. Unless, of course, you count the time in 1975 when I almost ended up.... Anyway, it was definitely the first wedding where I had never met either the bride or the groom and the first and last time I was ever allowed to show up in my pajamas.

Not since the birth of Little Ricky on *I Love Lucy* had a TV couple shared something so personal with me and the rest of the viewing public. It's true, these days, there's very little that has not been pulled out of the closet and trotted out in front of a television audience, but that was 1969. It made us feel like we were part of the family. Just like Lucy and Ricky Ricardo, Tiny Tim was someone we knew mostly from television, but he was more than just a fictional character. A character, definitely, but one who still existed even after we turned off the TV set.

Years later, Tiny would reveal to me how pivotal that moment was for him, accomplishing more for his career than anything before or after. In those days, most singers' careers followed a fairly predictable, connect-the-dots kind of course. Performers made records, got them played on the airwaves, and that in turn got people lining up and screaming to see them in live performances. For dear Tiny, who never did a single thing in his life in typical fashion, it happened like this. His one big smash, *Tiptoe Through the Tulips*, did well enough on the pop charts, reaching number seventeen, but it was his tuxedoed image taking his nuptials on television that generated enough interest in him that, for the rest of his born days, he somehow managed to eke out a living. Basically, the marriage to Miss Vicki put him permanently in the spotlight — and he rode that publicity horse for the rest of his life.

How could that one event have had such an impact on Tiny's career? Even Tiny couldn't say for sure. Maybe it was because, at the time, television itself was so young and innocent, and music still had the excitement of a rebellious teenager refusing to follow the rules. The new broadcast medium seemed to stand for a whole new set of possibilities — just like Tiny. You looked at TV and figured, hey, who knows what could happen next? You looked at Tiny and thought more or less the same thing. As a country, we were still more than capable of being shocked. It would be nearly thirty years before any of us could become jaded and say we had seen it all. Whatever the reason, it all added up to an unprecedented number of viewers tuning in to see the strange singer who we all assumed was gay and the pretty girl he had somehow managed to convince to marry him.

Since it was two years before Tiny and I would even meet, and a far cry from the point in time when I would consider him anything more than a national joke, I was just one more smart-aleck teenager happy to sit myself down in front of the tube and poke fun at the guy.

Maybe if he had been about to marry his bride in some out-of-the-way chapel with actual privacy and we'd heard about it later in the papers or on the news, no one would have cared one way or another. But, considering how much of a mystery he was to us, how bizarre it was that he was marrying a girl, and the best part of all — that we were going to get to watch — it made for a true media event. Safely on the other side of the television screen where Tiny and Miss Vicki couldn't hear us, we could laugh, snicker, second-guess, take pot shots and take bets about whether she would go through with the vows or run screaming off the set.

We all got to share in a national event that we could talk about the next day and for years to come. Like everyone else, I sat glued to the set that night, muttering under my breath and thoroughly enjoying the spectacle. What if there isn't going to be a real wedding? I thought. Maybe it is nothing more than a huge publicity stunt, like the time Lucy and Ethel posed as invading Martians on the roof of their apartment building just to boost Ricky's career. Only this time, the Martian was Tiny Tim, and he was about to marry an earthling. We all cracked our gum, cracked jokes, and held our breath.

Sitting cross-legged on shag-carpeted floors, I, and teens from coast to coast, heard our parents shouting over our heads from behind us on the couch, "Darling, move a little to the right. We can't see."

I heard that later calculations estimated that between forty and forty-five million assorted men, women, and children were craning their necks that night, scrunching up their noses, and squinting hard at their television sets, asking in unison, *"Him??? She's marrying him???"* It was one of the most widely watched events in television history. And I was there.

♦ ♦ ♦

Tiny was a frequent guest on *The Tonight Show*, and, as the story goes, it all started one day when Johnny Carson said something to the effect of, "Why not get married right here on the show? We could treat it nicely, do it with respect and good taste, have all the trappings."

Apparently, it went down something like this.… On the one hand, or should I say on the one arm, you had Tiny's paralyzing fears tugging at him. Pulling at his other arm were some very persuasive agents and managers and Tiny's own hopes and ambitions. "Tiny, baby, listen, your public wants you, and this wedding means National Publicity in capital letters. Think of all the hoopla. You'll be a smash. It will be a huge boost for your career."

The wave was cresting and heading right for Tiny Tim and he wasn't about to turn and run. So he closed his eyes, held his nose, and let the wave crash over him and carry him into the hearts and homes of the American public. As I said, everyone was right. The

TV wedding turned out to be like baptism in the fountain of youth and it kept his career alive long past its natural life expectancy.

♦ ♦ ♦

For Johnny Carson, the master of ceremonies and the deadpan king of the one-liner, it was anything but business as usual. Sitting in his black bow tie and tails behind his desk, he might have been interviewing a crown prince and the new princess instead of the newly married *clown* prince and his bride. Yes, the one man we all went to sleep to for so many years was interviewing the one man most women could never picture waking up next to in the morning. Wow, Tiny in bed with a woman — there was a thought! I had no idea at that moment exactly what was entailed in sharing a bed with Tiny Tim. But I don't want to get ahead of myself.

I remember Tiny sporting surprisingly black dyed locks for the occasion (Tiny always died his hair), a matching black tuxedo, and white shirt and boutonniere. He was a bashful groom that even in a tuxedo looked slightly off-kilter, and he was sitting in the hot seat next to the famous *Tonight Show* desk, smiling his signature crooked smile. Hand in hand with his new bride, he beamed. Beamed into nearly every living room in America, that is.

Beside him, the ever tranquil Miss Vicki held her husband's hand in one of hers, and clutched her bridal bouquet in the other. In front of her sat the customary tray filled with complimentary water glasses and pitcher. Not exactly what most brides fantasize about.... Was she wishing she had been swept away into a waiting limousine amid champagne toasts and raining rice? Missing the rice storm may be good for the hairdo, but I had to wonder how the bride felt about it. With the poker-faced Miss Vicki, it was hard to tell. How would you feel if you had just married a man like Tiny Tim? Not that he wasn't a sweetheart, but it's all the other things one might be worrying that he could turn out to be that could give a girl a bad case of the heebie-jeebies.

Her white veil was pulled back off her face and the long train bunched up around her ankles. There was no doubt about it that, as the new Mrs. Herbert Khaury sat timidly on the Ed McMahon couch, she cinched Tiny's career. Like him, hate him, wonder about him — one way or another, thanks to that unforgettable television moment, for the rest of Tiny's life, I and everyone else in the country would know his name. For over twenty-five years, everyone would come to his performances, wanting to see the outlandishly dressed oddity that they had watched marry Miss Vicki on TV.

The white-hot heat of the studio lights, sweaty palms, nervous anticipation, and a palpable excitement — the usual "Wow, I'm getting married today" emotions — this was what the cameras captured. The real story, as Tiny would tell me later, was what happened after the wedding, or more accurately, what didn't happen. The wedding night was quite a lukewarm affair, a non-event, actually. Then there was the fact that the wedding itself nearly didn't take place, thanks to another serious problem with low body temperature — frostbitten tootsies, otherwise known as cold feet.

♦ ♦ ♦

Tiny later told me he had met his bride at a gig. Sitting in the audience, the young Vicki radiated everything he had ever dreamed of — beauty, sweetness, purity, innocence. Had she floated up from her seat in a gauzy white dress with a halo around her head, he would not have been surprised, or any more smitten.

"She was a perfect angel, and I fell for her instantly," remembered Tiny.

"So, how did you go from love at first sight to wanting to back out of the wedding?" I wondered.

"Oh, in the beginning, it was wonderful, simply wonderful. She was my dream girl and I was every bit the gentleman. Romantic dinners, lovely dates. At first, I did not even try to kiss her, although I would sometimes tremble, I wanted her so badly. For what seemed an eternity, Mr. Plym, the most I dared to do was hold her hand and stare into her eyes. Then she began to speak to me about her dreams of a white picket fence… Oh, my Lord, she even imagined me outside mowing the lawn and shoveling snow. Me! Can you imagine?…" We both started laughing.

Tiny Tim in Bermuda shorts and T-shirt with his tie dangling loosely around his neck and his long hair pushed up under a baseball cap, pushing a lawn mower? Tiny Tim bundled up in huge snowboots, parka, and ear muffs? Or, better yet, one of those hats with the basset hound-type flaps hanging over the ears, his long locks peeking out from beneath the hat, and at the collar of the parka, a tie, of course, as he did the old heave-ho with the snow shovel? Sure, why not?

Why couldn't his wife expect a totally normal life?

For starters, because he was a traveling musical gypsy visiting from another galaxy, and he lived in a different hotel every week. And the most physical work he ever did was to pick up the phone and dial room service.

"Well, it was not long before I began to fear that, as much as I loved her, we were in for quite a letdown," Tiny continued. "She was sure to be disappointed once she truly got to know me better...."

It was the little things that began to gnaw at poor Tiny. Little things a woman might not completely appreciate. Like the fact that he always slept with all the lights on, fully dressed and wearing a tie. Huh???

"Tiny, why, man?" I asked. "Why couldn't you turn off the lights and sleep in your birthday suit for her?"

"We must always be on our toes, Mr. Plym. One never knows when the telephone might ring and summon me to a meeting. Something might come up," he explained.

Damn. Tiny Tim was right to be afraid. It wasn't overstating things to say he was going to be a handful for the inexperienced young bride who wanted nothing more than normalcy. On top of all his strange nocturnal habits, there were his obsessive bathroom habits — scrubbing the toilet thoroughly after each use, the hours he would spend applying lotions and creams, his refusal to dry off his body with anything but paper towels. So much for his 'n' hers towel sets. Let's face it — anyone looking for average, run of the mill is definitely shopping in the wrong aisle when they pick up Tiny Tim and put him in their cart.

Seeing himself the way Tiny worried Miss Vicki would begin to see him down the line, he knew his marriage was going to be a real crapshoot. And even more than not wanting to disappoint Miss Vicki, he didn't want to make a commitment to God that he would end up having to break. If he took his vows, he wanted to be very sure that the marriage would last 'til the bitter end.

Tiny's fears understandably grew bigger and his hopes for a successful marriage began to shrink. Had it not been for the allure of national publicity whispering in his ear, and his agents and managers screaming in his other ear, he might have simply slunk out of sight, never to bother the unsuspecting Miss Vicki again.

As their short courtship bounced along the bumpy road headed for matrimony, Tiny's mind raced in circles like a broken merry-go-round and the would-be groom began to bite his nails, even as the bride was picturing a Buick and two point five kids in a nice suburban home.

"In the end," Tiny remembered, "I simply gave it to the Lord and prayed like I had never prayed before. It was my only possible hope. My own brain was too confused to think straight, and every time I looked into Miss Vicki's eyes, all reason and logic left me," recalled Tiny.

On top of his fears of the marriage being doomed from the start, Tiny was plagued by the usual male resistance to the idea of being caged, restricted, never again to plant his seed in another garden. Plagued by the thought that forever, for the rest of his life, he would be making love to the same woman — or, in Tiny's case, forever, for the rest of his life, enduring many humiliating false starts and horribly premature finishes while trying to make love to the same woman.

He didn't back out, and even more miraculously, neither did she. The tapes rolled, the director yelled, the audiences cheered and jeered, and he said "I do" and she said, "Me, too." It was a done deal. It was for better — or as bad as or worse than he feared. It was for richer — or poorer, if he went the way of most novelty acts. And yes, it was in sickness — his sickness, that is, in all its various physical, mental, emotional and other strange forms, and in health — mostly hers.

It was no picnic.

◆ ◆ ◆

"What do you mean, you didn't sleep with her? On your wedding night?" I asked him, incredulous.

"How could we?" Tiny countered. "We had not yet gone through the preparation period. A couple must live together for seven days before sharing the wedding bed. Prayer, meditation, you know. You have to become spiritually ready before you have…" Tiny tucked his head down and gave me a shy smile.

"…*intercourse,*" he whispered.

"Wow, that's really something, man. And how did Miss Vicki like that idea?" I asked, trying not to sound too horrified.

"Admittedly, she was not exactly thrilled about the idea, but in the end, she realized that she had no choice but to respect my decision."

Or, you can lead a horse to water but if he won't take off his clothes and jump in, what is a girl to do? Tiny said she thought the idea was insane, but it takes two to tango.

♦ ♦ ♦

Once the self-imposed waiting period had elapsed and Tiny gave the green light for their first sexual experience together, Tiny said, "I was never so nervous in all my life."

"Oh, Mr. Plym, it was horrible. I was plagued by fears that I could not perform and could not last like other men. I wanted so badly to please Miss Vicki, but the more I worried about leaving her unsatisfied and anxious, the more anxious I became."

From all Tiny had told me about his past sexual experiences, he had every reason to be worried and nervous. His track record in that department wasn't exactly encouraging. When it came to sex, Tiny had a big problem with the gun going off long before the trigger was pulled. And that was with him fully dressed. The best chance he could hope for in running a long distance race, sexually speaking, was making it through the first long passionate kiss. One good, long, deep, wet French kiss and that was usually the end of it. He was flat on his face and out of the race.

"Yes, I am sorry to say, my past had shown me that one kiss was all it would take," he admitted, "for me to be done, over, completely satisfied, and utterly humiliated. My idea of foreplay was to fantasize by myself…"

I'm sure that didn't help his problem of being too quick on the draw. Tiny was determined that things with his new wife would be different. So he prayed and he meditated and he meditated and prayed and crossed his fingers and hoped that he would not disappoint his bride or embarrass himself.

"When the moment came, she was a vision, an absolute vision," Tiny recalled. "She looked so beautiful and so sexy that I could hardly contain myself. I was excited and aroused beyond description."

In Tiny's mind, the torch was lit, the crowds filled the stadium, the music played, and the Olympic champion assumed the position, ready to break his own endurance record. There was only one problem....

"As soon as I was on top of her," he cringed, telling the story, "I started shaking from head to toe. How I even managed to enter her without exploding, I will never know."

His own cheerleading section, he told himself, "It will be okay, you can do it, you can do it. So far so good." Then, he looked down at her gorgeous face and body, felt her warmth envelop him, and was overcome with the profound spiritual union they were sharing. Well, maybe sharing is too strong a word. One of them was feeling it, anyway.

"That was it for me, Mr. Plym. Within two seconds, maybe three at the most, it was over for me. I let out a giant gasp of air and looked down at my lovely new wife to see her reaction. You'll never believe what she said. She had her eyes wide open and looked at me with a little half-smile. Then she spoke to me wryly, between clenched teeth, and asked, 'Are you having fun, dear?'"

It's always like that, isn't it? The little tear in the fabric of a relationship that turns into a giant rip. The little snag that doesn't get repaired. It always starts that way and then just keeps getting worse and worse. Their first night in the marriage bed was, sadly, as good as it got. The thread kept unraveling from there.

Out of desperation, Tiny brought out the sexual aids. Sex toys that could never completely stand in for a husband doing his husbandly duty. Tiny described his sexual relationship with Miss Vicki as one that left her continually unsatisfied and unfulfilled. Not a good feeling for a man. The poor guy tried every trick in the book to correct his sexual dysfunction, but to no avail. It was simply no use. Tiny Tim was never, ever going to perform like Mr. Atlas, or even the average box boy in the market.

"Many times, I would get so worked up just looking at my beautiful Miss Vicki that the moment she touched me, it was all over," he admitted. "I fear that over time, my dear bride began to believe I was a … *homosexual,"* Tiny whispered. "A homosexual! Hah! Me!" Tiny lowered his eyes and shook his head.

"Oh, my, nothing could have been further from the truth. It was because I wanted her so badly, because of the effect she had on me … I would get so excited, I simply could not — well, get a grip on myself, shall we say! Ha!" We both burst out laughing.

◆ ◆ ◆

The other chapters in the story of their marriage were every bit as disappointing and tragic. He loved to travel. She preferred to be at home tending to all the little angels they didn't have. When he wasn't travelling, he loved to rehearse. Naturally, she craved attention he couldn't give her while he was busy with his music. Miss Vicki, his beautiful rose, was starting to wilt and he seemed powerless to keep their love alive. So many problems and they couldn't even look forward to passionate trips together through the tunnel of love. The tunnel of love was too brightly lit — thanks to his insistence on keeping every light bulb in the house brightly burning, and all his various idiosyncrasies were like buckets full of cold water thrown on their marriage. All in all, the marriage was terrible, and in terrible trouble. Every fear Tiny had at the outset of the marriage began to come to life. It was like the child who has recurring nightmares of monsters and then one day discovers they really do live under the bed.

♦ ♦ ♦

How he ever planted enough of his seed to grow a little flower, I'll never know, but somehow, from the union of Tiny and Miss Vicki came their daughter named — what else?— Tulip.

There she was, his very own offspring, a chip off the old block, a bundle that had tumbled down from heaven itself, but had she been the neighbor's cat, he couldn't have been less attached to her. How could this be? Loving, sensitive, gentle, caring, kind Tiny Tim completely indifferent to his own child? This remains one of the great mysteries of the world to me. Now, I had known that being around other people's kids made him nervous and skittish, but I guess I figured when he had one of his own, that would change. It wasn't that he didn't like children, but they definitely unnerved him for some reason.

Now, when I say Tiny was indifferent to Tulip, I don't mean the nineteen-fifties kind of indifference where a husband returned from work in the evenings and spent a little bit of time with his daughter before she went to bed. I'm not even talking about today's version of indifference where, somehow between racing through our hundred-mile-an-hour schedules that we call living and the kid's scheduled play dates, the father squeezes in some so-called quality time. I'm talking complete and absolute indifference.

It was and remains utterly baffling to me. Believe me, I tried to get him to explain himself. Whenever I brought up the subject, Tiny became so squeamish and squirm-ish, so completely uncomfortable, that I never could get an answer to the riddle. Eventually I gave up. I never brought it up again. Neither did he.

All I can tell you are the facts as I know them, based on the monosyllabic answers of a man who couldn't bring himself to even consider the question. He admitted he was not a very loving or caring father, that he believed looking after a child was woman's work, and tending to his career was his job. He never had more than very little contact with his daughter, and eventually it dwindled down to no contact at all.

Who knows what went wrong inside of him or when it happened. Maybe his bonding mechanism never formed, the way that some people are born without the right number of teeth or toes. Maybe the weird kid who grew up in Brooklyn estranged from other kids and locked away in his room never learned how to relate. Maybe if his little girl had been seated at a safe distance from him in a chair in the audience, he could have expressed his affection for her from onstage, like he did with his audiences. He always was more than a bit reserved in one-on-one interactions. Or, perhaps she was just a living reminder of all the dreams he once held dear that went down the drain when the marriage to her mother finally hit the inevitable skids.

◆ ◆ ◆

Since I wasn't actually in the room when it happened, I can't say for sure that Vicki was unfaithful, but Tiny said she was, and I wouldn't find it surprising. I wouldn't even blame her. After all, she was living in a parched desert at home, sexually speaking, and if she eventually ran across an oasis of water that was more than a mirage, most people in her position would have stripped naked and jumped right in faster than you could count to ten.

There were a couple of feeble attempts to try to put the marriage in the garage and tinker with the engine, but they never could get it running again, and between the sputtering and the smoke that came out of the hood every time they tried, they eventually called it quits.

I had a friend who had a Spanish-speaking grandmother and whenever the subject of marriage came up, she always used to say, "En el camino arreglamos las cargas," or, loosely translated, "Trying to fix the luggage while you're already on the road." In other words, you've got to try to catch these things before the marriage gets rolling. Now, I don't speak Spanish and if I hadn't written it down on paper,

I wouldn't be able to share it with you, so if I accidentally said something like "your mother is a goat," please forgive me.

For Tiny, he said the day he gave up hope was the day he saw his wife beautifully lit and laid out completely in the buff on the pages of a girlie magazine. Tiny was funny like that. On the one hand, because of his sexual problems, he assumed the entire responsibility for the end of their marriage. On the other hand, he didn't hesitate for a minute to judge her in the way he imagined God would, tossing around phrases like "disgrace... selling her body for money..." and praying for her repentance and God's forgiveness of her sins.

"Miss Vicki always used to tell me she had nothing to wear," Tiny would say to me with a pained smile. "I never believed her until I saw her posing without any clothes."

Knowing he could never ask for a divorce without committing an unpardonable sin against God, Tiny let his wife do the honors.

"I never divorced Miss Vicki. Absolutely not. I never gave her a divorce. The state of New Jersey did," he rationalized. Somehow I doubt that God sees things in that read-the-fine-print kind of perspective, but who am I to say.

"Without the marriage to Miss Vicki, I would have been out of work after *Tiptoe* went off the charts," he would often remind me. "And, of course, I did love her. Not the way she needed me to love her, but I did love her in my own way."

Over the years, Tiny took his pain over his marriage to Miss

Vicki and found a way to laugh over it. He turned it into a standing joke between us. Sitting in a bar together, he would sometimes look over at me, clench his teeth and say,

"Are you having fun, dear?"

♦ ♦ ♦

"Thank you, thank you, ladies and gentlemen," Tiny often joked with his audiences. "I haven't gotten a standing ovation like that since the day I announced to Miss Vicki's friends and family that we were getting a divorce."

Huge roars of nervous laughter would always follow. Ha ha ha. Always leave 'em laughing, no matter how much it hurts inside. That was Tiny Tim — estranged father, ex-husband, but always first and foremost, a consummate entertainer. In Tiny's heart, God, music, and his audiences always tied for first place in his affections. If you were going to marry Tiny Tim, you'd better know how to play second (or third or fourth) fiddle.

Written In The Stars

Tiny Fact: Tiny Tim was a great baritone singer,
with incredible stamina and range of style.
The high falsetto voice was a gimmick and
diversion he used for effect.

From that fateful night in 1971 when I had my first close encounter with Tiny Tim, a meant-to-be, no-way-around-it, written-in-the-stars kind of friendship was set into motion. And just as there have been times in my life when I tried to be extra charming, talked myself blue in the face, did my best song and dance and a backflip for good measure, and it made absolutely no impression whatsoever on the person I was trying to get close to, with Tiny, I could tell right off the bat that there wasn't much I could do to make him change his mind about me.

He was sold on me and that was that. It wouldn't have mattered if we talked one time a year or fifty, or if I happened to be cranky, hungover, hard to get along with, or my usual irresistible self. The fact was, Tiny was an extraterrestrial creature visiting our fair planet and there was no place I could hide — his spacecraft was programmed to find me — and over and over and over again, find me he did. Not that I'm complaining. Not for a minute.

For reasons I'll never understand, the Man In Charge had

me in mind as one of the earthlings whom Tiny would come to call family — and eventually call upon for everything. Though it is true that over the years, there were countless times when we said see ya later, hung up the phone, and went back to running in separate directions, as surely as the sun finds its way back to the horizon by sundown, we eventually crossed each other's paths once again. It wasn't long before we were a fact of each other's lives, and although between us, throughout the years, success, fame, public adoration, public humiliation, and a bunch of wives appeared and disappeared, somehow, through it all, there was always Tiny and me.

I can't speak for Tiny, but as for me, when they finally dress me up in some itchy, uncomfortable suit and lay me down in a wooden box — or throw me in big clouds of ash into a good strong breeze — it will certainly be my friendship with Tiny that was one of the biggest factors in making me who I am today. Inside, where it counts. After all, I love money but if you can believe what a bunch of penniless spirits have to say, you can't take it with you.

What I'm getting at is this: no matter what else goes well or might get shot to hell in this life, one really good friend can make all the difference — maybe even more than thousands of cheering fans.

That reminds me of a story someone once told me about an older writer in the twilight of his life. His young, cocky whippersnapper of a grandson — ah, a man after my own heart — who had recently discovered he also had a gift with the pen, came to his elder one day to get a few of the big life questions answered before the old man kicked the bucket.

"Grandfather?"

"Yes, my son?"

"How many readers does a writer need to have in order to be considered successful?"

The kid paced back and forth and checked his watch and waited what seemed to be an eternity for an answer. Finally, the old man spoke.

"Four is good."

Maybe it's true. Maybe four is enough, and maybe the same thing is true with friends. I was also thinking of that great scene in Frank Capra's movie, *It's a Wonderful Life*, where the Jimmy Stewart character is stumbling through his home town, unrecognized, hopeless, and completely miserable, feeling like a total failure. Then he gets to see what the world might have been like if he'd never been born. I know there were many late nights where Tiny sat alone in the dark — probably eating walnuts and throwing the shells on the floor — wondering if his life amounted to anything, feeling like a failure, and sometimes making the hair on the back of my neck stand straight up by ringing my phone at ungodly hours and scaring me half to death. In the light of day, it's easier to manage a brave smile, but in the privacy of his own mind, a man can think some pretty strange thoughts. Not that I have any experience with long, endless nights of teeth gnashing. Nosiree, not me.

Anyway, in the movie, Clarence the Angel showed Jimmy Stewart how much he was loved and all the little ways he had touched the lives of the people he had known. At the end of the movie, the angel gives him a book in which he has inscribed the phrase, "No man is a failure who has friends," or something to that effect.

All washed up, over the hill, a throwback to the sixties — whatever people said about Tiny over the years, I know that he knew that for me, my family, and whatever wife I happened to be married to at the time, our lives would have been much less full, less meaningful, and a lot more boring if he had never been born. Maybe Clarence was right.

Anyway, a lot of years came and went between our first meeting and actually setting up camp together in the middle of Nowhere, USA. During those years, the phone company strung a permanent telephone line between Tiny and me. Thanks to the phone, we could hear each other over the wild 1970s and the disco '80s, and not even the gale force winds of fate or the ice storms that make up a normal day in the entertainment industry could blow us out of each other's universe.

Life was doing its usual pin-the-tail-on-the-donkey routine of blindfolding us both, spinning us around, and then letting us stumble into our destinies, but Fate was making sure that Tiny and I never strayed too far from each other's orbit. While I couldn't have said at the time that any of it was leading anywhere, hindsight really is twenty-twenty. In looking back, I can see that not a moment too soon or a moment later than it was meant to happen, Tiny and I were thrown smack into the middle of each other's lives and that's where we stayed until the good Lord called him home.

One day, one good puff of wind was all it took, and like Dorothy, we flew head over heels and landed with a thud in the heartland of America. For that is where, near the end of Tiny's life, we came to spend as much as twenty-four hours a day together as the hourglass dropped the grains of sands that would eventually carry the strange fish called Tiny Tim back out to sea.

♦ ♦ ♦

Just to retrace our steps a bit…. You remember that in 1969, the newlywed couple stunned the nation with their TV wedding vows. As I've told you, Tiny and Miss Vicki rode off into a very gray sunset with a huge wet blanket thrown over their not-exactly- sizzling-to-begin-with marriage. Two years later, as you know, the very-proud-of-himself young hotshot that I was booked Tiny into a tiny little hole in Waterloo, Iowa, and that's where we met. Then I started chasing after carrots, brass rings, my tail — and every rainbow that might possibly have a pot of gold or silver at the other end — an activity that kept me pretty damned busy for nearly two decades.

Before we left the club that night, I had said, "Hey, Tiny, I don't want to be out of line, but if you feel like staying in touch, here's my number. I enjoyed your show a lot and it was cool getting to hang out with you." You know, just a friendly gesture.

"Oh, yes, yes, that would be wonderful, Mr. Plym, I would be delighted to stay in touch." With that, he scribbled his number on a scrap of paper also and gave it to me, and I gave him my number.

Then I returned to the business at hand — finding the one and only, never before discovered, astronomically talented so'n'so who I could claim as my own discovery or creation.

♦ ♦ ♦

I doubt that anyone watching my erratic movements between 1971 and the twenty years that followed could have imagined that all my detours through the maze of life would have amounted to any kind of sense at all. I was a restless guy who was ready at a moment's notice to pack up my world and take it on the road if I thought that would get me closer to — what, exactly, I don't know. It's not like I had a clear sense of what I was looking for. All I knew was that I loved to travel and spent a great deal of time standing on my tiptoes trying to figure out if the grass really was greener on the other side of the fence. Tiny and I both had that gypsy spirit and it wouldn't take much to lull me out of my complacency and my own zip code. Before I knew it, I would be tailing one more moving van into a new suburb with a brand new welcome mat and a mailbox with my name on it. I was always in search of new opportunities and, let's face it, I had ants in my pants.

If I'm totally honest, I have to admit that it was more than that — more than restlessness, more than opportunism, more than the fact that I got bored if I stayed in one place for too long. No matter how many hairs I got on my chin or how much of a so-called adult I became, I was never too far removed from the kid in the band who wanted more than anything on earth to be a part of the exciting world of entertainment.

Yes, I confess. Behind the stay-at-home dad who loved nothing more than taking my kid to the ball game and cooking dinner, I was and am today a show biz junkie. Pure and simple. An addict hooked on the attention. If there was a 12-step meeting for people like me, it would go like this: "Hi, my name is Steve and I'm an attention junkie." (And then everyone in unison would say "Hi, Steve.")

I need the applause. I crave the adoration. Just like when I was a kid, I live to do the one-liner-lampshade-on-my-head-dog-and-pony show. Sure, all that adoration is only fleeting — the adrenaline rush, the feeling of your hair being blown back by the sound of a crowd that's really on fire. I know the feeling doesn't last for more than a minute. Yeah, but it's a hell of a minute. So that's what was driving me. Hmmm, so maybe I had more in common with Tiny Tim than first meets the eye? Now you're getting the picture.

◆ ◆ ◆

If I couldn't be the one on stage making everyone clap and scream, then I had to be the guy behind the guy on stage. I don't mean literally, of course, like a roadie doing a poor job of hiding in the wings. I wanted to be a starmaker. I wanted to make a real difference in the life of a performer — to groom, build, develop, and mentor someone so that I could go to bed at night feeling like I'd left my mark on the world.

So I spit-shined my shoes, followed the glint in my eye, and set out to conquer the world. Surely in all of America there had to be a single fabulously gifted budding talent just waiting for someone like me to come along. And like Sherlock Holmes or Phillip Marlowe with the big magnifying glass, I put my nose to the ground looking for clues. From that moment on, the driving force in my life has never changed. I have been as devoted as any astronomer spending hours with his eye to the telescope. My life had become my own personal star search.

◆ ◆ ◆

A couple of months after meeting Tiny Tim, my phone rang.

"Hello?" I said.

"Mr. Plym?" said the voice on the other end.

Mister? Now how many people call me Mister anything?

"Tiny? Tiny Tim, is that you?" I responded, somewhat shocked to be hearing from him.

"I just thought I would telephone you. It was such a wonderful engagement and I hope I am not interrupting anything..."

"Oh, no, no, not at all."

We started out as the picture of politeness with each other and soon relaxed into a comfy cozy conversation that must have gone on for two hours. What did we talk about? The meaning of life — and death. Why we were here — on earth, and in our specific spots of the planet. You know, your usual small talk.

It wasn't long before he got in the habit of calling me when he'd get off the road. Then from the pay phone outside the gig. Soon, from the pay phone by the bathroom at the gig, the phone in his hotel room, the phone at the 7-Eleven on the way home from the gig.... Or, at other times, he would vanish for awhile. I'd leave him a message and wonder why he wasn't ringing my phone off the hook, and just to make sure I didn't start thinking he was becoming predictable, he would wait to return the call until he was back in town. Sometimes I'd find a note from him in the mailbox. There was never any thought in either of our minds of me managing him or booking him. I just liked the guy.

◆ ◆ ◆

1971, 1972, 1973, and still looking. Managing acts, booking acts — I was manager and agent extraordinaire but I had discovered no pop phenomenon about to pop. Then in 1974, I finally got lucky. Oh, yeah, I got lucky all right. Just remember, there are two kinds of luck, one kind you find like striking oil and one kind hunts you down. Her name was Carrie McDowell, she was ten years old, and she could sing like Barbra Streisand. Best of all, she was my very own discovery. *The Tonight Show* had us on three times, we did *Merv Griffin* and *Sonny & Cher*, and she even played with George Burns and Liberace. I was basking in the sunlight of success, and even the reflection of the ocean off the pearly sands of Bermuda couldn't have looked any brighter to me.

She was called Carrie McDowell and her band was the Love Train, consisting of eight or nine other kid wonders, and I had on my engineer hat and was blowing that train whistle to beat the band. Success was about to be mine. I could almost taste it and it was so sweet, it was making my pancreas hurt just thinking about it. I could hear it now. "Ladies and gentlemen, here are the next Osmonds! Or, the white Jackson Five (actually, the Jackson Nine)!" There was only one teensy weensy little problem, and that was — to continue in the train metaphor — the gigantic freight train was running out of control and about to jump the tracks. Alcohol, greed, insanity, stage mother, and a crooked money man — and I'm not talking about me.

It all amounted to a helluva train wreck and I had the bruises to show for it. By the time it was over, I was three years older and I don't know if I was any wiser but I sure had a bad taste in my mouth for the schmooze and the schmaltz of showbiz. I was ready for a change.

All the while, right under my nose, there was someone who was everyone's star and no one's, and telephone conversation by telephone conversation, I began to give him the very thing I needed so badly to give, and in so doing, to get back the kind of satisfaction I had always been seeking. Never for a second thinking it was, or ever would be, about business.

◆ ◆ ◆

"So what are you up to, Tiny?" I would always start the ball rolling.

"Well, Mr. Plym, I am back on the road again…" and I could hear it in his voice — the resignation, the feeling that the road ahead was an endless dreary, predictable, lonely place, filled with tumbleweeds and broken-down abandoned cars. He felt like he was doomed to drag his flagging career along behind him down the dusty road like a tramp with a bundle on a stick. And he was resigned that he had no other choice. He was a performer and perform he would — even if the audiences, the venues, and the populations of the towns kept shrinking until he sometimes needed a magnifying glass to find them.

I wasn't going to stand by and let him sulk.

"Just think, Tiny…" I would quickly slip into my pep rally cheerleading voice. "Most of us poor slobs are just ordinary everyday civilians. Day after day, we get out of bed and go in to work and for most of us, no one hardly even knows we're alive. Now you, on the other hand," I would pause for emphasis, "you, Tiny, are really blessed, man. God made you a star. Everyone around the world knows your name."

Never mind that they weren't exactly banging down his door. It was true, they did know his name. I wasn't lying. Exaggerating, yes.

I became the King of Hyperbole. I offered myself as the emotional gas station where he could stop to fill his tank with kind words and support, with exaggeration and positive thinking, with any damn thing I could pull out of thin air.

"I know that Brownsville is just a small town, Tiny, and you didn't get a very big turnout at the gig, but just think. Every time you walk into a restaurant, everyone turns around. You never have to stand in line, man! How cool. You are never really alone. Doesn't someone come up to your table nearly every time you're out in public?" I was really reaching.

"Well, Mr. Plym..." he would become very still and contemplate my words very seriously. "Yes, yes, I suppose they do," his voice becoming light again. And he would let the weight of my encouragement sink in.

I wanted to believe in happy endings, to believe in a world where the glass could be half full. So I became the Spin Doctor. Even though God hadn't yet seen fit to send me my own Big Deal, He had sent me Tiny Tim, and I'd be damned if I wasn't going to do everything in my power to brighten his day and give him the little push he needed to pick himself up and get from the middle of Backwards, USA, to Nowheresville, if that's the only place that would have him.

"You are so right. You are so right," he would admit. "I must be thankful. The Good Lord has blessed me, indeed, and who am I to question..."

Whew! So what if I didn't have my own Big Shot. Here was a star who was down in the mouth and down on his luck, and I had found a way to make a difference in his life. Whenever Tiny called and I could offer him some kind word, I slept a little better at night. I made him feel like he was still someone, and in so doing, I wasn't invisible anymore, either. In some small way, I was making a difference.

♦ ♦ ♦

In 1977, after I had finally recovered from watching the crash and burn of my dreams of breaking the next Shirley Temple, I picked myself up and dusted myself off. Then, true to my nature of letting the road lead me in its own direction without first checking the bus schedule or worrying too much about where I was going to end up, I promptly got myself involved in the business of sports.

It all started with a conversation with a buddy of mine who was living in Los Angeles. Basically, my friend was a promoter, who would book NFL football bigwigs to play against local teams all over the country. The way it worked was like this. He would take some of the players from the Rams, for example, and book them in some city that happened to have a local college basketball team. So you'd have Mr. NFL Star competing against Mr. Local Yokel — in any sport other than the one in which Mr. NFL Star had excelled.

How well would a Minnesota Vikings safety do on the basketball court against Cincinnati's finest college basketball center? I had no idea, but according to my friend, there were plenty of people willing to pay to find out. Family sports shows, he called them. Sometimes we'd have the football stars come and play against local teams made up of police or fire department heroes. Local heroes versus the NFL's finest. One thing I learned pretty quickly about Americans — there was never any shortage of people willing to turn out to root for the underdog. Years later, the biggest underdog of them all was going to throw me a big fat bone by agreeing to stand in the middle of one of my stadium shows and howl at the moon. But for now, it's still 1977, so back to my story.

♦ ♦ ♦

1979 turned me into Mister Las Vegas, booking shows on the strip. Then in 1983, I went to work in the Big Apple for a big agency and handled Jake La Motta — as much as anyone can handle a raging bull. When 1987 brought the death of the mother of my then-wife, Julie, we both wanted to get as far away as we could — and ended up in the middle of the flatlands. Houston, Texas. It took all of a year for me to be ready to hang myself.

In every town I hit, and every stone I overturned looking for my payoff, there was one thing I could always count on. I knew for sure that some night when I'd been up too late and had smoked too many cigarettes and seen too many green olives floating in a martini glass and my head was about to split, and all I wanted to do was sink into the pillow and never get up again, Tiny Tim would call me at four o'clock in the morning.

"Tiny, man, imagine what it's like to be us ordinary people. No one recognizes us, and every day is a humdrum day." Even in my sleep, I knew my lines by heart. "Now, you, on the other hand.... By the way, I saw that picture of you in the paper. Is that a new face cream you're wearing? Man, I swear it's taken ten years off your life!" I said, looking for the silver lining.

"Oh do you think so?" He'd brighten. "Do you really think so?" And the hope in his voice made it all worthwhile. It wasn't like I was full of baloney. It's not like I didn't mean what I was saying. I wanted it to be true, and so did he.

One day, my friend, Mike, could hear the dust in my lungs from too many days in the middle of Texas and he said, hey, how about The Rams versus the local police or fire department? Whaddya think? So, I did it. I moved from dusty Texas to beautiful downtown dusty Pomona, to book more football shows and look at a place that had hills. At least I was in California. The Land of Dreams. A place where anything could happen, and often did.

What happened for me in California, between arranging to have a lot of guys running over Astro Turf and throwing each other into heaps of muddy muscles, was that the fine court system of Los Angeles saw fit to grant my request to turn me into the single parent of my baby son. It looked to me like the itsy-bitsy drinking problem my first wife had came out of the closet when she lost her mother — and it wasn't so itsy-bitsy after all. She seemed to be out of control and I was now living in Pomona, California, the only parent of a rather small little boy who shared my name.

Hmmm, I'm thinking. All alone in a state where I know nobody with a tiny little fella and now I'm wifeless. Hey, mom and dad would love to see their grandson more, wouldn't they? I was desperate. They said yes and I said Des Moines, Iowa, here I come.

Nearly twenty years had elapsed since I'd started looking for my own little mound of clay to help mold, my own piece of marble to coax into a work of art, and now I was going home empty-handed. Unless you counted the tiny little guy who was counting on me for everything.

And of course, there was Tiny Tim, the roaming vagabond, bravely following his fan base from small town venue to small town venue, stopping at every phone along the way to drop a quarter and bend my ear.

Maybe I was needed, after all.

Alien Shoots For The Moon, Lands In Midwest

Tiny fact: Tiny Tim ate lots of walnuts in the winter.
"Squirrels eat them to keep warm,
and I'm going to do the same," he reasoned.
From November to February, his floors were
covered in walnut shells.

Like the superhero my kid thought I was, every day I would leave home, slip into the nearest phone booth, change out of my Mister Mom outfit, and emerge as the fast-talking, adrenaline-pumped ringleader of the Greatest Shoe on Earth. In my mind, anyway. In real life, I was not exactly the King of Show Biz. But someone once said if God gives you lemons, you may as well make lemonade, so that's what I did.

The bright lights of the big cities hadn't panned out for me, and now I was in a whole new ballgame. Literally. I had to make it work for me and for my son. From my own little out-in-the-middle-of-nowhere plot of earth commonly known as Des Moines, Iowa, I became the Master of the Midwest, filling stadiums in four states, and keeping food in the mouth of my miniature namesake, Steve Plym, Jr., or "S.P.," as I call him.

It was 1989 and I was right back where I started from, in good ol' Iowa. All my years of chasing my muse around, and coming so close to swinging from that proverbial brass ring, and where in the world do I end up? Within rock throwing distance of the nest where my dreams of rockin' and rollin' were first hatched. Go figure. I had left as a kid with big dreams of star-catching and I had returned without a big star, or even a little one I could call my own. I was, however, the head of my own full-fledged entertainment promotion office — alarmingly close to my old house, my old school, my old haunts, and at least two or three ex-girlfriends.

So what if I didn't have my own Big Shot and the mind-numbing success I was after? At least I had the sweet smell of family and roots.

♦ ♦ ♦

One day I was planning an upcoming baseball event and I needed a guest celebrity host. It was an easy gig. All the celebrity had to do was give a brief speech, shake hands, and say cheese for a lot of cameras. The worst thing that could happen was that the star would end up with carpal tunnel syndrome from signing too many autographs or blind from too many flashbulbs. Hmmm… maybe I'd better look into liability insurance.

I started scratching my head and thinking. Now, who could I approach? In the past, I had booked the Lone Ranger, and everyone from Smokin' Joe Frazier to The Beaver, otherwise known as Jerry Mathers. Who on earth was I going to get this time? That line of thought — who *on earth* — kept me from coming up with the answer right off the bat.

To really boost sales, it was going to have to be someone different. Someone really different, completely outside the mainstream… I followed my tail around and around…. Where could I get someone who was novel and unique but wouldn't cost me a fortune? After all, I may have been trying to pull off the Greatest Shoe on Earth, but I was doing it on a shoestring budget. I really wanted someone wild and zany, a guest host who would positively shock people. Shock people? Wait a minute…

"Oh my God!" I thought. "Tiny Tim!" He had all the ingredients I needed.

♦ ♦ ♦

I picked up the phone, dialed Tiny Tim in New York, and after we got caught up, I got to the point.

"So, whaddya think, man?" I asked.

"Oh, Mister Plym, Mister Plym, I simply could not be more thrilled. It just so happens that you are speaking with an avid baseball fan!"

"That's great, Tiny, glad to hear it. It will be a blast." It looked like I had my host. Wow, that was easy. Yeah… too easy.

"…I know every statistic about every one of the fine players on the Brooklyn Dodgers. Ask me anything," he replied.

I quizzed him, and to my utter amazement, the sonofabitch really did know everything there was to know about his favorite team, down to what kind of deodorant those guys liked to wear. He was full of surprises. Two hours later, he had worked himself up into such a lather of enthusiasm, I felt like I was talking to a little kid who had spotted Santa Claus hovering outside his window with a bag full of toys.

Time to close the deal. "Then, you'll do the show?"

"Do it? Mister Plym, you could not keep me away!"

"Great! Great! Now, we're going to have to…"

"This will give me the chance of a lifetime!" Tiny interrupted. I had given him the ball and before I could stop him, he was on the field and running as fast as he could — in the wrong direction.

"…At last, I will have the opportunity to play baseball with real professional athletes. I cannot wait! What position would you like me to play?" he bubbled.

Huh??? What position did I want him to play?

"I would be delighted if I could pitch," announced Tiny Tim.

Pitch? Tiny playing baseball? I had to nip this weed in the bud. "No, no, you've got the wrong picture. I just want you to show up, shake hands, and greet the fans. You're not going to actually play ball, man! Are you nuts?"

There was dead silence on the other end of the phone.

"Tiny, are you there? You know, photographs and autographs. I thought those were two of your favorite things."

"I thought you wanted me to play in the game." The picture of Tiny Tim wearing a baseball cap and mitt, spitting chewing tobacco on the ground, was too much to take. If he hadn't sounded so heartbroken and dejected, I would have burst out laughing.

"I want to play baseball. I must play!" Even over the phone,

I could see him pouting — and it was a pitiful sight.

"Please, Mr. Plym, this is so exciting for me, a real dream come true. It would be my opportunity to relive a lost childhood dream." He was really pouring it on.

My God, I thought, Tiny Tim playing baseball? This is insane!

"I will never forgive you if you do not let me play…"

Wow… was there any way I could let this happen?

Tiny sensed a tiny opening and he went barreling through. "I will even play for free. Honestly, no charge. This is my big chance. If you are my friend, you will let me play."

My back was against the wall and short of hitting him where it hurt, there was no way out. "Okay, okay, Tiny. You're on the team, man. But look, you're no spring chicken. You've got to take it easy…"

I had done it now. I had given him plenty of rope and in the hours we spent on the phone he had worked it into a nice little noose and tightened it around my neck.

"It will be really hot and humid and I don't want anything to happen to you. Do you know what I mean?" Maybe he would listen to reason. Or threats of death.

"I will be fine, really." He wasn't about to budge an inch. It was hard to blame the guy. After all, we were talking about America's greatest pastime. Or second greatest, anyway.

♦ ♦ ♦

"What???" My business associates looked at me like the

61

insane person I was, like the guy who had, somehow, over the course of one long conversation with Tiny Tim, caught his insanity.

"Let me get this straight. He is appearing as guest host, *and playing in the game?*"

What could I say?

"You're out of your mind, Plym…" It was unanimous. They all agreed that Tiny Tim's involvement in a celebrity sports event in the Midwest was a sure-fire failproof guarantee of disaster and humiliation.

"Everyone will laugh at you. You'll lose your ass on this show, not to mention your reputation and credibility. No one in their right mind wants that queer-lookin' Tiny Tim at a ball game!" Their voices reverberated in my head like broken stage monitors blasting so loudly that my ears were starting to hurt. My mind was racing around and around…

They concluded, "You want a flop, you've got a flop." Disgusted, they shook their heads, looked at each other with raised eyebrows, rolled their eyes, and left me alone in the office to contemplate my upcoming public flogging.

Fine. If God had brought me back to the Midwest only to meet the hangman and witness my own demise by embarrassing myself on my very own home turf — or Astro Turf as the case may be — then so be it. If that's the way it was, I was going to have my last meal, smoke a dead man's last cigarette, stick my chin in the air like the adolescent rebel I had always been, and face my fate.

Tiny Tim was counting on me and I wasn't going to let him

down. Coming back to the Midwest was all about family, wasn't it? Well, somewhere along the line, the great hospital in the sky had put my name on his I.D. bracelet and entrusted him to me, and one way or another, this overgrown alien baby was mine. And damn it, if I had anything to say about it, he was about to play ball.

I was ready to meet the firing squad.

◆ ◆ ◆

Amazingly, ticket sales went through the roof. The fine people of the country's heartland showed they had a lot of heart, gave the big thumbs up, and ate up the idea whole. I can't explain it.

Old fogeys, young 'uns, in-between folks. The only ones who didn't buy a ticket were on all fours and didn't carry a wallet — they got made into wallets.

It was so over the top, so wild, so extraordinary, that it couldn't fail. Crowds poured in, and so did the money.

◆ ◆ ◆

It was ninety degrees outside and Tiny Tim was wearing a tuxedo. With Mickey Mouse faces all over it. I mean actually wearing it on the playing field. Center field, to be exact. It was quite a sight. Hot enough to roast a pig on home base and he's got the full tails on and, of course, a tie.

I had my finger on the phone ready to call the paramedics during the entire game. Between all the clothes he was wearing and the fact that he absolutely refused to drink from any cup that might have been filled from the Gatorade thermos because — horror of all horrors — it might contain a germ or two, we were taking bets as to whether he would have an all-out heart attack, a stroke, or just pass out dead from heat exhaustion.

Batter up and… Crack! The batter would hit the ball, the ball would hit the sky and sail, sail, sail 'til it got right over Tiny's mitt, just waiting to drop neatly inside. Instead of trying to catch the ball, the second it got anywhere near him, Tiny would lift his tuxedoed arm up to cover his head and face and then…duck. Just like a little girl. This was the center fielder, ladies and gentleman. Yes, that's right, the world's all-time greatest athlete.

"Tiny, baby! Catch it, catch it! Put up your mitt! Catch the BALL!" Thank God, the players were so good-natured and, frankly, so amused, they just couldn't get mad at him.

Like an instant replay gone bananas, Tiny kept repeating the same play over and over again. A player on the other team would hit the ball right to him, he would cover his face and duck. Once he felt the danger had passed, he would mosey on over to the ball, pick it up and … to say he would throw it might be overstating the case.

Picture a five-year-old girl. Then put a baseball in her hands. Now watch her throw the ball. Straight down into the dirt, probably. Maybe, if she's really good, and extra lucky, she might throw it six or seven feet in some wild direction. Now imagine that same kindergartner with a broken arm, and you're getting close to Tiny's throwing arm. Spastic throwing and phobic terror of baseballs are not great qualities in an outfielder. Plus, there was the problem of Tiny being frail and melting in the noonday sun. When I say melting, I mean melting. Given the grand occasion that it was, of course, he wouldn't be seen without his stage makeup. So, not only was he dressed in formal attire, but his white face was dripping onto his shirt. He was quite a sight. And quite a trooper.

Wait a minute! How about letting him catch? We figured at least he would get a little less direct sun if he was behind the plate. Tiny, Mickey Mouse, the tie, and a catcher's mitt. Only, where was he? If you strained your eyes, you could almost see him standing way, way, way back behind the plate because... Yep, you guessed it! He didn't want to get anywhere near the ball. The pitcher would throw, Tiny would scoot out of the way really fast and cling to the left side of the catcher's net, shaking, giggling and panting.

"Tiny, baby, the ball! The ball! THE BALL! CATCH THE BALL!" It was useless.

When his team was up, it was just as bad. Batter up! Tiny would take the bat and hold it so loosely it looked like a big limp drooping candle. The pitcher would take aim, throw, and of course, Tiny would jump out of the way. The pitcher got a little closer, threw a little less aggressively. Tiny still cringed. Finally, the pitcher got within three feet of Tiny Tim and gave him the gentlest underhand toss. Somehow Tiny's bat made contact with the ball.

"Tiny, run! Run, man! Run!" We were hysterical, cheering him on.

In little stutter steps, completely off balance, he tried to run. Exactly like a baby first learning to walk. Up goes the leg, back and forth goes the body and then, and then, and then... In slow motion, down goes one foot, and then the other, until the baby is stumbling like a drunk, half running, half falling, half walking. There wasn't a single tulip on that field, but he sure was tiptoeing. On tippy-toes, taking little baby steps. He could not have run the bases if there was a jackpot waiting for him at the other end. Suddenly, I felt S.P.'s little hand tugging at my shirt.

"Daddy, Daddy!"

"Not now!"

"But Daddy…" Okay, okay. I bent down and gave my kid my ear.

Great idea, kid. He gets his brains from me. I whispered to the coach. The pitcher got eye to eye with Tiny, gave him a light underhand toss, Tiny hit the ball, and ran — or speed-stepped. Out of the way, that is. Ran right back into the dugout. S.P., meanwhile, ran the bases for him.

I know what you're thinking. Tiny ruined it. I let him play and he blew the game, not only for himself but for all the other players. You would think so, wouldn't you? But you'd be wrong. He was an unequivocal smash. If I had gotten Bozo the Clown himself to suit up and take the field, it could not have been any funnier, or any more entertaining.

The players laughed themselves sick, Tiny had a great time, and we all praised him, saying, "Great job, Tiny, great job." The entire stadium of fans had the best time they had had since Aunt Eunice tried to get fresh with the prize bull at the fair. Or maybe it was the bull who made the first move… In any case, it was an unqualified success. And I'm just talking about the game. The aftergame was equally wonderful, as the people fell in love with Tiny, up close and personal.

Every time I turned around, people were mobbing him, swarming him like a bunch of bees, all trying to get at the same flower. I hadn't let Tiny down, and he didn't let me down, either. He shook hands, cooed, said oh, you are too kind and oh, you are so wonderful. He grinned and laughed and signed his name. So many cameras went off that it could have been a big movie star at a red carpet premiere in Hollywood instead of an off-the-wall pop star in a sports arena.

"Damn!" I thought. "If this worked this time, could it work in all my venues?" Maybe I was on to something. Or in other words, sure, this one time was a big success, but would it play in Peoria? Yeah, yeah, I know, for all intents and purposes, we were in Peoria, but that's just a rumor. All small towns are *not* the same.

It didn't take long to get the answer to my question. I decided that in order to avoid a real medical emergency, Tiny should confine himself to more appropriate duties. Leave the ball playing to the ball players. Thank God, he'd had his big day and as he said, now he could die happy, and that was good enough for him. I didn't have to twist his arm to convince him that a star as refined and downright spectacular as he was belonged in the spotlight, not out there sweating on the field. In the name of dignity, good buddy, in the name of dignity, stick to your hosting duties. Not that you weren't great on the field…

We did it. We booked him at dozens of my sports events and every single time, he was a huge smash. It was a no-lose proposition.

Here were the basic facts: every time he ever opened up his own closet, Tiny made a serious fashion statement. He never combed his long crazy hair, he never left home without wearing two bottles of cologne and his exaggerated face makeup, and when he opened his mouth to sing, he was as campy as they get. When you add, on top of all that, the fact that Tiny Tim absolutely, genuinely, wholeheartedly loved people, spoke like he was the King of England and you were royalty, too, and adored being adored, there you had it — the kind of recipe that makes the perfect dish every time. And dish they did. Any publicity is good publicity and Tiny and I agreed — at least people were talking about him again.

The two-headed man, the tightrope walker, the flame eater, the fat lady, and the vertically challenged — there wasn't a circus performer alive who could draw a crowd like the curious Tiny Tim. Everyone wanted to see him, touch him, talk to him. Maybe if we had played Manhattan, Chicago, and Los Angeles instead, he would have looked like any other oddity on any other street corner anywhere. Maybe.

As it was, the salt-of-the-earth people in the middle of our great country were pure gold and they made Tiny Tim feel like meeting him was the single greatest event of their entire lives.

At first, they wanted to watch him, smell him, examine him. Was he made of green cheese, like the moon? Did he eat like normal people? Did he dance, drink, think like an earthling? Once they decided that he really was some form of human creature, they always relaxed a little and got friendly. Real friendly.

How was he? How did it feel, meeting those other celebrities? Where did he learn to sing like that? Would he mind signing their autograph book and addressing the message to so'n'so? Was Tiny Tim his real name? What was it like getting married on TV? Where was Miss Vicki? Was he for real? For Tiny, it was like having a hit record. Attention, attention, adoration and more attention. Put a colorful tulip in a field of flowers, and nobody notices. Plant it in a field of dirt and everyone notices. Nature. Human nature.

◆ ◆ ◆

The more shows we did together, the more time we had to talk, and what I was hearing about the way life had treated Tiny Tim was tearing me up inside. From all those years on the road, on the downhill slide of his popularity, he was dog tired, depressed, and resigned to it all.

"Tiny, man, you've been beat up, rode hard, and put away wet. Hearing these stories makes me sick. You need a manager who really understands you. Don't you know of anyone who's worth a damn?"

"You, Mister Plym, are the only one who really understands me."

"I know, I know, we're friends, but I'm talkin' about business, Tiny. You need someone who understands you so they can take charge of your career and try to turn it around."

"You are the only one who understands me… Perhaps you

could manage me."

It may sound strange to say that the thought had never occurred to me. Sure, Tiny had become my son, my brother, my pal, my own personal E.T., not to mention a great friend, but manage him? No way.

"Why not, Mister Plym? Can you think of one good reason why you should not manage me?"

He was a has-been. His singing career wasn't likely to yield anything greater than the prize at the bottom of the Cracker Jack box. He was all washed up. These were just a few of the perfectly good reasons. Of course, I did not say any of this to Tiny.

"Tiny, how would we make money? I'm not sure you'll be fortunate enough to have another hit record."

Not sure? I was dead sure. There was no question about it. He would never, ever, ever have another hit record. We looked at each other and shrugged. If I threw all my good sense to the wind and said yes, I would manage him, how would we make money? If I drew a line down the center of a page and divided the pros and the cons, the down side was obvious.

On the plus side, the guy had unquestionable name and face recognition. He was one hundred percent famous. No question about that. When he hosted my sports shows, he was always mobbed. Everywhere we went together, people swarmed, grabbed, and crowded him. It was like he carried his own spotlight around with him wherever he went, like a moon that shone only on him. It wasn't much, but it was all we had. How could we make it work for us?

Suddenly, the tumbleweeds in my head began to roll, the winds kicked up, the dust was cleared away and ... Bingo! I had a brainstorm. Hadn't everyone, in every state where he had appeared as celebrity sports host, foamed at the mouth at the idea of having a real celebrity pass through their town? Well, what if he wasn't just passing through? What if the weirdest, most avant-garde cat on the planet actually planted himself right in the middle of Iowa? Not just for a vacation, but for real. A mailbox, an address, a couple of shirts at the local dry cleaner. Showing up at the local Wal-Mart and the meat 'n' three for lunch.

I knew what I had to do. If I didn't want to find Tiny someday with a white sheet over his head, lying across four seats in one of the many airports he called home, I had to get him close enough for me to keep a good eye on him and get him a career transfusion.

I can talk a good game, but this time the stakes were high and I wasn't going to try my snake oil salesman routine on Tiny. My heart was breaking for him and I had to be brutally honest, make him see the truth. I would be honest, all right, honestly begging and pleading and doing some old-fashioned arm-twisting if that's what it took. Considering the fact that he had heavy mileage on his poor old out-of-shape body, and wasn't exactly in prime health, the truth was that this whole matter really was beginning to seem like a matter of life and death.

The fact was, there was no fortune to be made. Those days were long since past. It was, after all, 1992 at this point. Tiny was still a household name but his anxiousness to perform coupled with his willingness to take crumbs for the effort had brought his price down so low that it was never going to rebound back to where it had been. I would have had to be a full blown psychotic delusional, instead of just the neurotic paranoid that I am, to see him as any kind of fatted calf. *Rowan & Martin's Laugh-In, The Tonight Show,* the good old days of Tiny Tim the Moneymaker were long gone.

Managing my old pal was not going to line my pockets with gold or put a Cadillac in my driveway. It was purely a labor of love. In the same way that looking into the face of my son straightened out my motives and my priorities real fast, when it came to looking after Tiny, I was driven by a whole different kind of fuel. I had one goal, pure and simple — whatever was best for Tiny. We both needed to eat but I wasn't in it for the big payoff.

I had an idea. Why didn't we move Tiny to Iowa?

"Tiny, play along with me for a minute. You are the biggest character this town has seen in twenty-five years. What if you packed up and set up camp here? In Iowa. Near me."

"Here, Mister Plym? Here in Des Moines? Are you suggesting I move here?"

"Yeah, why not? It's not a hit record but it may be the next best thing. The press will go nuts. Can't you just see the headlines? 'Big City Singer Goes Country.'"

Headlines? I had him going now. "Yes, yes, it is brilliant, really…"

"They'll eat you up, man. 'New York City Pop Star Moves to Midwest.' It will put you back in the papers, Tiny. The press won't be able to resist it. Then, in the midst of the hubbub, we use all the publicity to jumpstart your career…."

"The move is just what you need," I explained, "National attention. Positive publicity that will generate mass public interest. Some way to get your name and face in the media again…."

"I know, I know. Every word you are saying is true. I will do it," Tiny agreed.

Expecting an argument, I just assumed he'd given me one.

"…I'm tellin' ya, you're too kind, man. Too sensitive and everyone's taking advantage of you. One way or another, I am going to help you, because frankly, you're being shafted!"

"Mister Plym, I said I will do it. I will move to Iowa." He smiled.

Wow, he was sold! Just like that. It was the easiest sale I've ever made in my life.

All I had to do was get the press hot on his tail, and then piggyback on the coattails of the buzz. Get some new bookings. What did we have to lose? I crossed my fingers, remembering that even a blind dog gets a bone once in awhile.

If we could just get his name on the lips of the American public again, we could ride the wave into promising new territory. Uncharted shores. Or quicksand. Either way, I was willing to roll the dice, and so was he.

"It could be a comeback, Tiny. Just think…."

He smiled, pretending not to be worried. I worried, not bothering to smile, and we shook on it. I was now Tiny Tim's manager. And Tiny now belonged to Des Moines, Iowa.

Tiny Tim and Mister Plym. It had kind of a nice ring to it. I felt like we were the cannonball and the crazy guy who rides the cannonball, closing our eyes, climbing into the dark barrel of the big cannon and letting it shoot us into space toward an unknown destination. We counted to three. Even if we landed with a thud, we planned to enjoy every second of the ride.

He was the same guy I had known for so many years, only now I was flying his spacecraft.

"UFO Sighted. Alien Lands in the Midwest." Now all we needed was a couple of locals with a telescope and a telephone to call the news in to the press.

David and Goliath, Part Two:
Gentle Giant Outwits Mental Midget

"The show must never seem scripted.
You must leave room for spontaneity."

--Tiny Tim

Before I became Tiny's manager, his career had become an endless game of hopscotching all over the country for nickels and dimes. Thanks to his incredible business savvy and some very financially creative and enterprising handlers pimping him, he pocketed less than a hooker with a heroin habit. He did one-night stands in small dingy venues. His willingness to work hard was continually being turned into an obligation to perform — sometimes as many as three or four shows a night.

What did he get for his trouble? A couple of bucks and a slimy pat on the back before his handlers stuck the knife in again.

"I hate to admit this, Mister Plym, but half the time I did not even know how much money I was being paid," Tiny said sheepishly.

I couldn't believe my ears. "What??? You're kidding, right? How could you play without asking how much the purse was? Don't you fight for what is yours?"

"These fellows were a rough bunch, if you know what I mean,

and I was frightened and intimidated. I lived in a whirlwind, never knowing where I would be from one week to the next. I just did as I was told. I did not wish to rock the boat when things were going so well…"

"*Well?* How were they going well, for God's sake?" I was incredulous.

"I was a big star," he explained. "Everyone wanted my autograph. I had all I had ever dreamed of and I was afraid if I raised too many questions, everything would be taken away from me."

It was easy to dig up some of his old contracts for past gigs, and what I saw made me sick to my stomach. Tiny worried that everything would be taken away but it seemed to me like everyone had pretty much already taken whatever they wanted to take. Even at the height of his career, he was treated like a five-year-old — he never knew how much money he made and he lived on a kid's allowance. Even when he was so hot that people were lighting their cigars on the tip of his nose, he still got taken to the cleaners.

"Standing room only. I will never forget it. Playing Las Vegas, earning sixty thousand dollars a week. Sixty thousand! And how much did I ever personally receive?"

I was cringing, covering my ears. I didn't want to know.

"Two thousand dollars, my room, food, drinks, and a limousine — which I have to admit was beautiful — at my disposal. Two thousand dollars out of sixty. I am not a mathematician but there was definitely something rotten in Denmark."

It was the oldest story in Tinseltown. He had worn a groove in the road, running around in circles like a trained monkey, and the cycle was killing him. Every month more miles, new airports, the same heavy luggage, the same embarrassing paycheck stuffed in his pocket when it was all over. A nonstop frenzy to keep his commitments, and for what? Just to end up back in New York City again, worried, broke, and kicking himself for taking the abuse.

In Tiny's mind, it made sense that no one let him handle his money. He figured he knew nothing about money, so how could he argue?

"I simply decided to leave the business matters to the professionals," he said.

Oh, yeah, they were professionals, all right. Professional shysters, thieves, manipulators. He was a perfect mark for hustlers, charlatans, grifters, confidence men. I can hear them now. "Oh, sure, we'll take care of *everything* for you…Don't worry about a thing. We'll invest your money for you." And invest it they did, right into the local Savings and Loanshark.

Here was how it worked. An agent would sell Tiny Tim to a club for twenty-five hundred per week. Only he would tell Tiny that the purse was only fifteen hundred dollars per week. Tiny didn't know the difference and the agent had an extra grand to play with. On top of screwing Tiny, he would then take his fifteen percent of the fake amount he had quoted Tiny! Unbelievable. Nice guys.

Tiny was a crooked agent's dream. Because of his name recognition, he was easy money. Any club owner would be willing to book him because his name brought in crowds and, more importantly, he would play for peanuts. The agents loved it because they could keep the price down for the club owners and ensure a return gig, while keeping whatever money was made for themselves. All Tiny ever knew was that he was being given the chance to play.

It was an unsolvable problem as long as the clubs kept offering him crumbs and he kept taking them. You can't hide desperation — it's more pungent than cow dung and people can smell it from a mile away. It's not generally a good bargaining chip (speaking of cow dung).

If Tiny ever did speak up, his goons would say, "You'll get better money next time, Tiny. We promise. Just this one time, you better take what they are offering before we lose the date and you have zero money this week. You don't want to make anybody upset, now, Tiny, do you?" God forbid.

Clearly, his old strategy for making a living had cost him more than he made, and, at his age, it was more than he could afford to pay. Things had gotten so bad that before I agreed to manage him, I'd started having nightmares where Tiny was one of those tired old players who stands in a doorway with a tin cup at his feet, holding a guitar with broken strings, or whistlin' a sad old tune in the town square and sleeping on his coat with his hat pulled down over his eyes.

"At some of these terrible engagements," he remembered, "I felt like I had slipped back in time to the beginning of my career when I was playing in Greenwich Village for pennies, or performing on the street for tips. I suppose that I played dumb to their thieving ways out of fear that I would return to that awful situation. At least I had work. And then, after awhile, I simply did not care anymore."

Tiny never held a grudge. He just gave up.

But now he had a new lease on life. "Traveling Troubadour Abandons Starving Gypsy Routine For Steady Gig as Fish Out of Water."

◆ ◆ ◆

We had done it. We had gotten Tiny Tim his first consistent gig in years and the headlines to prove it. He was now the unofficial Ambassador of Absurdity, Urbanity, and Culture to the fine state of Iowa. He was local royalty. All he had to do was put one foot in front of another and walk down the street, and he caused a ruckus. He was a walking weather machine, always causing a stir.

"Tiny Tim Eats Lunch at Local Diner, Clouds Gather to Watch. Crowds, too." If Tiny stopped in to a nearby drugstore for lotions and creams — as he often did — a tornado of people descended on aisle five, sending products flying off shelves. He was like Pigpen in the Charlie Brown cartoon strip, or the cartoon Tasmanian devil. If Tiny was anywhere in the vicinity, he was turning things upside down and sending them rockin' and rollin'.

Helping him keep a high profile in town was the fact that he genuinely loved hotel living and had no intention of renting an apartment or a house. So I put him up at the Savery Hotel, a place not too unsavory, with a rich history of being home to who's who in this and that.

"Look at it this way," I said, leaning over the front desk of the hotel and speaking in a low confidential tone like I was giving a tip on the horses. "You get Tiny Tim telling every reporter he talks to that he lives at the wonderful Savery Hotel, and we get the opportunity for him to enjoy your fine establishment."

They gave us the room at half rate. Not just a room — a suite. True to my prediction, Tiny's presence at the hotel did bring in tons of business. Sadly, the hotel didn't look too kindly upon all the walnut shells on the floor and the fact that the King of Cleanliness in the showering department was the King of Filth when it came to his clothes and his room. Even with maid service. Before too long, we had to move him to the Fort Des Moines Hotel. At that point, though, it didn't matter which hotel he was living in — he had gotten the attention of the press. After that, it was pretty much a cakewalk. All he had to do was be Mr. Big City Oddball in Des Moines and the rest pretty much took care of itself.

The man who had been running around in circles for so long he had a permanent case of motion sickness now had all the attention he could want right on his own doorstep.

Tongues started wagging, heads started shakin' in disbelief and amazement, and we were off to a good start. We had created a buzz and now all we had to do was work it for all it was worth. A strategic announcement here, a well-placed press release there, and soon Tiny was big news again. From the shores of sunny California to Tiny's beloved Big Apple, reporters wanted to talk to Tiny Tim and ask the inevitable question: Why??? Why move from the bright lights of New York to Anonymous, U.S.A.?

As soon as the story broke, the personal appearances started pouring in. Pouring! Now, the money didn't come close to the *Tiptoe Through the Tulips* days or the kinds of paydays he saw after the *Tonight Show* wedding, but it was nothing to sneeze at. Oh, sorry, I forgot my grammar. It was nothing at which to sneeze.

"I feel like I have returned from the dead!" proclaimed Tiny. The spring was back in his step — and speaking of sneezing, it was also in his sinuses, causing quite a series of allergy attacks, but that's another story — and the color, or what little color he ever had to begin with, was back in his cheeks.

He was getting five times as much money as he had been getting, playing respectable venues, and he even had a full-time assistant.

"This is wonderful, Mister Plym. You truly are the best. Aahhh, yes, Tiny Tim is back." He was downright thrilled. "It's so good to be back on the national scene once more!"

"Sixties Star Long Thought To Be Dead Found Resurrected in Midwest."

◆ ◆ ◆

One night, Tiny was booked at a telethon at Adventureland, our local theme park. For some reason, we both found it hilarious that a little theme park in Iowa had such an ambitious name. Standing at the window of the hotel that night at about three or four in the morning, Tiny looked down at the place and it suddenly struck his funny bone.

"To think, all these years and all my travels looking for the one great adventure, and I never would have thought to look here in Iowa! At last, Adventureland! Ha ha ha!"

After that, all it would take to get us hysterical was for Tiny to look around him and say, "My goodness, my dear Mister Plym. Look where I have ended up!" In unison, we would say, "Adventureland!"

♦ ♦ ♦

My method of madness had worked. Thank God. There was only one little catch, and it was kind of funny. True, Tiny's move to Iowa had gotten him back on track, both personally and career-wise, but it wasn't like he moved to Iowa and resuscitated his career by actually *playing* in Iowa. Nosiree. We found out that, while everyone fell all over themselves to get near him, we couldn't seem to get the local townspeople to shell out two cents to come see him perform. It wasn't going to happen. It was nothing personal. Even the Doc Severinsen Orchestra barely filled one quarter of the venue where they played when they blew through town.

Face to face with the highest profile guy in town, people wanted a piece of him. They just didn't want to pay for the honor.

Though he caused pandemonium by merely peeking his head out the front door of his hotel, Tiny's appearance at the Adventureland telethon was one of his only Iowa gigs. Tiny generally thought the situation was funny, and took it all in stride.

One day, in a pensive mood, he looked at me and said, "I know that it was my own actions and inactions that put me in a position to be vulnerable and used. That is all in the past. Being in Iowa is like the sixties all over again, like the good old days for me. The God-fearing people of Des Moines have really made me feel loved again. It is a wonderful feeling, and I love them for all the love and attention they are giving me."

So what if they wouldn't go see him play.

"Another thing about Iowa," Tiny whispered, "is the girls. They certainly are a testament to clean living. Just look at the huge, uh, lungs on them, shall I say. Look at what I have been missing!"

If Tiny had found a steady gig as the local Fish Out of Water, I was a shoe-in for Fisherman of the Year. Around town, I was the legend who had somehow pulled that big fish out of our small pond. Actually, I had planted him in the pond and then fished him out to put him on display, but luckily no one was splitting hairs.

I had the respect I'd been craving and, while I wasn't exactly wearing thousand-dollar sharkskin suits, we were all getting by. Me, my little kid, and the big overgrown one eating walnuts in his room at his hotel in beautiful downtown Des Moines. My home state had, in its own backwards way, given Tiny a new start.

♦ ♦ ♦

Tiny-ism: "The Good Lord made us each unique."

♦ ♦ ♦

"Mister Plym? Mister Plym, is that you?"

Of course it was me. It was always me, but Tiny had to ask. Just to make sure the pod people hadn't taken over my body right before I picked up the phone, I guess.

"Oh, hey, Tiny. Is everything okay?"

"Mister Plym, it is five o'clock and this is eerie … no screaming cab drivers, no bumper-to-bumper traffic crawling down the streets, no insanity, no horns blaring," he continued. "How in the world can a person be expected to relax?"

After we got done laughing, Tiny said, "You know what I could use right now, Mr. Plym? A nice slice of Miss Betty's lemon pie."

The first time he ever took off his tie, signed it, and presented it as a gift to Miss Betty, Tiny Tim and my mom formed a mutual admiration society, and it was still going strong.

"…After all," he continued, "we do not need to worry about fighting the traffic…."

No, we didn't need to worry about fighting the traffic. There were plenty of other things to fight once you got outside the city limits.

◆ ◆ ◆

As we pulled into the illustrious budget motel that my mom and dad owned, we saw the usual suspects. God-fearing, family-value-respecting people who would be right there if you ever needed them, but turn their back on you in a second if you fell short of their idea of how a person ought to act. You know, just for your own good. Just to turn you around and get you back on the straight and narrow. Real devoted manly type men who would work themselves into the ground eighteen hours a day just to make sure there was food on the table — but would shoot a freak on sight if they passed one on the road. A man's got to have limits, after all.

Considering that Tiny Tim definitely did not fit into anyone's category of how a person should look, much less act, he was starting off with a great big handicap the minute he set foot out in public. One look at him and some people saw a man whose soul definitely needed to be saved from the fiery pits of hell. Or thrown right in if he didn't want saving. It was his choice.

Tiny was finally getting to see the lovely Mir-a-Mar Motel, the pride and joy of Edith and Archie — Des Moines' version of the Bunker family and the best parents I ever had. I threw the car into park and we headed toward the lobby. The air was filled with that wonderful feeling of breathless anticipation — like right before a lynching or a town hanging.

I have to admit that to see Tiny standing in that motel parking lot out in the middle of the boondocks was bizarre. It was like walking along in a field full of tumbleweeds and coming upon a full grown Christmas tree planted in the ground with all the ornaments hanging from the branches.

Sauntering along at Tiny's granny pace, the two of us watched as we were passed by teenage girls cracking their gum, zipped tightly into cut-off shorts and staring at Tiny from underneath permed and teased big hair and blue eye-shadowed eyes. Tiny was in Heaven, watching Iowa's finest grain-bred, apple pie-fed chicks. He grinned charmingly and shyly at them from under the Veronica Lake wave of hair that fell over his eyes, and I could feel his heart starting to trip all over itself.

"Tiny," I whispered. "Don't even think about it. Some of these guys around here would just as soon shoot you as look at you."

He tried not to look but it was a lost cause. He was making me nervous because in that neck of the woods, guys take their firearms very seriously. And they carry them matter of factly, like a spare set of keys.

Tiny, bless his heart, wasn't scared. He walked through that parking lot like the entertainer he was, happy for the attention. Decked out in matching Mickey Mouse pants and jacket with a bright red checkered shirt, orange tie and face make-up, he was quite a sight. And in the eyes of this particular audience, first cousin to the anti-Christ.

We saw faded jeans-wearing, tobacco-chewing, beer-belly-toting truckers, and believe me, they saw us, too.

We saw vigilante Old West-type guys who had seen one too many Clint Eastwood movies, looking at Tiny from underneath cowboy hats and baseball caps. All of them were clenching their jaws and grinding their teeth. Greasy-haired guys snarled their lips doing bad Elvis Presley imitations.

Guys with dull looks in their eyes and thick leather belts with huge buckles walked a little too close to us. The kind of guys whose hair stands up on top, is shaved close around the ears, and hangs in a rattail down their back. They were wearing steel-toed boots and looking Tiny over with a challenging look in their eyes. They didn't know what the hell he was, but they knew he was some type of bug they ain't never seen before, and they were ready to squash it.

And, like always, there was Tiny Tim, smiling. Not scared. Oblivious. I was doing a poor ventriloquist imitation under my breath, "Shit, Tiny, move it! Come on, hustle! Step it up! If we can just make it to the lobby, we'll be okay..."

A couple of guys looked at Tiny's hair flying wildly around his face and down his back, and then they saw his shoes. His red, white, and blue tennis shoes with silver and gold stars on them. That was the last straw. I felt my pocket to see if I had my two-inch-long sissy Swiss Army knife — in case things went badly and I needed to commit suicide. I was staring at Tiny's shoes now, too, but I had something else on my mind. I was wondering how fast Tiny could run.

◆ ◆ ◆

At last we reached the promised land. The lobby. As we were walking in, Texas was walking out wearing a ten-gallon cowboy hat. They say everything is bigger in Texas and they aren't kidding. The entire state of Texas was stuffed into this trucker's jeans and beneath his hubcap-sized belt buckle. When this guy swung around to look at Tiny, he definitely gave himself a case of whiplash.

In a Southern accent thick as Sunday gravy, the guy said, "Bah God, bo-ay! Ya look jest lahk that... uh, whut's iz nay-um? Uh, uh... Ahh, she-yitt! Whut in the hay-ell is that gah's nay-um? Yew know, that Gawd damn cry-zy nut on tay-vay. Dat Tim guy... Yeah! LAHK TINY TIM! Mah Gawd, yer his double, Ah sway-ear it!..."

I was standing back a little, watching Tiny like a hawk and praying like I had never prayed before.

"Ladies and gentlemen, in this corner, weighing in at 175 pounds of pure unexercised muscle-free wimpy-ness, we have the great big weakling, Tiny Tim, and in this corner weighing in at 300 pounds of solid concrete, we have the famous Peter Bilt Truck..."

"...Yew really are his twee-in, Ah swear it! Anybody ever told yew that b'fore?" the guy continued. "If you ain't his twee-in, thar ain't a cow in Texas, Ah swear to Gawd!"

I was holding my breath, hoping I'd told everyone I knew I loved them, and kicking myself for not making up a Last Will and Testament when I still had the chance.

Without missing a beat, Tiny looked the guy dead in the eye and in a perfect Southern-fried accent, he responded, "Now, hold on, pardner. Them's fightin' words where Ah come from! Ah hear that Tiny Tim is queer as a three-dollah be-ill. Now, yew wouldn't be calling me no damned queer, would ya?"

There he was, Mickey Mouse suit, patriotic tennis shoes, orange tie, white face paint, standing right up to this guy who made most professional wrestlers look like stick figure drawings.

The guy jumped back, shocked to hear that voice coming out of Tiny's mouth, Tiny took advantage of the element of surprise and just kept right on going. He was on a roll.

"You sayin' I'm a switch-hitter type? Huh, buddy? Is that what yer sayin? Ah swear to yew, Ah been smokin' that dad-gum marijuana all day, and this is really freakin' me out. Yer really bringing me down. I'm about fit to be tied!…"

"Er, well, it's jest that Ah… Ah didn't mean…" Before the guy could recapture his composure or equilibrium enough to get a complete sentence out of his mouth, Tiny put on his fiercest pout, puffed out his chest, and announced, "That's it. Ah can't stand here and take this. Ah'm goin' to the car fer mah gun!!!" And true to his word, Tiny marched right out to my car with fists clenched, playing out his impromptu role to the hilt.

I stood in the corner by the front desk and watched the guy watch Tiny. I was about to wet my pants.

And then, that oversized brick wall ran all the way to his truck, the ground shaking beneath his feet like we were having a five-point earthquake. He hit the motel parking lot exit like a rocket, the truck smoking and spitting gravel all the way to the main highway! Just like a Bugs Bunny cartoon where Bugs sneaks up on a huge monster who's ten times his size, tiptoes up to his shoulder and yells Boo! and the monster screams and runs for his life.

Tiny and I stood with our arms around each other's shoulders doing instant replay, blow by blow, and falling down laughing, as my mom kept dabbing at her eyes with a handkerchief and laughing all over the pie she was slicing.

"Oh, Tiny, man, you were something else! If only the press had been here… Can't you just see it? 'Macho Man Runs From Tiny Tim, World's Most Harmless Weakling.'"

Suddenly, the adrenaline wore off and the reality of what

had just happened struck Tiny.

"Miss Betty! When I said what I did… I mean about going for my gun. Oh, oh. What if that man would have struck me?…"

My mom took her napkin, wiped the pie off Tiny's cheek. and teased him. "Just remember, Tiny, the good Lord looks after fools and little children."

"… That really could have happened, you know," he went on, suddenly deadly serious. "I could be lying right here in a pool of my own blood. He could have killed me on the spot. What's wrong with me? I cannot believe what I said… what I did!"

"Just like David with Goliath. You had faith and you felled the giant!" chimed in Miss Betty.

My mother always knew the right thing to say to Tiny. One good quote from the Holy Bible could always turn him around.

"Yes, Miss Betty, yes, you're right. I suppose the Lord was on my side…"

Then Tiny suddenly stood up in mock macho fashion, sucking in his gut, snarling his lip, and posturing. In the same Southern accent, he said, "Bah golly, yew mess with the bull, yew get the horn!"

You tell 'em, Tiny. You tell 'em.

Wrestling With First Class

"You always fight for your place in the sun."

--Tiny Tim

It all started when the World Wrestling Federation announced that they were going to blow the lid off Veterans' Auditorium in Des Moines.

"Oh, please, please, please say we can go…" When it came to something he really wanted, Tiny could out-whine, out-beg, and out-charm the best of them. In the wide-eyed, childlike enthusiasm department, my little S.P. — an actual child — had nothing on Tiny Tim.

"I simply cannot miss this opportunity to see the world's finest wrestlers," he continued. "How often are they right here in Iowa?"

Tiny was right. There was no guarantee that the greatest show on earth would ever make a second appearance here. Hell, the fact that the WWF was planning to show up in Des Moines at all was so remarkable that the wrestlers could have set up a card table in the middle of the ring and played Old Maid and the locals still would have loved them.

Not that Iowa, herself, was exactly blameless. As I said, whenever a big name did actually come to town, said big name was often greeted with an embarrassingly sparse auditorium, so who could blame them if they thought twice about playing here?

Just like Cinderella, we watched our popular stepsister cities get all the attention. Chicago, Minneapolis, Omaha, and Kansas City all saw ten times more action than we ever did. What did they have that we didn't? Probably ticket buyers. Unlike Cinderella, most of us couldn't have walked two feet in a pair of glass slippers and couldn't dance worth a damn, but so what? We wanted to go to the ball, anyway, dammit. And now we were going to have our chance. The WWF had graciously decided to include us on their itinerary, and this time the Iowa townsfolk didn't think twice about dipping into the cookie jar and coughing up the price of admission. No one was more anxious to go than Tiny Tim.

On sheer showmanship value alone, it was no surprise that wrestling would tickle Tiny. Those WWF guys are all about theatrics and exaggeration and Tiny was not exactly Mister Understatement.

So the biggest clown in the music world got spiffed up and ready to go see the biggest, baddest clowns in the sports world. Tiny took five or six showers, shredded two or three rolls of paper towels drying off, drained an extra bottle of cologne onto his neck, got out some fresh diapers, and put on his best tuxedo. If I didn't end up asphyxiated behind the wheel from the overwhelming cologne scent, we were in for a great time.

As I was starting the car, Tiny hedged. "You do not think the

Good Lord will mind, do you? I mean wrestling could be seen as somewhat — violent, right? Ooh, but I could not possibly pass it up. Could I? It is not as if it is going to be me in there striking anyone, right? So it will not really be a sin, will it? It is going to be so exciting!"

"Tiny, relax, man. What's the harm? A guy needs to cool his heels sometimes. Don't worry. It's good clean fun…" What was I saying? It is not good clean fun. Oh well, in any event, it is fun, and that was what we needed. I pulled out onto the street.

"Oh, do you really think so?"

"Sure," I said with a straight face. That's right, Tiny, just take that guilt, throw it down on the mat, and pin it there. Eventually, the voices will stop screaming in your head. Trust me.

♦ ♦ ♦

When we got to the auditorium and took our place in line at the box office, a wonderful, miraculous thing happened. Tiny's name was definitely not on the marquee, but the way the crowds went wild, you never would have known. In some small way in Tiny's mind, the attention they gave him that night made up for the insult of not coming to his gigs.

People lost their minds, screamed, and swarmed all over him It was a beautiful thing — like thousands of pubescent girls going crazy over the sight of the mop-topped guys from Liverpool. Only these weren't darling teenage girls. Tiny didn't care. He was a love junkie so he was happy anyway — smiling, signing autographs, offering his hand for handshakes and his cheek for kisses. The way people were swooning over him, I was starting to wonder why I had left the smelling salts and ammonia at home.

It made perfect sense, really. A crowd of wrestling fans is a crowd tailor-made to fall in love with Tiny Tim. Other than brute strength, cunning, muscle tone, brute strength — did I mention that? — and a couple hundred pounds of solidly packed aggression, what was the difference between Tiny Tim and your typical wrestler?

"Tiny, man, we've got to get you inside," I urged him away from the crowds.

"Do you suppose there is any way we might get backstage? It would mean the world to me to meet the fabulous World Wrestling Federation stars," he whispered.

I found the obvious guy wearing black — the one who looked like the thickest cut of steak and had the most trouble smiling. He had to be the guy in charge.

"Are you the event manager?" I asked, and took his monosyllabic grunt as a yes.

"Oh, hey, I'm Stephen Plym. You know, Tiny Tim's manager? Anyway, the guys and gals told us to be sure to pop backstage and say hi when we got here." I donned that extra casual, we-do-this-all-the-time voice you use when you're trying to convince someone in show business that you're from the same fraternity. I told myself it was not like I was lying, exactly. Surely, if they had known we were coming down, they would have wanted to meet Tiny Tim, right?

To my amazement, it worked. Like Samantha on *Bewitched*,

I just wiggled my nose — or in my case, wagged my fast-talking tongue — and poof! We were backstage.

Backstage? Uh-oh. Wait a minute. We were backstage, all right… with a big bunch of the most macho men you could ever hope to find. The WWF brand of macho made your average bodybuilder look like a sissy boy. Even the WWF women were macho, for Christsakes.

How would they respond to Tiny Tim being in their inner circle? If you wanted to get technical, it was not like they had invited us. I just said that to get backstage, like any other groupie.

"I am feeling a little bit like Daniel," Tiny whispered, walking very close by my side and trying not to be too obvious about holding on to my sleeve.

"Daniel? Daniel who?" I snapped. When I get nervous, I get a little snippy.

"You know, the lions' den."

"Yeah, you ain't the only one, believe me."

But as sure as the meanest hillbillies standing vigil on any Tennessee porch will put their shotguns down, wipe off their scowls, and put on a big pot of venison stew when their kin come calling, those wrestlers opened their arms to us and gave us a hearty welcome. With bear hugs. I mean big-tight-ouch-was-that-a-rib? kind of bear hugs.

They loved Tiny Tim! Maybe they saw in him a fellow rebel — a guy who, like them, would push the envelope as far as it could go. In any case, they circled him, sniffed him out, and decided that he was one of them. So what if he sang like a feline and they growled like bears? The point was, they all got on stage and made a helluva ruckus.

"So, how about a couple of tunes, Tiny? Come on, whaddya say?" They started chanting his name in unison and of course, he couldn't refuse. He hadn't brought the ukulele, so he sang *a cappella* and they loved him. They were hooting, hollering, cheering. They were Tiny's kind of audience, not shy about their excitement. If Tiny had fallen into the lions' den, it turned out that he was the lion — happy as could be lapping up their adoration like a giant bowl of warm milk.

◆ ◆ ◆

"And now, Ladies and Gentlemen," the announcer began in his most dramatic voice, "we have a very special surprise guest for you, all the way from Brooklyn, New York, by way of downtown Iowa. Yes, it is true, Des Moines' own Tiny Tim has agreed to sing the national anthem for us. Let's hear it for Tiny Tim!!! Give him a big hand!"

They welcomed him like the major star he used to be, and the sound was deafening, the roar of a thousand trucks barreling through a dark tunnel. Enough to make even a veteran entertainer run screaming from Veterans' Auditorium with a serious case of stage fright.

"Oh, Lord, oh, Lord in Heaven. What in the world am I doing? Why did I say yes? I am not at all prepared! Oh, Lord, if ever I needed you to hear my prayer, please keep me from making a complete fool of myself…"

Tiny heard the announcement, heard the crowd go wild, and promptly began to stumble down the wrong aisle, wondering "How do I get into the ring?"

The room was a terrible combination of too dark in some places and too light in others and Tiny's brain turned into such a scrambled mess that he could not steer around the obstacles. The auditorium had become a maze and he weaved in and around, backwards and forwards, trying to figure out how the hell to get himself inside the ring. Watching him, I was reminded of those huge indoor malls where, after you're done standing like an idiot in front of an incomprehensible directory staring at a picture of a stick figure marked "You are here," you spend the next four hours wandering around the mall, lost.

"Come on, Tiny, come on!" I was screaming, as if he could hear me over the roar. "You can do it. This is your big moment. Get inside the damned ring, already!"

"Please, Lord, please, help me…." Tiny was praying.

Lost and confused, Tiny completely missed the entry to the ring and found himself up against the ropes. "Fine," he thought. "At this point, I do not care how I get inside, just save me from this nightmare."

He hoisted his big out-of-shape body up and tried to climb through the ropes. Of course, he stumbled, lost his balance, and fell through the ropes, flopping onto the mat with a big thud.

Yay! Wha-hoo! Wha-hoo! The crowds thought it was

absolutely hilarious. They howled and hooted and shoved their fists in the air in victory. Tiny was a natural clown, and even his mistakes tended to be funny.

Dazed, Tiny slowly rose from the mat like a cartoon character with a ring of stars around his head. "Huh? They are clapping? Wow! The crowd liked that?" he thought, surprised and delighted. He stood up and gave the audience a low bow and a huge confused grin.

Meanwhile, I was thinking, "Unbelievable! They loved it! Little did they know this was not an act." I was thinking how incredible it was that Tiny always landed on his feet, so to speak. I was also praying he hadn't hurt himself too badly and hoping we had remembered to pay his health insurance premium.

Like the consummate performer he was, he reached down inside of himself, pulled up his best baritone, and sang, "Oh, say, can you see?…"

Yeah, damned good question. I wish someone had bothered to ask Tiny that question before he had headed off, half-cocked, to try to find the ring.

"…By the dawn's early light…" He was fully in charge of himself now, and he had the crowd eating out of the palm of his hand. I don't think either one of us will ever forget those wonderful leotard-wearing, pumped up, overblown giants with tears in their eyes and their hands over their hearts as Tiny sang our national anthem.

♦ ♦ ♦

"Tiny, what in the hell happened out there? Was it the

spotlights?" I asked him later, over drinks.

"Yes, it was the lights… and the large wad of cash in my left shoe!" He said, smiling an embarrassed smile and looking at me sideways.

"What? You're kidding me, man." He was too much.

"Do you remember that when I lived in New York, I developed the habit of carrying my cash in my shoe to make it harder to mug me? Well, I had so much money in there tonight that I could hardly walk! I completely lost my balance…"

"You are something else, Tiny. A true original." We had a couple of drinks and a good laugh. We also had an invitation to host an upcoming WWF event in New York City that would be broadcast on cable television.

◆ ◆ ◆

When the day came to go to New York, I had a bad taste in my mouth. Driving with Tiny to the airport, my heart sank. I didn't want to say anything to him, but frankly, the whole business of flying coach was really eating at me. Damn! I thought. We may as well just hang a banner on the side of the airplane that reads, "Tiny Tim Not Big Enough Star to Sit With Big Boys in First Class." It was downright humiliating. Not for me — other than the fact that back in coach when you order a stiff one, you have to drink it out of a plastic glass, I was perfectly fine sitting with the general riffraff. I was right at home.

It was Tiny that I was worried about. It just didn't look good. There we were, trying to tweak the publicity machine so it would stop spitting out the rumor that Tiny Tim was a has-been and start generating renewed interest in his Everlasting Star status and where do we end up sitting? A hundred miles — I mean aisles — from the Star Zone, all the way back in Row Y. That is spelled W-H-Y. That's what I kept asking myself... why, why, why?

The horror began from the second we walked onto the plane. Since we were flying into La Guardia Airport in New York, every musician within a thousand-mile radius had decided to fly from Iowa to New York. Great. Just perfect.

"Excuse me, pardon me, excuse me, pardon me." Tiny ducked and moved through the first-class section, forcing a smile from ear to ear, trying not to feel bad about where we were sitting. I, on the other hand, was right behind him trying to cover my face with my sleeve to avoid eye contact.

"Huh? Isn't that Tiny Tim?" Half the people shook their heads and decided that no, of course it wasn't him because what the hell would Tiny Tim be doing flying coach?

"Poor sonofabitch, can't afford the first-class fare..."

I was really getting pissed but what could I do? It was true. Even though Iowa had been the shot in the arm that Tiny and his career had needed, it was just that — a shot in the arm. In order to fly first class, we needed something much bigger. Of course, the coach fare was often included in the contract for a gig, but if it wasn't or if we wanted to sit in first class, that was our tough luck.

When it came to money, tough luck was the only kind Tiny ever had. There was no way around it. Tiny and money were a bad chemical mix, like oil and water or Democrats and Republicans. No matter how you tried, they just didn't blend together well. It wasn't like Tiny did anything in particular to lose money, it was just that they were two magnets with opposing polarities. So, until some mogul decided to bankroll us, we had to work with what we were given — tough luck.

So what was a manager to do for his poor dark-cloud-carrying artist? We couldn't afford to fly first class, but on the other hand, we couldn't afford not to, because, hey, that's show biz. If we didn't make Tiny look like he was at the top of his game, he wouldn't stand a chance in hell of ever being treated well. You know, you've got to have a girl to get one and you've got to have one job before you can get a better one.

♦ ♦ ♦

There we were in our dinky little seats, once again feeling like poor relations. Or like teenagers who wait in line all day to get into a concert and then have to sit so high up they can't see anything. Yeah, I thought. That's exactly what it felt like — we were seated in the airplane equivalent of the nosebleed section at a concert! To make matters worse, there were the usual fan club types coming over to us to ask for Tiny's autograph and shoot the breeze. It was great but it was also drawing attention to our location. Location, location, location — at that moment the cliché was true. Location really was all that mattered.

So, we sat on the tarmac waiting for takeoff. The longer we sat, the more I steamed. Tiny wanted to talk to me, to cheer me up and tell me not to worry, but I was in full-blown growling mode and he knew enough to leave me alone when I was like that. Tiny occupied himself by trying to wish himself shorter.

"Tiny Tim's Recent Popularity Surge Apparently Over For Good, According To Sources At Airline Who Spied Him Seated in Coach." I was miserable and I was making up miserable headlines again. I was also making a mental note to go talk to a professional when we got home. Just in case I needed a rabies vaccine or something to protect me from all the squirrel-caging I did — you know, going around and around and around in my head like a rodent on a wheel and never getting anywhere.

♦ ♦ ♦

Eventually the squirrel-caging paid off. Wait a minute, I thought. What is the best way to get treated like a king? Act like a king.

I whispered to Tiny, "Wait here, I'll be right back."

I leapt up and found the head stewardess. I can say that because in those days they were still plain old ordinary stewardesses. When I say plain old ordinary, I don't mean they weren't pretty. I just mean that if she had been a "flight attendant" like they are now, who knows what would have happened.

Giving her my most penetrating look and the Steve Plym version of a smile, I said in my lowest, sexiest voice, "Excuse me, Miss, could I see you for a second behind that curtain?"

She was blonde and pretty in that bright-eyed and bushy-tailed kind of way. Perfect. Bright-eyed and bushy-tailed was going to work for me much better than brittle and jaded.

"Do you know who that is over there?" I asked her confidentially, pointing Tiny out from behind the curtain.

"Oh yes," she announced, proud of herself. "I certainly do." She smiled. "That, of course, is Tiny Tim. So great to have him on board. Do you think he would mind," she began, and now she was the one speaking in a confidential tone, "if I asked him for an autograph later? I was really young at the time, but I still remember seeing him marry Miss Vicki on *The Tonight Show*."

My whole body relaxed. This was going to be easier than I thought.

"Absolutely no problem," I assured her with a huge grin. "You know, this is kind of embarrassing, but I need to ask a huge favor for Tiny Tim… It seems that in our hurry to get to the airport to make our next gig, we forgot to look at our tickets."

I stiffened, and braced myself. Maybe she could read minds. Maybe she was trained in espionage and carried lie detector equipment in her bra. She could have seen right through me and known that I was as full of baloney as a fifty-cent tabloid. She might kick me in the shins. I searched her face for a sign, listened for the whistle from the sidelines calling penalty or foul. Nothing. So far, so good.

"As I'm sure you realize, Tiny Tim always flies first class… there must've been some kind of mix-up… If there is anything at all you could do, just this once…"

That's right, lady, come on… just a little scoot up to first class.

"Tiny will be so appreciative of your sensitivity. I can tell you're the kind of person who instinctively understands the importance of the…" Here I paused for emphasis and effect. "You know, the *image thing.*"

"Of course," she said in a sympathetic tone, touching my hand like a doctor who had been reading up on good bedside manner. "Let me go speak to the captain and I'll be right back."

She was going to speak to the captain. Unbelievable. Back in my seat to wait for the verdict, a game show theme song started playing in my head. I saw myself as a contestant in the final *Jeopardy* round. Tick-tock, tick-tock, tick-tock, tick…

"Okay, players, time's up. Let's see how much Mr. Plym knew about our subject today, 'Lying and Manipulation for a Good Cause.' What did you wager, Mr. Plym? Oh dear, I'm sorry, that was not the right answer. Jay will tell you about your lovely parting gifts and escort you off the plane."

I fidgeted in my seat, contemplated biting my nails, remembered I don't bite my nails, and started picking lint off of Tiny's jacket instead. Within a few minutes the stewardess came over to me and whispered in my ear.

With a smile and a wink, she said, "Don't worry about a thing. It's all been taken care of. You get Tiny Tim up to first class where he belongs."

Where he belongs. You're damned straight that's where he belongs. Yes, yes, yes. I breathed a huge sigh of relief. Tiny knew something was up and even though he wasn't sure what it was, he was definitely enjoying the cloak-and-dagger game I seemed to be playing.

"Oh, and one more thing," the stewardess continued, "don't forget my autograph."

♦ ♦ ♦

Drinking whiskey out of real glasses, picking at a wonderfully artistic plate of food that was starting to look blurry, and dabbing at the corners of our mouths with starched linen napkins, Tiny and I stretched our legs and let out contented sighs. I was playing with Tiny, avoiding eye contact and generally acting casual, like the whole thing was no big deal.

"So? Are you planning to share with me how exactly you managed this miracle?" Tiny was chomping at the bit.

"They just love ya, Tiny. What can I say? They just love ya."

"Mister Plym, I do not know how you accomplished such a magical feat, but you are wonderful! Simply wonderful!"

The best part of all was that we took that same act on the road and over and over again, and used it to great success. It never failed and we never again flew coach.

Looking out the window at the Manhattan horizon, we both started to get really amped. Tiny was going to host a WWF show! Every teenager's dream.

While the pilot made the announcement asking the stewardesses to prepare the cabin for landing, Tiny and I were both hit, instantaneously, by the same thought. Like an asteroid crashing through the window, it struck us right between the eyes. In unison, we gasped, looked at each other, and said in horror, "Oh no! Miss Jan!!!"

We were so excited about the upcoming event, we had not given it a thought. But the odds of running into Tiny Tim's second wife at the gig were almost as good as spotting the Statue of Liberty sitting in the harbor.

'Til Death Do Us Part, Take Two:
Miss Jan, The Second Wife

Tiny-ism: "I trust you, I just don't trust the devil within you."

As I write this, I can hear my mom saying, "Stephen, if I've told you once, I've told you a thousand times, if you can't say something nice about someone, it's better not to say anything at all." Well, I sure hope Mom will forgive me for what I'm about to do because, hey, what choice do I have? The fact is, I am writing a book here. If I hold my tongue and say nothing, this chapter is only going to be one paragraph long — the one you just finished reading

Now, before any of you legal types out there start foaming at the mouth and sharpening your fangs and pencils for libel and slander suits, let's get this straightened out right off the bat. I am unequivocally, absolutely, expressly *not* saying that Tiny Tim's second wife, Jan, is now or ever was any of the rotten, lousy, disgusting things I saw when I looked at her. Who am I to cast aspersions? Just because I would rather pass a kidney stone than be around her, I am sure that's my problem, not hers. I'm sure the truth is that Jan is a perfectly lovely person with many wonderfully redeeming qualities and I'm just too damned shortsighted to notice. Yeah, that's it. Let's just say I'm a blind, intolerant, unforgiving sonofabitch incapable of perceiving her finer points. Okay?

Let me also make it very clear that I am not speaking for Tiny Tim when I say horrible things about his wife. I can't speak for Tiny, and since he's not here anymore, he can't speak for himself. And I know there are two sides to every story. Just because he never knocked me upside the head for bad-mouthing her doesn't mean he shared my feelings. He just wasn't a knockin'-upside-the-head kind of guy, that's all. Obviously, for a man to stay married to a woman for ten whole years, he has to have some pretty deep feelings for her. Yeah, yeah, I know — he didn't believe in divorce, but believe me, I happen to know she had him wrapped around her pinky finger. Plus, I was there the week after their divorce was final and I saw him cry. I mean really cry, like a baby. More waterworks than the usual hour-and-a-half showers he used to take.

So, now that we've gotten that out of the way…

◆ ◆ ◆

As the driver loaded our bags into the trunk and we piled inside for the ride to the Plaza Hotel, I turned to Tiny and asked the question I'd asked him so many times.

"Why in the hell did you marry that bitch, anyway? Of all the women you could have hitched your wagon to, why Miss Jan, for God's sakes?"

It was a rhetorical question, a routine, really. The answer was obvious. She was the kind of woman that made you trip over your tongue and fall all over yourself just to get her to smile. She was a certain kind of good-looking girl. The kind that only had to walk by a construction site and distracted construction workers would go tumbling to their deaths. And men being the way they are, once Tiny had fallen under the spell of her beauty, he was a dead man.

There was no logic on earth that could have swayed him from his urge to capture that fox and spend the rest of his life admiring her and stroking her fur.

"Mister Plym, I will thank you to keep in mind that, technically speaking, she is still my wife. And as you know, she is not without her charms." And then, contemplating some of her less charming qualities, he nervously asked, "You do not honestly think she will be waiting for us at the show, do you?"

"Nah, probably not. Why would she? It's only the most exciting photo opportunity to happen to Mrs. Herbert Khaury in ages. I'm sure she won't even be slightly interested. She's probably at the hobby store right now buying a bunch of yarn so she can stay home crocheting potholders instead."

"I was just hoping that perhaps, just this one time, we might get lucky. Lord, I pray she does not cause a scene," Tiny said, nervous as hell.

From what I could tell, the honeymoon phase of the relationship between Tiny and wife number two was about as powerful and short-lived as your run-of-the-mill Los Angeles earthquake. It seemed to hit fast, pack a helluva wallop, turn Tiny's world upside down, and leave him shaken, skittish, and waiting for the inevitable aftershocks. While the initial courtship was over as quickly as it started in 1984, the marriage was still legally in force for another ten years after that, and the aftershocks kept coming — like clockwork, every time Tiny's name was up in lights.

After their vows, Tiny told me they spent about ten minutes under the same roof together, but she must have had that women's intuition thing going because she never did completely give up her own place and move in with Tiny. Let's just say they became estranged in record time. When I say estranged, I do mean estranged, as in rarely seeing each other. Hell, Tiny even moved across the country by himself, leaving his wife in Manhattan.

If every marriage partnership is a deal that is negotiated from the second the couple first sets eyes on each other, I couldn't help but wonder what Jan Alweiss thought she was going to get by wearing Tiny Tim's wedding ring.

"What do you think Miss Jan stays in this marriage for, Tiny? She doesn't really think she's going to get her hands on your millions, does she?" I joked.

"Smell that?" he said, too in love with the city to hear me, his head stuck completely out the window of the limousine the WWF had been kind enough to send to fetch us. "New York City. There is nothing and nowhere on earth quite like it. I smell the best pizza in America … and Chinese food … and if I am not mistaken, coming from that Polish kitchen is the smell of my favorite soup — mushroom and barley… Did you ask me a question, Mister Plym?" Tiny pulled himself back inside the car, his hair even wilder than usual from the wind.

"What do you think it is that keeps Miss Jan hanging around, Tiny? Do you think it's your millions?"

"Oh, yes, quite definitely. It is undeniably, undoubtedly, indubitably my considerable wealth," he joked in a droll voice, perfectly British, with one eyebrow raised and the side of his mouth pulled down in proper highbrow form.

"Yeah, in her dreams," I said, and we had a good laugh over that one. Only the world's worst prospector would go digging for gold in the mines of Tiny Tim's bank accounts.

"I confess, Mister Plym," Tiny said with a mischievous grin, "I may have allowed my beloved wife to believe that I did indeed have a fortune stashed away in some mysterious hiding place."

"No!" I said in mock surprise. "You? Tell an untruth? Tiny, I'm shocked…"

"Yes, I know, it is hard to believe that a God-fearing man of my caliber… But I did not lie. Not exactly," Tiny rationalized. "I did not want to lose her. So I chose not to disavow her of her hope that the fortune I never made might be hidden in the backyard — or the hills of South Carolina. It was like a game… a game of hide and seek. She would try to figure out where the treasure was buried and, just for fun, I would play along."

"Tiny, listen, when couples play hide and seek, they usually do it in the bedroom and it's not gold they're looking for, it's the family jewels!"

We were cracking up and the limo driver was eyeing us suspiciously in the rear-view mirror.

"Anyway, man, you're just being modest," I teased. "It's common knowledge why Miss Jan won't let you go. Everyone knows you are the world's greatest lover. Or is it the world's fastest? Maybe that was it — the world's fastest lover. Ideal for the woman on the go."

"Like instant pudding! I only take three minutes!" There was a lot of room on the floor of that limo and we used every inch of it, taking turns falling off the seat and rolling on the carpet, clutching our stomachs from laughter. Tiny let me tease him because he knew I loved him. If anyone else said a bad word about him, they would have to answer to me.

After we recovered from our laughing fits, we started to seriously worry. I lit a cigarette instead and exhaled out the window.

If Miss Vicki was the demure, soft-spoken type, Miss Jan was an opera singer, speaking her mind with a definite dramatic flair and plenty of volume. Now here we were on the very streets of New York City where she lived, preparing for one of the biggest gigs in Tiny's resurgent career, and we were imagining her arriving on the set like a wildcat.

Tiny was no lion tamer and definitely did not have what it took to handle her. "What if we get into another screaming match?" he worried.

"Tiny, listen, you've really been looking forward to this gig, right?" I said.

"Yes..." he agreed.

"And it's exactly what your career needs, right?" I continued.

"Yes, definitely," he admitted.

"Then, come hell or high water, no matter how pissed off, how hot under the collar, how furious you get, you will keep your cool, right? You will remember all we have gone through to get you back on track and we will not let anyone — not even that... that... Damn! I can't stand that woman! We're not going to let her ruin this night for you. Deal?"

"It is a deal." We shook on it and then we each turned to our respective windows and stared out at the city rolling by, imagining the worst.

◆ ◆ ◆

Blame it on that shortsightedness I mentioned, but as she

breezed onto the set, I didn't see Miss Jan's best qualities. I saw a classic film star like Bette Davis or Marlene Dietrich acting her ass off. She wasn't wearing a feather boa around her neck or holding a six-inch-long cigarette holder, but you get the idea.

Oh, it was sooo good to see him. She threw her arms around Tiny's neck. Kiss, kiss, kiss, air kiss. She'd missed him so much! She was so sincere, flashing her to-die-for smile around the room. Yep, she was the picture of the dramatically devoted wife. I was getting nauseous. Probably the smell of the pizza, or the Polish kitchen we passed on the limo ride.

Oh, no, he wasn't planning to wear that awful thing, was he? No, no, no. It would never do. You! Over there! What else do you have? She summoned the wardrobe guy and gave him the benefit of her expert opinion, as Tiny and I gritted our teeth and bit our tongues. I doubted that she had even seen the inside of Tiny's closet in years, but here on the set, you would have thought she had helped him get dressed every morning of his life.

There we were, just the three of us — and the USA cable network and every gossip columnist and newspaper reporter within miles. God knows, Tiny and Jan weren't the first couple to fake it in front of the press.

"Mister Plym, here is the way I see it. I have no money to give her and I am terrible at sex. Let her have some glory. It is all I have to offer…" Tiny said under his breath.

So we all froze our faces into smiles and got along as famously as the Hatfields and the McCoys during the ten minutes it took to reload their ammunition. Miss Jan was the perfect celebrity wife, publicist, press agent, and photographer all rolled into one ball of fire. Like a machine gun, her camera went off constantly and when she wasn't on one side of the camera, she was on the other, flashing her pearly whites with her arms draped around the big strong wrestlers.

◆ ◆ ◆

For the life of me, I can't remember the name of the venue where the wrestling event took place, but it looked like Madison Square Garden might look after it had been left in the dryer too long.

At last the excruciating schmooze was over, and, finally, it was showtime. If the Iowa crowd had been enthusiastic, the New York crowd was turbo-charged. They grunted and yelled and put every bit of urban angst into their voices as they welcomed Tiny Tim back to his hometown.

"You warm an old man's heart," Tiny said over the microphone. "I do not even have words for how delighted I am to be back in the bosom of New York City, the only woman who has never let me down."

"Whoo, whoo, whoo, whoo, whoo…" the crowd hooted in response, lighting matches.

It was a general lovefest, with Tiny welcoming the crowd to the one and only Super Duper Extra-Spectacular World Wrestling Federation Extravaganza broadcast live over USA cable network. The crowd, in turn, was throwing roses at his feet and hugging him with their voices. Tiny took a bow and disappeared for a few rounds.

After a few rousing bouts of stomping, posing, growling, slamming, and flying through the air, the World Wrestling Federation brought Tiny out again.

"You! You call yourself a man? What in the hell is this?" In a staged skit, the wrestler, pretending to be horrified by Tiny's effeminate appearance, flicked Tiny's long hair with his fingers.

Tiny, right on cue, put his hands on his hips and began to pout.

"And who calls themselves 'Tiny,' anyway? What kind of a freako are you?" The brute poked his finger into Tiny's chest and Tiny fell backwards against the ropes in an exaggerated motion. Tiny picked up his ukulele and started to imitate the guy, grunting and stomping in circles around him, wielding his ukulele like a club.

"So, you want a piece of me, huh? Come on! Come and get me!" The wrestler grabbed the ukulele and smashed it into a million pieces while Tiny looked on in horror, screaming.

Tiny then threw a perfect fit, falling onto the mat and kicking his legs and screaming like a child having a tantrum.

"Boo! Boo! Boo!" The crowd went nuts, screaming in defense of Tiny as the wrestler continued to berate and harass him. It was hilarious. Tiny was thrilled, New York was thrilled, the WWF was happy to have him there, and the wrestlers had great fun toying with him.

◆ ◆ ◆

I was so grateful that we had survived the evening, but I had no intention of hitting the pillow. I had lived in New York for about four years myself, and I was itching to get back into the clubs. That was my first impulse, anyway. Before the evening was out and after several martinis, I was going to end up with a whole different agenda.

Sometime before morning, after I was good and liquored up, I would tell myself, hey, if Tiny won't listen to logic when it comes to Miss Jan, maybe I can come up with something no man can ignore. Proof.

See, it all came down to the core difference between Tiny Tim and me. We both believed in God, but when The Man Upstairs didn't answer my prayers quickly enough, I was not above taking matters into my own hands and trying to force the chess pieces around the board myself. Okay, so I am not a patient man, especially after a few drinks and that fire hits my belly. I am a fix-things-by-sheer-force-of-will man of action. Once in awhile it actually pays off, and even when it doesn't, the results almost always make for a good story later.

Sitting in our suite back at the Plaza, I was nursing a Scotch and water and, as I knew he would, Tiny started to yawn and droop. Yep, I thought, any minute now, he's going to announce that he needs to hit the sack right at the same moment that Jan is ready to hit the clubs and make the morning papers. I didn't care about getting my mug in the *Post,* I just wanted to see the city.

Sure enough, the fireworks began right on schedule. He was going to bed. What??? Why didn't he want to take her out? He never took her anywhere, dammit all. Was it too much for a girl to ask that her husband, who lived in another state, for Heaven's sakes, might be able to rise to the occasion and take his wife out on the town once in a million years? It's not like there was any m-o-n-e-y, you know. She didn't ask for much. He was never there for her, he was a terrible provider, and now here he was in the Big Apple for a change and he couldn't drink a damned cup of coffee and wake himself up?

"Absolutely not," Tiny said, refusing to budge. There was a

seductive sandman waiting for him in his dreams and that was all the audience Tiny wanted at that point. It had, after all, been a long night.

So the next thing I knew, Miss Wonderful, who knew I was not exactly her biggest fan, said to me, "Come on, let's go out to some clubs."

Huh? Me and her? I couldn't stand the sight of her and I knew she hated my ass. Not just my ass, but every inch of me. And the feeling was mutual.

"We won't have to stand in line. I never have to stand in line," she continued. "Everyone knows I'm Tiny Tim's wife. Come on, it will be fun."

"Imagine that," I said to her, as we climbed into a cab. "Wonder how on earth everyone figured out you're Tiny's wife. Seeing as how you keep it so quiet and all…"

What were we doing? Tiny was knocked out at the hotel, deep in dreamland, and I was riding through the streets of Manhattan with his wife — a woman I couldn't stand. We hit club after club and I downed drink after drink until even dancing with the girl I thought of as a snake seemed like fun. Two-faced? Guilty as charged. I was loaded and going with the flow. No one and nothing was going to keep me from enjoying New York. Forty-eight hours later, when I was out of there, I could pray for forgiveness, kick myself, and give myself a proper tongue-lashing. The night was still young.

Sometime near closing time and last call, I became a dog with a bone, a man with a plan, Phillip Marlowe out to crack the case of the phony wife. We were in some bar, somewhere in New York City — things were a little fuzzy then and even fuzzier now —

and neither one of us was feeling any pain. I've got her, I thought. She's drunk and opening up to me and I'm going in for the kill. I'm going to set a trap and watch her fall right in. At last, I'll have bona fide evidence to prove my belief that Mrs. Khaury Number Two didn't see her husband as anything more than a meal ticket. Which was funny, really, because when it came to Tiny's finances, a meal ticket from him is likely to land you right in the soup lines on skid row.

She was as guarded as an armored truck and I had to summon up my best fire-breathing techniques to melt her shell.

"Come on, baby, let's cut the horseshit. We've never liked each other, but maybe I've been wrong about you. I'm sure deep down you really do care for Tiny, right? I know being married to him can't be a picnic." Come on, sweetheart, come on, you can level with me. Come on, dammit! Spill the beans!

It took me about sixty seconds to go postal on her. How dare she try to trade on his name and notoriety? So what if that was all she had to work with because his name was all he had given her? So what if being married to Tiny left her totally unfulfilled emotionally and physically? Who cares if all she had to do was breathe on him and he was finished sexually?

I went totally ballistic. I know, I know, it was completely unfair. I set her up to trust me and the second she did, I let her have it. I completely unloaded on her. I told her I was wise to her, called her every gold-digging, trampy name in the book, and I finished by telling her she was a user and a bitch and ought to be ashamed of herself.

Completely out of line and totally out of control, I was fueled by my fierce devotion and loyalty to Tiny — not to mention that hundred-proof fuel called alcohol. I was like a papa bear who had caught someone messing with his cub. I had her pinned and I was mauling her with my words.

On top of everything I held against her personally, like the fact that I just flat out didn't like her and I felt she wasn't loving Tiny the way I thought he should be loved, I unloaded on her for every moment of weakness that Tiny himself had ever had. Furious at him for not sticking up for himself with promoters, agents, managers, and every parasite who had ever taken advantage of him, I took it all out on his wife. Like a hot ball of lava, my anger boiled up inside and I spewed all over her.

"If Tiny wasn't so whipped by you, he would've given you the boot a long time ago. But no… you just bat those eyelashes of yours and he gives in to you. What the f— is wrong with him, anyway? He forgives you, he prays for you, and around and around you two go on the merry-go-round from hell…"

I was looking at her but I was fighting for every underdog who had ever gotten the short end of a bone.

She was a cool one. Just like Lauren Bacall, she leveled a cold stare at me, and told me to f— off and go back to the Midwest where I belonged. Then she calmly ordered another drink, said yes to some stud who walked by and gave her the once-over, and out onto the dance floor they went.

Damn! Shit! Piss! I ran through my artillery of cuss words and could not believe that even my worst insults had bounced off her like bullets off Superman's chest. I had made no impression whatsoever. She was not even upset. I was itching for a fight but she wasn't biting.

Hopping mad, I wanted something I could use, something I could run with — or stumble, anyway — all the way back to Tiny's room at the hotel. I wanted to be able to shake him until he woke up, and say, look man, I can prove to you that she's every bit as fake as I thought she was. She doesn't give a damn about you.

As if Tiny didn't know what they did or didn't have going for them. As if I knew squat about what went on between the two of them or any of the complicated reasons any two people anywhere ever get, or stay, together.

The committee in my inebriated head was egging me on. Telling me I could find the proof I wanted, I just hadn't been looking in the right places. I needed proof. Solid, not squishy, pwoof. Yep, tha's what I need. Tiny'll lissen to real pwoof. And, dammitall, I'm gonna get some. Some what, again? Oh, yeah, some ev'dence. Then, at las', Tiny'll see he doesn't haf to baby her anymo'. He can stan' up like a man and not be manifulated anymo'. Gotta find somethin'. Hard ev'dence that would make Tiny dwop this pafetic 'scuse of a relationship once and fer all!

When I got back to the hotel, I managed to focus my eyes long enough to see the dial pad on the phone. I picked up the receiver and rang Miss Jan's apartment.

"I'm so sorry, Jan. Yer so bootifull… I so sorry, maybe you forgive me? Truf be known, I admire you, always have. Yer so purdy… Maybe I jus' jealous of what Tiny has…" I was gagging on that last line. Yeah, right. I was drunk but not that drunk. I was about as jealous of her as I'd be of a really bad case of poison ivy.

Maybe she would like to come over to the Plaza, let me get

her into bed, and then lie there nice and still while I ran, in my birthday suit, down the hall to grab Tiny and show him what his two-timing wife was doing while he counted sheep.

She was too smooth for me, warming up to me on the phone, whiling away a good half hour. Thinking back, she was probably rolling her eyes and thinking, how stupid does this guy think I am, anyway? She was probably filing her nails and balancing her checkbook while she let me think I was getting over on her.

Thinking maybe she was missing my subtle invitation, I spelled it out for her.

"Why Steve, you know I can't come over there and go to bed with you, silly. You're married! Not only that, but Tiny would not approve of your behavior, either. Not that I'm not flattered. Thanks for the offer," she stated flatly.

Damn! The room was spinning, my brain was melting and she had seen right through me.

"Besides, how do you know I'm not taping this conversation?" She teased. "Bye bye now."

Taping me? Wait a minute... that was the last thing I needed. I imagined the tape arriving in a brown paper wrapper, one copy to Tiny's room, one copy to my dear wife, back home in Iowa. Oh, no, not my wife. The same wife God had seen fit to send me after three years of being a single parent.

Oh Sandra, Sandra, you're going to kill me, aren't you? Will you ever believe the whole thing was a setup? What about Tiny? Would he think I had turned on him, too? Oh God, they would hate me, dump me, dropkick me as sure as my name is Mud.

I fell over with a plop and passed out on the bed.

In the morning, the whole nightmare woke me up and in addition to the thousands of little wooden piano hammers knocking out *Heart and Soul* in my head, there were the squirrel-caging voices. "You're screwed now. Your best friend, your wife — they're going to toss you out like yesterday's eggshells, like old coffee grounds. What in the hell were you thinking?"

Jan was on her way over to the hotel to say goodbye to Tiny before we left for our next gig.

What was I going to do? Help! I was only acting! I swear it wasn't real. Tiny and my wife would see, right? Wouldn't they see? My intentions were pure. And by the way, did anyone have any aspirin? As I was saying, my intentions were pure. Surely they would understand, right?

Bang, bang, bang. Oh my God, she was at the door of his hotel room where we were hanging out.

Cool as a cucumber, she swooped in like last night had never happened. "Goodbye my dahling, precious husband, my love. I'll miss you and think of you every second you're away. I love you so much. Be well, my love," she cooed.

I wanted to vomit, but I was too nervous to even spit. Oh no, she was headed right for me!

"It will be our little secret," she whispered as she air-kissed me, Hollywood style.

"Well, at least for now…," she teased.

♦ ♦ ♦

I'd gotten it all out on the table and I was waiting for the reactions of my wife and my best friend.

They raised their glasses in a toast to me. "Here's to lost

opportunities," Sandra and Tiny joked, when I finally told them the whole story. "And to think what might have been…" They let out an exaggerated sigh, pretending to pity me for blowing the chance to see Miss Jan under the covers. Then they laughed themselves silly. Oh well, you can't blame a guy for trying to save his best friend from himself. I couldn't ever seem to do a damn thing to save myself from my own demons, but I was perfectly willing to suit up in my dragon-slayer outfit and try to fell the big ones that Tiny couldn't handle on his own.

In 1994, Fate finally took its course and marriage number two went in the dumper. I'm talking about Tiny's marriage, not mine, although mine didn't last more than another year or two either, but that's a story for another time. Tiny officially felt like a failure. It was the longest week of our lives. Tiny wept morning, noon, and night. He gnashed his teeth, moped around, cried some more, and felt terrible when he wondered how he and Miss Jan would get along without each other. Whether I hated her or not, Miss Jan was his wife and divorce is no laughing matter.

Tiny took it hard.

As for me, I had the courtesy to do my celebrating behind his back. How sad to think there would be no more late-night arguments between them on the phone. My heart was breaking. Oh, how I would miss all his guilt trips over her. Yes, it was a sad day, indeed. No more night terrors wondering if she would show up unexpectedly at a gig. Yeah, I was downright heartsick, hearing a full-blown marching band in my head and dancing a jig. It killed me to see Tiny hurting, but I was deliriously happy.

After that agonizing seven days, Tiny left his grief behind

him and experienced a miraculous rebirth. Suddenly, he was keeping up with me on the drinking, staying up past midnight, and sowing his wild oats.

"Mister Plym, I am free! If I had known how good it would feel to be free to be me, I would have done this years ago."

Sexcapades

"…I bought Godfrey's book called
You Too Can Learn To Play Ukulele and taught myself.
It's a very romantic instrument.
You can take it on a canoe."
--Tiny Tim

"Mister Plym," Tiny would say to me, "I am the world's worst lover. All someone has to do is touch me, and I am finished. What can I do? Please help me." Tiny asked me this over and over again.

"Well, Tiny, do what most guys do. Think about something else. Think about a boring card game or some ugly chick you wouldn't want to have sex with. Anything to take your mind off your pecker," I suggested.

"Really, Mister Plym? Really? All right. Thank you. I will try it. Thank you, thank you so much. You are simply wonderful." And, as happy as a kid with a buck in his pocket for ice cream, he skipped off. It wouldn't be long before he'd be back, sulking.

"I simply could not do it. I could not take my mind off how wonderful it felt…," he said in anguish. "Three minutes, Mister Plym. That is all I could last."

Tiny decided that if he practiced enough by himself, maybe he could learn how to keep himself from exploding too early. Like a boy with a science project, he took this self-assigned experiment very much to heart, determined to get an A on the test.

"Mister Plym! Mister Plym! I have invented a new technique that may help with my — you know — my problem," he whispered.

"Yeah, man? What is it?" This guy was too much. There was nothing he wouldn't say to me.

"I discovered that if I simply switch hands when I'm touching myself, it is like I am with two women at once," he said, excitedly.

"That's great, Tiny, really great. I'm happy for you. But how is that gonna help you last longer? I don't get it," I said.

"Well, I have not yet figured that out, but it feels incredible. Two women at once! Twice as exciting."

Ultimately, no matter what he tried, he was still Quick Draw McGraw, he was still heartbroken, and his women were still frustrated. And he would always come to me looking for the answer.

I would tell him, "I wish I had a magic pill you could take, pal, but I don't know what the hell to tell you. I know it's tough, man…" My heart went out to him, but how could I help? All a girl had to do was brush up against Tiny anywhere below the belt, and that was the end of that. And we're talking with all his clothes and the lights still on. Before his date even knew what happened, the evening of lovemaking she had been fantasizing about would turn into a three-minute solo by Tiny, Junior. It was over before it even got started.

Not only did I get to hear about every girl Tiny Tim went to bed with, or tried not to go to bed with, but he would then describe every move he made, what he was thinking while he made the move, what position he was in, how it felt in that position, what she said, and what I thought she really could have been thinking in case what she said she was thinking wasn't really the whole truth.

There we would be, sitting outside his hotel room, it would be late and I'd be yawning, hoping he'd catch the hint that I was exhausted. I'd say goodnight to him and hope he'd hop out and run into the hotel. And then it would start. The long drawn-out blow-by-blow (no pun intended) playback of his latest sexcapade.

He would do a complete analysis of the whole scene, just like a sportscaster trying to reconstruct the latest game.

"Aw, too bad! Tiny Tim was dribbling a little bit too fast, and dropped the ball halfway down the court. Oh, well. And the game was off to such a promising start, too. What do you think, Bill?" That's what I would be hearing in my head as Tiny did his play-by-play for me.

"Oh, you're right, Rick, he had shown such promise last season, but wait, what is that under his shorts? Maybe that's the problem right there! That isn't a *diaper*, is it?" Then both of my imaginary announcers would be craning their necks and squinting their eyes.

"Yes, Bill, I believe you're right! Oh my God, it is a diaper! The greatest player in the league is actually wearing Depends. Unbelievable! This explains everything!"

This is how my mind would wander as Tiny was wondering what his latest girl meant when she said blah, blah, blah and what she thought he might have been thinking and how it felt when he did the old standard move with his eyes closed, and so on.

Trust me, I did not begrudge him his sexual peccadilloes or whatever the hell they were, but after a long, hard day, three hours of that crap was more than I could take. I wanted to scream, tie him up with the seat belt, rip his diaper off, and stuff it in his mouth. He drove me nuts. But, hey, I loved the guy, so I bit my tongue and I listened and listened and listened. And I nodded and gave my two cents worth and prayed it would end soon, as I watched the afternoon turn to night and the sky fill up with stars.

I knew, as hard as it was to be his prisoner during his tirades, it was harder to take the temperamental, depressed, sulking blue mood I was bound to find him in if he couldn't get this stuff out of his head. He had to talk, so I had to listen. At least when he was done talking, I could go home. At least I didn't have to live inside his head. That must have been hell. My own squirrelly brain was a bad enough neighborhood, but at least I was only visiting his brain. He actually had to live there.

♦ ♦ ♦

When it came to Tiny and sex, you never knew which side of him was going to win the battle — the pious religious man or the sexaholic. So many times I saw him make a Herculean effort to resist and it was always a sight to see, and no matter how painful, always hilarious.

There were so many events and so many women, they have all blended together in my mind, so I'm hoping you girls forgive me if I get you mixed up in my memory… Anyway, the story I'm about to tell you could have happened all on the same day or I could have borrowed a blonde from here, mixed her up with a redhead and a brunette from there, and piled them all up together, but one thing is for sure — this kind of thing happened all the time.

At a celebrity softball game one day when he was still married to Miss Jan, Tiny turned to me and said, "Oh, my goodness, Mr. Plym. I do believe these young lovelies have s-e-x on their minds, and now it's on my mind, too, not to mention other vital areas."

He was laughing and exaggeratedly spelling out the word sex for me, like he always did. Leaning his shoulder into mine like a teenage boy, he was whispering confidentially, all the while keeping his eyes fixed on a threesome of undeniably stunning girls in their twenties who couldn't take their eyes off of him.

"Ah, yes, it is definitely s-e-x. I can see it in their eyes," he would say, getting a crazed look in his own eyes. "Lord help me, for I simply must resist, but, oh, dear, did you notice the redhead? I have always had a weakness for redheads. Do you think I might be imagining things, Mr. Plym, to think that such luscious young beauties would be lusting after me?"

"No, Tiny, I'd say you're right on. They're definitely looking your way," I responded.

"Mmmm, they are intoxicating, are they not? Oh no, I cannot believe it — the blonde is signaling for me to go over there. Oh, dear, what shall I do? Lord above, save me from myself..." He was fanning his face with his hand.

The blonde, who could have been any cheerleader from anywhere, waved flirtatiously. Fidgeting in place, Tiny smiled shyly and gave her an impulsive Hollywood-style finger-wiggling wave. Holding the girl's gaze, he reached into his pocket like a man desperately searching for a clove of garlic to ward off vampires. He took out his wallet and, sighing with relief, removed his most precious possession. It was a small picture of his beloved Savior, Jesus Christ. He tore his eyes away from the young girl, looked at the picture for a long time, and then held it close to his heart. Like Samson trying to resist Delilah.

He looked back at the incredible temptresses. You know, just for a minute to make sure they were still looking. I could feel them luring him, tugging at him like the tide. Then he tore himself away again and looked at Jesus. Then he looked back at the girls, then at Jesus.

"Forgive me, Lord, and deliver me, for my flesh is weak." He was struggling, big time. And believe me, it wasn't the first time.

There was only one thing Tiny wanted more than to run right over to those girls, scoop them up in his arms, cover them in honey and whipped cream with cherries on top, and make a meal out of them. He wanted so badly to be good, to do the right thing in God's eyes. Just picturing his shoes under some little darling's bed, he saw the sky raining hellfire upon them both.

"If those girls have their way, I am about to become an

adulterous sinner," Tiny declared, dramatically. "An adulterer, Mr. Plym, just like the book about Hester Prynne wearing the Scarlet Letter. Marked for life. It is a shame that they are not just a little bit less lovely... Oh, but I really must not..." Tiny Tim fanned his face with his hand, his voice trailing off down a guilty path, no doubt thinking of Miss Jan back home.

One of the more enticing creatures blew him a kiss — like he, himself, had done so many times on stage. This girl wasn't kidding. His radiator was overheating so he loosened his tie.

"Oh, my, oh dear. I am doomed. The Lord is going to strike me down and I will burn forever. Oh, but how can a man resist when they are so willing and so very delicious?"

On the other hand, there were plenty of times when he didn't resist. And those were the times when he had to figure out how to get from wanting and courting a girl to actually being able to keep himself in check long enough to put a smile on her face. Here was a classic scenario.

"So, there she was," he would tell me, "looking like the perfect Southern belle, sitting so ladylike on that barstool, flirting with me."

"That's great, man, great. Then what happened?" And each time I would hope that maybe this time, Tiny would get the happy ending.

"Well, Mister Plym, for some reason, when I got her up to my room, she seemed to become very upset, and before I knew what happened, she had walked out of the hotel." He would always be the picture of innocence in that moment, the kid who had just robbed the liquor store swearing to the cops he had no idea what happened, as Tootsie Rolls and Snickers bars fell out of his pockets.

"Tiny, come on, man. Tell the truth. You did your usual, didn't you?" I knew him too well.

"Why Mister Plym, what do you mean?" He would ask me, pouting.

"You know, Tiny, your usual. Quoting Bible sermons to the chick and running down your list of all the great reasons you really shouldn't be doing the do. You know, your usual." I said.

At this point, he would always start giggling. "I was simply reminding us both why we should not engage in fornication…"

"F—ing A, man. And you wonder why she ran out of your room? That's some foreplay, Tiny. You're a smooth one, all right." I shook my head.

Tiny would just give me a shy smile and giggle. He was a total flop in the Casanova department.

♦ ♦ ♦

One day Tiny asked me, "Do you think I should talk dirty to women, Mister Plym? Do they honestly like that? And what kinds of things should I say?"

"You know what, pal? Anything you say has gotta be more of a turn-on than reading scary scriptures from the Bible. What exactly are you reading anyway?" I was afraid to ask.

Here's what would happen. Tiny and some little kitten would

end up in his hotel room. He would tell them that it was against God's laws for them to have sex and that absolutely under no circumstances was that going to happen.

"I do not wish to go all the way, but perhaps I could give you a massage...," he would offer. With one hand, he would pour lotion on the girl's back and begin massaging her. With the other hand, he would grab the Bible and in dead seriousness and earnestness, he would share with her the religious basis for why fornication — if he was single at the time, or adultery, if he was married at the time — was evil, sinful, and wrong. Well, okay, maybe just a bit of touching and maybe taking off just one pants leg or undoing her bra....

Believe me, no one was more surprised than Tiny when they actually ended up having sex — or his Evelyn Wood Speed Climaxing version of sex, anyway. He honestly never, ever planned to "go all the way."

After his quick performance and whatever he could dream up to try to make up for the woman's or girl's sexual frustration, he would top off the date in a most memorable way.

"Well, now we have done it. We are both going to hell. I am afraid you must get dressed and leave immediately." This was his standard pillow-talk line. So much for a hug and a cigarette afterwards.

"What???" The poor naked girl would say in disbelief.

"The devil is among us now. The spirit of lust. You must get out of here at once. I can never see you again," Tiny would declare.

Shocked, the chick would say, "You've got to be kidding

me. We've just slept together and now you're telling me we can never see each other again and throwing me out? What in the hell is the matter with you?"

"It is not that I do not like you, I do. That is precisely the problem. We have just proven that we cannot resist our attraction to each other, and I must never see you again. That is the only way I can be sure not to fall into temptation again." It made perfect sense to him.

♦ ♦ ♦

To make matters even worse, Tiny was absolutely stark raving madly in love with females. And everywhere he went, they were all over him — constant reminders of the one feat he could never accomplish, the one performance he could never really perfect. They fell from the trees, jumped from cars, leapt from barstools and landed in his arms, ready to be serenaded and swept off their feet by a real live celebrity.

"I know it is not because I am good looking," he would say to me. "I know how awful I look. They just want to get next to my money and fame. I may have fame, but if they are looking for money, they have disappointment in their future."

We'd have a good laugh over that one. Underneath the laughter, my dear friend was in agony. All the poor guy wanted was that pounding-your-chest-with-your-fists-like-Tarzan kind of feeling a guy gets when he's sent a woman through the roof sexually.

Poor Tiny, so taken with women, so many of them to choose from, and absolutely incapable of any kind of follow-through. He was like a man with a sweet tooth waking up every morning with his hands tied behind his back, his teeth missing, and every cheesecake, chocolate mousse, cherry pie, and scrumptious dessert you can think of just sitting on his table. Close enough to smell and taste, but knowing there wasn't a damn thing he could do about it.

By the way, when I say women, I don't necessarily mean the adult version of a female. The women Tiny loved most of all were just the other side of puberty and not quite over that line they call legal. Fifteen-, sixteen-, seventeen-year-old girls. He was the kind of guy Nabokov had in mind when he wrote *Lolita.* Tiny loved them fresh, innocent, and completely inexperienced. Of course, he hated himself for it, and prayed for deliverance, only to find himself over and over again intoxicated by the allure of some girl who may or may not even be old enough to get her driver's license.

"It is a curse, I know, but no matter how I pray, I cannot seem to help myself," he would admit.

One day he decided the only possible solution was to go out and purchase marital aids. A dildo soon became as much a part of his relationships as candlelight, soft music, and roses would be for a woman who was with any man other than Tiny Tim.

◆ ◆ ◆

Tiny Tidbit: On the one hand, Tiny wouldn't have sex
with anyone who used birth control and refused to use
it himself because he believed that the only kind of sex
that God did not forbid was sex for making babies.
On the other hand, he absolutely did not want to be making

any babies, so every time he had unprotected sex,
he would pray as hard as he could that their sinful
sex act did not result in a pregnancy.

◆ ◆ ◆

It was like Tiny Tim had an angel on one shoulder and a devil on the other, and his entire life was spent in the middle of a shouting match between the two. Usually, he replaced God's voice with the scary voice of whatever fire and brimstone televangelist happened to be on TV that day, telling him he was going straight to hell if he spent one more minute listening to the devil. More than anything, he just wanted to cover his ears so he couldn't hear either voice. All he ever wanted was a moment's peace, and I'm not sure he ever got that much.

Something hit me the other day. Maybe Tiny's sexual obsessions, his sexual performance problems, and his religious fears and convictions were really three different faces of the same beast. It makes perfect sense if you think about it. Let's say you're Tiny Tim and at the deepest core of your being, you believe that a fiery lake of damnation is going to become your permanent home if you give in to your sexual obsessions.

Maybe Tiny's body was just responding to his soul and that's why he couldn't last more than a few seconds. Maybe it wasn't his body that couldn't last more than a few minutes during sex — maybe it was his tortured mind and soul. Believe me, if I literally took a mental trip through hell every time I got excited by a chick, I'd want it over with as quickly as possible, too. It would sort of take the fun out of it, don't you think?

See, there was some sort of beautiful sense to it all. His body had figured out a way to rescue him from himself. His psyche had come up with a system where he could meet Miss Sexually Desirable, alternate between torture and guilt for awhile, and get off instantly. It sped up the process so he could get right on to the remorse and repentance part of the program. That way, after fifty or sixty showers to wash off the guilt, he would feel normal again. At least until the next female caught his eye.

♦ ♦ ♦

Honestly, considering how attached Tiny was to his clothes, especially his suit jacket and tie, it's a miracle he ever got naked with a woman. He was not just shy, he was deathly afraid of ever being seen totally nude. In the twenty-five years I knew him, he never once let me see him without a full suit of clothes on. Don't get me wrong, it's not that I was interested, but you know, in the normal course of life, two guys who hang out together a lot would probably end up catching a glimpse of each other in their underwear, or in this case, in his diaper — coming out of the shower, running to answer the phone, you know.

Not with Tiny. I'm not joking when I say I never even saw him without his tie. Any guy who sleeps in a tie must be a regular laugh riot in bed with a woman. Can't you just imagine this scene...?

Tiny Tim has some little vixen waiting for him on his hotel room bed. She has slipped into something more comfortable and is posed seductively on the bed...

137

He sidles over to the bed, John Wayne style, unbuckles his belt, drops his pants and there he is in all his glory. His long stringy hair, his beer belly, and his long legs poking out of an oversized plastic diaper.

And with a whip of the hand, he would fling his diaper off, toss it into the air, watch it land on the light fixture, smile at the girl, and say, "Thank God for Velcro."

Remember, Tiny Tim was a professional. Don't try this at home.

Tiny Tim is stricken during 'Tulips,' dies

The last thing he heard was applause, says the widow of the falsetto-voiced crooner.

Minneapolis, Minn. (AP) — Tiny Tim, the ukulele-plunking crooner who bemused and amused millions by trilling the whimsical "Tiptoe Thru' the Tulips," died after falling ill while singing his signature song.

The singer, who had a history of heart trouble, was stricken Saturday night during a benefit for the Woman's Club of Minneapolis. His widow, Susan Khaury, said he cut short "Tulips" and told her he was not well. She was trying to help him back to their table when he collapsed.

"I don't think he had time to feel pain," Susan Khaury said Sunday. "He died singing 'Tiptoe Thru' the Tulips,' and the last thing he heard was the applause, and the last thing he saw was me."

Tiny Tim died at a Minneapolis hospital late Saturday. A hospital spokeswoman said the cause apparently was cardiac arrest, but a final determination was to be made later.

Tiny Tim said a few weeks ago that he was born April 12, 1932, making him 64, although over the years he had sometimes hedged about his age. The World Almanac lists his birth date as April 12, 1923, which would have made him 73.

Born Herbert Khaury, Tiny Tim built his career on his single hit song in 1968, his stratospheric falsetto, an asexual and childlike stage persona and a flair for self-promotion.

The 6-foot-1-inch entertainer with

LIVED IN DES MOINES

Tiny Tim lived in Des Moines in the early 1990s, staying downtown at the Savery and Fort Des Moines hotels and performing at such nightspots as the now-closed Holiday Inn South on Fleur Drive.

Tiny Tim, who moved to Iowa at the urging of his Des Moines management team, said he found the city to be a peaceful place and "a God-fearing community."

The most memorable event of his stay may have been the time one of his trademark ukuleles was taken during an October 1992 appearance in the Court Avenue district.

A Des Moines woman found the ukulele the next day. She got a phone call and $100 reward from the entertainer.

long, frizzy hair was given his stage name in 1960 by an agent who had been working with midget acts. He made his first national television appearance on "Rowan and Martin's Laugh-in."

His 1969 marriage to Vicki Budinger on Johnny Carson's "The Tonight Show" attracted 40 million viewers. They had a daughter, Tulip Victoria, before they divorced.

After Tiny Tim and Susan Khaury, his third wife, were married in 1995, he moved here from Des Moines. His funeral will be here Wednesday.

Tiny entertains a captivated audience at Steve Plym's home in Des Moines, Iowa

Signing autographs after a show. "Sammy Davis, Jr."
look-alike followed Tiny around all evening!

Tiny and Steve's dad were great beer-drinking pals

Tiny listens intently to Steve's mother about taking care of his health

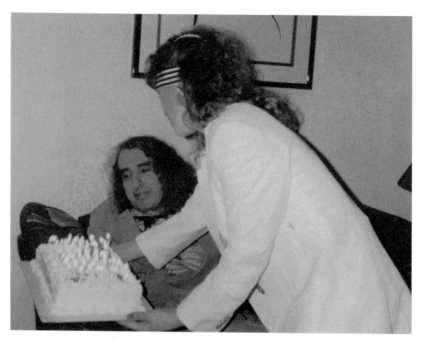

Tiny gets his birthday cake from Steve's "ex"

How many candles are there on Tiny's Birthday cake?

"Miss Sue" walks
down the aisle

Sculptured "Uke"
at wedding to
"Miss Sue"

Herbert Khaury marries
Sue Gardner:
Tiny's third go-round --
Sue's first time

Mr. and Mrs. Gardner...
"Miss Sue's" mom
and dad

"Miss Sue" and Tiny recite vows

Seven wedding cakes

Presenting ... Mr. & Mrs. Herbert Khaury!

"Miss Sue" and her proud father

"Delight yourself in the Lord
and He will give you the
desires of your heart."

The Marriage Ceremony
of
Susan Marie Gardner
and
Herbert Butros Khaury

Friday, August 18, 1995

Immaculate Heart of Mary Church
Minnetonka, Minnesota

Tiny telling show-biz stories till the
wee hours of the morning

Tiny in his favorite chair at Steve Plym's home,
posing with Steve's dad, mom, sister, and Steve

Tiny chatting with Steve's daughter, Chyenne

Tiny hanging out at the
Plym home

Tiny with Steve's son, S.P.

Tiny, with beer in hand, gets in the mood for Santa's visit

Tiny's Birthday Party

Tiny, straw and glass of wine, a dangerous mixture

TinyTimTimes

APRIL
1994
#9

THE OFFICIAL NEWSLETTER OF THE TINY TIM FAN CLUB

MISS JAN SEEKS DIVORCE!

This year marks the 10th anniversary of Tiny Tim's marriage to his second wife, Jan Alweiss, but on March 15, Miss Jan formally announced that she wants a divorce. In an exclusive interview, Tiny Tim told the TIMES about this recent development: "She called me up less than an hour ago and said to me, 'We'll soon have our divorce, dear.' I said, 'I beg your pardon?' And she said, 'Yes, I think we should get our divorce to avoid the expenses that the lawyers are going to charge.' Well I said to her, 'Look, I am not getting a divorce. I did not give one to Miss Vicki, and I am certainly not going to give you one.' When Miss Vicki filed for divorce in 1977, I was living in Florida at the time and couldn't afford to to come up and contest it, so the state of Jersey gave her the divorce, not I... If Miss Jan wants to send me a subpoena, she can go ahead and send it, but I am not giving her a divorce, because once I divorce her she can say, 'See, no matter what the reason, he quit.' Besideds, as you wrote in the last issue, if I can't be true to Miss Jan then I can't be true to Miss Stephanie or anybody else... If she wants a divorce, she'll have to let the state of New York give it to her." Tiny continued his diatribe by comparing his wife to an old song: "Miss Jan reminds me of a song called What Do You Do Sunday, Mary?, written by Irving Ceaser & Stephan Jones, and sung by the late great Billy Murray of the American Quartet in 1920. It goes:

'Mary you have not been so kind, Mary, there's something on my mind. Gladly would I believe you, dearest, if I but knew of all the things you do. What do you do Sunday, what do you do Monday, Mary?

What do you do Tuesday, what do you do Wednesday, Mary? When it's my payday, deary, you can be found. But what do you do Mary, all week 'round?' etc. Now I could insert Miss Jan's name in place of Mary, because these are the same questions I've been asking her since 1984."

With Miss Jan: After Miss Vicki

Whereas Tiny's first marriage to Miss Vicki was viewed by an estimated 40 million people, Tiny and Miss Jan were wed at the Imperial Palace hotel in Las Vegas by a justice of the peace. They were married on June 26th, 1984, just six months after first meeting each other at a 1983 Christmas party. The marriage showed signs of trouble during its first year, and the couple have been living separately for the last several years. Miss Jan is a graphic arts designer, residing in New York.

Tiny Tim Times JANUARY 1994 #6

THE OFFICIAL NEWSLETTER OF THE TINY TIM FAN CLUB

Greetings

Welcome to a New Year and a new issue of TINY TIM TIMES. Formerly the newsletter of the Lawrence, Kansas Tiny Tim fan club, T.T.T. is now the official newsletter of of the international Tiny Tim fan club in Dallas, TX. Several months ago I received a letter from Tiny Tim's Australian producer, Martin Sharp, who wrote, "Somehow we have all got to pull together to give Tiny our best support... I don't know how we can do this; perhaps we should hold a convention or develop some effective network." It is my hope that an effective network can be established through the Tiny Tim fan club, by having the newsletter serve as a connecting point for the various Tiny Tim fans scattered throughout the country and the world. I hope that through TINY TIM TIMES we Tiny fans can get better acquainted by sharing our thoughts, feelings, and reminiscences about Tiny Tim. Therefore, I encourage Tiny fans everywhere to keep the contributions coming. This month I happily received enough submissions to make another 8-page double issue! The cover photo was sent to me by Nick Bougas of Burbank, California, and inside is a newspaper clipping from Chicago, and a lovely tour review from Boston. Thanks

to all who contributed, and special thanks to Charles Brown for his careful editing work.

One of the things that the new TINY TIM TIMES will be featuring is a monthly schedule of Tiny's upcoming shows, so that we can know in advance when & where to see him. Unfortun-

ately, all of his January shows have been cancelled, as Tiny is currently rehearsing a new act. We'll keep you posted. Also, I'm hoping that the new T.T.T. can continue to be 8 pages or more per issue, so I'm counting on you readers to keep sending new material. If there is anything you wish to contribute, send it to: TINY TIM TIMES, 1432 Brook, Lawrece, KS 66044. For fan club information write to the Tiny Tim fan club address, which is printed on the back. Let's give Tiny Tim our collective support and help make 1994 his biggest year since '68. Thanks. Gregor P. Brune

Mr. and Mrs. Steve Plym

*T*here's nothing nicer
to be said
To a special pair like you
Than to wish you more
of the joys you bring
Each other all year through,
So enjoy your anniversary
To the fullest while it's here,
And may you find it starts you
On another happy year!

Sincerly

Tony Tan

Dec 19 1994

HOWARD STERN'S NEW YEAR'S EVE PAGEANT

Mr. Herbert Khaury   December 17, 1993
C/O Steve Plym
8992 Carpenter Circle Drives
Desmoines, Iowa 50265

Dear Tiny Tim:

Thank you for your participation in the Howard Stern New Year's
Eve Pageant. We are looking forward to an exciting and memorable
show!

Enclosed find yours and Steve Plym's airline ticket and travel
information for your involvement in the show.

While in New York, you will be staying at:

        Michelangelo
        152 West 51st Street
        New York, NY 10019
        212-765-1900
        212-541-6604 Fax

Your rooms are booked under Herbert Khaury & Steve Plym.

You will be met at the gate upon your arrival into Newark Airport
by a talent escort.   They will be holding a sign that reads "New
Year's Eve." Your escort will bring you to the hotel, and will
give you your rehearsal schedule.

Everyone appearing on the show will be wearing black tie. We
will be providing one for you unless you choose to bring your own
(must be black). Steve does not need to wear black tie but
should dress accordingly.

If you have any questions, please feel free to call either of us
at 212-730-4827.

Have a safe trip, and we look forward to meeting you.

Regards,

Karen Tasch-Weiss
Elise Frankovitz
Talent Coordinators

Tiny poses for fans outside a Des Moines nightclub

Tiny, all smiles, just had a great show

Tiny poses in Las Vegas with Buddy Ebson from *The Beverly Hillbillies*
and *Barnaby Jones* fame.
Tiny's first comment: "Where's Miss Ellie May?"

The Hagar Twins from *Hee-Haw* and some cute dancers
meet up with Tiny in Vegas

APRIL 8 1993

DEAR MR STEPHEN FLYN

Thank you for your
very nice Birthday Card
and money gift.

I will never forget
your kindness.

Thanks again

Mrs. Betty Plym

For all the thoughtful things
That you so often say and do,
This brings a world of special thanks
Especially for you.

Thanks again for
the beautiful pillow you
made me.
love Tim

APRIL 14 1993

Steve and Tiny with Stan Reynolds, President of Variety Clubs International

Tiny stars in Iowa Variety Club Telethon, the largest
showbiz telethon for children

STATE OF KANSAS

JIM CATES
REPRESENTATIVE, 52ND DISTRICT

STATE CAPITOL
TOPEKA, KANSAS 66612
(913) 296-7692
6850 Aylesbury
5800 W. 31ST TERR
TOPEKA, KANSAS 66614-10
(913) 272-7616

COMMITTEE ASSIGNMENTS
MEMBER: COMMERCIAL AND FINANCIAL
INSTITUTIONS
ELECTIONS
FEDERAL AND STATE AFFAIRS

TOPEKA

HOUSE OF
REPRESENTATIVES

1-18-93

Stur + Jany,

Wanted to drop you a note on Tiny
Tim appearance in Topeka. On a
scale of 1-10, the evening would score
a solid 10.

Cold Sweat was well received.
Tiny received warm standing ovations
through out the evening and the owners
found him to be a delight to work with.
His willingness to sign autographs, stand
for pictures etc throughout the evening made
it a very pleasurable experience for
every one.

Also, if a 3rd party reference is ever
needed regarding a Tiny Tim performance, don't
hesitate to contact me if I can be of
assistance.

Hope will be in contact again

Jim

January 21, 1993

Stephen Plym
Entertainment America of Iowa, Inc.

Larry King Show--

Dear Stephen:

This will confirm the appearance of Tiny Tim on the
Larry King Show.

The Larry King show will be broadcasting from "Duke
Zeibert's Restaurant at 1050 Connecticut Avenue N.W.
on Thursday, January 28th.

We will be celebrating 15 years on the Mutual Broadcasting
Network... Tiny is confirmed for 11:45p.m segment..

If you need to reach me please call 703-413-3475...

Please tell Joe thanks for all his help..

Regards

Judith Thomas
Associate Producer
via fax 515-287-6836

ROWAN & MARTiN'S LAUGH-iN

25th Anniversary Party
Friday, January 15, 1993
Loews Santa Monica Beach Hotel
1700 Ocean Avenue, Santa Monica

Lobby
Cocktails at 5:30 p.m.
Ballroom
Press Conference at 6:30 p.m.
Dinner at 7:30 p.m.

Say hello to old friends and exchange
wonderful memories with the original cast and guest stars.

RSVP Tera Yahm, NBC (818)840-4661

NON-TRANSFERRABLE

Entertainment
America
_{of} **Iowa, Inc.**

mo Plym

Keep on Smiling

Tiny Tim

Oct 7 1992

First promotion package Steve put together for Tiny when he moved to Iowa

INTERNATIONALLY ACCLAIMED
RECORDING & TELEVISION PERSONALITY
"TINY TIM"

MANAGEMENT
Stephen M. Plym
515-221-1748
515-266-1866

From Steve's first promotion package for Tiny when he moved to Des Moines, Iowa

Tiny Tim marries Miss Vicki on *The Tonight Show*

Here's Johnny, one last time

The Associated Press

BURBANK, Calif. — Johnny Carson ended his 30-year reign on late-night television Friday, choking back tears as he closed his final "Tonight Show" by telling America, "I bid you a very heartfelt good night."

Longtime sidekick Ed McMahon yelled the traditional "Heeeere's Johnny" at the start of the show, and Doc Severinsen struck up the NBC Orchestra. But little else was the same during Carson's farewell broadcast, with no big-name guests and an invitation-only audience of family and staff.

Carson, 66, began by introducing his wife, Alex, and sons Chris and Cory — and remembering his son Richard, who was killed in a car accident last year.

Carson delivered his last monologue sitting on a stool instead of standing on the star that marked his spot on the floor of NBC's Studio One. Then came clips from memorable interviews.

He told the audience that the best thing to come of his final broadcast was that, "You won't have to see or read one more story about the end of this show. . . . The end of the Soviet Union didn't get this much press."

At the end, the audience rose to its feet. Many cried. The band played "I'll Be Seeing You."

Preliminary ratings indicated that 23 million people — 42 percent of the viewing audience at that hour — watched. The highest rated "Tonight Show" was in 1969, when 45 million saw singer Tiny Tim marry Miss Vicki.

Tiny Tim Meets The King

Tiny fact: Tiny got the name "Tiny Tim" from an
agent of his early in his career in New York City.
There were auditions being held for midgets.
Tiny — a big man at six feet, one or two inches tall —
went to the small people's audition under the
new moniker, Tiny Tim.
He got the job, and kept the nickname.

It was all over the papers. The King was going to be holding court, and that could only mean one thing. It was going to be the world's greatest schmooze, and everyone who was anyone would be coming to bow at the King's throne. Show business royalty, political heavyweights, and every mucky-muck from Hollywood to Washington, D.C. was sure to be there.

The night promised to be a twenty-four-carat event, complete with the favorite indoor sports of the rich, powerful, and famous. You know — hand-shaking, double-talking, boot-licking, elbow-rubbing, and more fake smiling and air kissing than your average run for the Presidency. The event was Larry King's Fifteenth Anniversary Radio Show and, for Tiny Tim, it was a photo and publicity opportunity to die for. I was foaming at the mouth just thinking about getting Tiny in the same room with all the different luminaries that were scheduled to appear.

Not only did it promise to be a night to remember, but considering the serious mingling possibilities, who knew what else could come of it? When you get that many powerful people in a room and give them a little bit to drink, you can make handshake deals that will change your entire future before you can even get that tiny little fork with the shrimp cocktail into your mouth.

If I could just get Tiny on the bill, it might result in the kind of payoff that just keeps on paying off. Domino number one? The show itself. Get that in the bag and, with a little luck, all the other dominoes — credibility, national exposure, gigs, and m-o-n-e-y — would fall into place without us having to lift a finger. Those were always the carrots we were after. Any time we had the opportunity to capture all of those elusive things at the same time, it was like having your horse come in first.

Like I've said before, Tiny was a guy who couldn't hold on to money if it was glued to his hands, so we were always looking for more. Where did it go? What did he have to show for it? How did he lose it so fast? No one could say for sure. He would just look at me innocently and then shrug, with thousands of dollars worth of cologne and French youth lotions and potions dripping from his body.

♦ ♦ ♦

For the Larry King Anniversary Show, Tiny and I were in that position that sets your teeth on edge and makes you cringe. It's a position every manager and artist tries to avoid at all costs — when you realize the powers that be are not knocking on your door and you're going to have to figure out how to ask for something without looking like you care one way or another whether or not they give it to you. Or worse, like you need it.

Here's how it works. In a perfect world, they are ringing

your phone off the hook, plying you with plane tickets and hotel suites. They send you baskets of orchids and Godiva chocolates and specialty foods that are so rare and expensive, you never open them because you have no idea what they are or what will happen if you open the lid.

It was Heaven when that happened, but that kind of Heaven hadn't happened to Tiny Tim in twenty years. That's A-List treatment. And although he still had a certain amount of clout and name recognition, by then — I think it was 1993 or so — Tiny was definitely further down in the alphabet than the A's — closer to the c-a-t-s and d-o-g-s. That meant we were going to have to take whatever we could get.

I had no choice but to pick up the phone.

Anyway, I figured, what the hell? Once you've been locked in a room with monosyllabic, patent-leather-shoe-wearing mafioso type guys that have the pin halfway out of a hand grenade (you guessed it — a business deal gone bad), you realize there's fear and then there's fear with a capital F.

I held my breath, and rolled the dice. "Um, yes, this is Stephen Plym... you know, Tiny Tim's manager?"

Once it was determined that I was fine and they were too and that it was indeed great weather we were having, I started to put on the squeeze.

"The reason I'm calling is that the huge Fifteenth Anniversary Radio Show Larry King is planning is all over the press and we just wanted to say that we love the idea. You must be so excited..." I paused to let her show her excitement.

Nothing.

"Well, anyway, I'm not sure if you realize this or not, but

Tiny Tim happens to be one of Mr. King's biggest fans. He has nothing but respect and admiration for him. He thinks Mr. King is the greatest…"

She said all the right things and was the picture of politeness, but I knew that she knew I was working her. She was waiting for me to get to the bottom line.

"Tiny is probably his number one fan." I kept repeating the same sentiment, thinking come on, dammit! Take the bait! I wasn't exactly being subtle.

All I got in return were some polite um-hmms and phrases like "how sweet" and "isn't that nice!"

"It would be such an honor for Tiny Tim to be able to show his respect for Mr. King. It would be a real thrill…" I was running out of patience.

They said they would have to give the matter some thought.

Over the next week, I kept calling and they kept passing the buck around the office. They eventually threw us a bone — no plane tickets, no hotel room, no limousine or car service coming to pick us up, just a bone. Basically, if we wanted to show up, they wouldn't slam the door in our faces. Big of them.

You know what? I didn't care. Even their lack of enthusiasm, lack of respect, and begrudging invitation couldn't spoil the fact that Tiny was going to be downright slaphappy when he found out the news. His excitement was reward enough for me.

♦ ♦ ♦

Just as I knew he would be, my pal was completely ecstatic when I told him the news and I would have sooner cut off my right arm than tell him that they had been lukewarm in extending the invitation to the gig.

"Mr. Plym, you are wonderful, wonderful, simply the best. How did you ever get me on this program?" Tiny asked me this with his eyes wide and an equally wide smile. He was genuinely shocked. "Are you certain they really want me?"

I assured him, saying, "Of course. Absolutely. No question about it. When Larry King heard that you were going to take the time to attend and help him celebrate his fifteenth anniversary... well, Tiny, he was speechless." Yeah, that's for sure. No one said much of anything. "Everyone knows what an original you are and how much sparkle you will add to the cast line-up. You know everyone loves you, man."

♦ ♦ ♦

All that stuff I had told Larry King's office about how highly Tiny Tim thought of him — every word of it was true. Tiny really was a huge fan. The fact that he was going to meet Larry King — by personal, sincere, heartfelt invitation, or so he thought — meant so much to him.

"Do you realize what a great gift he has, Mister Plym? Mr. King is truly a genius, a consummate interviewer and host. And oh, that speaking voice! Such resonance," Tiny pointed out to me while we were in the air.

"Yeah, a regular modern day Howard Cosell, isn't that what you always say? He's a tell-it-like-it-is kind of guy."

Tiny laughed. "Yes, that he is. That he is."

We had no idea exactly how candid he could be.

♦ ♦ ♦

We arrived at Duke Ziebart's famous Washington, D.C. restaurant, the site of the whole gala affair, at about 8:00 p.m. Tiny wasn't supposed to be on the air until much later but we wanted to get a head start on the evening and make sure we got ringside seats for the dog-and-pony show.

Walking through the main dining room, we were greeted by the Duke himself. He was very warm and gracious to us, extending his hand and his hospitality. He got the whole shindig off to a good start by gushing over Tiny, saying he was a big fan, and kidding around with him a bit. Duke Ziebart was a class act all the way.

We were then escorted to the back of the restaurant where a buffet table was overflowing with drinks and a veritable tapestry of gastronomic delights.

As we lingered around the food and drinks, the guests started to turn their heads. Soon, the entire room was staring at Tiny Tim. One by one, they recovered from the shock of seeing him and started to move in his direction, waving, smiling, and calling his name. Did he know they had seen him marry Miss Vicki on Johnny Carson? Ah, Johnny Carson. What a wonderful man. They all looked at each other and nodded and got dreamy-eyed thinking about how they had all grown up watching Johnny. Anyway, what a television moment Tiny's wedding was, wasn't it? They put their arms around his shoulders and asked, where was the lovely Miss Vicki, anyway?

Oh dear, the marriage was kaput? What? How many years ago? Well, they were awfully sorry to hear that, but if it wasn't too personal, just out of curiosity, how long did the marriage last anyway? Anyway, as it turned out, nearly every person there had always been a great fan of Tiny Tim's. Imagine that! It was hard to believe but hey, everyone said they were his biggest fan, and we all know that Hollywood types never, ever say anything they don't mean.

Tiny was in his element. He smiled and drank in their compliments like a tulip drinks in the sun. He did his best eyelash batting, head lowering, and blushing.

There was Tiny at a table, surrounded by all his favorite things — adoring fans, plenty of incredible food, and a trick bottle of wine that filled itself back up the minute it got empty. With everyone hanging on his every word, he was on fire.

Right on cue, he would grab his brown grocery bag and say, "Wait! That reminds me of a beautiful song." Then he would produce his famous ukulele. Everyone would ooh and aah to see his legendary instrument emerging from a paper bag. "I must give you a snippet of the song. Would you mind terribly?"

Mind? In fact, they insisted that he play them a tune. The hours ticked down and nobody noticed. Everyone was shocked and amazed when they heard that baritone voice coming from the most famous falsetto in the history of pop music.

On evenings like that one, he would always ask me later, in a confidential tone, How is it my absolute biggest fans have never been to even one of my live shows?" And we would laugh and shake our heads.

♦ ♦ ♦

Eventually, I had to drag Tiny away from his adoring mob. Left to his own devices, he would have kept everyone sitting at that table for a week, asleep in their cocktails, their evening wear wrinkled and wilted and their hairdos drooping. A *Washington Post* reporter had just gotten my two cents worth and now he wanted to talk to Tiny Tim. The reporter was not disappointed. Tiny was at his best. He talked a mile a minute, infusing all his words with charm, humor and eccentricity and, as he talked, a circle of onlookers gathered around him, until he was again, literally, the center of attention.

As Tiny was finishing up the interview, the King himself

walked by. I figured I'd better nab him and introduce him to Tiny before the cat got out of the bag and Tiny figured out that maybe Larry King had not personally requested his presence after all. Seeing my chance, I pushed my way to the front of the crowd.

After I'd shaken his hand, Larry King turned to Tiny Tim, looked him up and down, and half-heartedly said something to the effect of, "Yeah, Tiny Tim, how are ya?" Suddenly I was sorry I hadn't leveled with Tiny about what I'd had to go through to get him on the bill.

After shaking hands with Tiny, Larry King quickly turned around and as he did, the evening turned around, too. As King walked away, it became perfectly clear that I'd better dismiss any delusions I'd had of a warm and fuzzy interview between Tiny and Larry King. Tiny just stood there, all six foot two of him, watching Larry King walk away, like a little kid who can't understand why the bigger kids won't let him tag along.

Tiny gave me a hangdog look that just killed me, a look I knew really well.

If there was one thing I knew for sure, it was that I had to get that expression off Tiny's face before his brain caught on and started doing cartwheels and backflips. If I didn't get him back to thinking and feeling positive pronto, he would wear those bad vibes all night — like long pieces of last night's spaghetti clinging to the front of his shirt.

Suddenly, I saw the perfect solution standing by the bar.

"Tiny, don't look now," I whispered in urgent tones, "but that just happens to be a very important politician over there. And you know what, man? He's dyin' to meet you."

Tiny perked up a little. "Honestly, Mister Plym? Where?"

"Over there, Tiny." I pointed. "It's George Mitchell. Do you know who he is?"

Nope, Tiny didn't have the faintest idea. I quickly clued him in. "I don't think you realize how well known and well respected he is. He's a major national figure."

"And he truly wishes to meet me?" Tiny was, understandably, a little bit suspicious at this point.

"Yeah, Tiny, I swear. Anyway, listen, it's important you remember that he's a Democrat, got that? Don't screw that up because it'll be very embarrassing if you do. When it comes to mixing up which political party they're in, these guys have no sense of humor, okay?"

"Yes. Right. A Democrat. Yes, Mister Plym, I will remember." Tiny promised.

"Now," I said, as we walked in the direction of the senator, "he's from Maine. You can break the ice by mentioning that."

So, I stood them face to face and said, "Tiny Tim, I'd like you to meet Senator George Mitchell…"

Tiny Tim extended his hand and made me proud. "Senator Mitchell, it is so wonderful to meet you, one of the nation's Democratic standard bearers from the great state of Maine. It is truly a pleasure. And how I love Maine, one of my favorite places to visit. This is an honor, truly an honor."

Wow. I couldn't believe it. I guess I had misjudged Tiny's state of mind. Maybe Larry King's grunted hello hadn't spun him after all. Just as if they were old fishing buddies, Tiny and the senator talked for about fifteen minutes. Someone suggested a photo and the senator politely cooperated, and, to this day, I've got that photo of Senator Mitchell, with one arm around me and the other around

Tiny, hanging on my wall.

Later, Tiny joked to me, "Wait until the good Senator's people back home in Maine see him posing with the one and only Tiny Tim. I hope he's not up for re-election soon."

"Re-election? After a photograph with you, he'll be lucky if they don't run him out of town. You know, Maine Senator mysteriously resigns. News at eleven." We had a good laugh over that.

Next thing we knew, we were standing next to Bernard Shaw, correspondent for CNN. Then we met Pat Buchanan. They were both very warm and cordial to Tiny and me, and Tiny seemed to have forgotten all about the earlier King disappointment. Thank God, the incident hadn't done any real damage.

I pulled Tiny aside and said to him, "Look, man, Senator Mitchell, Pat Buchanan, Bernard Shaw, they all love you. I'll bet Larry King was just in a hurry, or maybe even in a bad mood. Can't you just imagine all he has on his mind tonight? Everyone here has come to see him and they all want a piece of him. He's gotta be under a lot of pressure. But see, everyone loves you!"

One of the great things about Tiny was that he was always willing to see the glass half full. As long as that little troll that liked to run his brain wasn't wreaking havoc, Tiny didn't take much prompting to see the sunny side of life, as the song goes.

"You are probably absolutely right," he agreed. "He was undoubtedly just in a rush. I bet it was nothing."

"Yeah, that's the spirit, Tiny. It was nothing. I just know you'll have a great interview with him. I have a really good feeling about it," I lied. I wasn't sure whether I was trying to convince Tiny or me, but I decided to just continue with the theme of the evening which was "think positive."

As Tiny was waiting in the wings for his turn at the microphone, Don Rickles called in to congratulate Larry King over the airwaves. Rickles got wind of the fact that Tiny was up next and true to form, he started razzing Tiny about his age, saying, "How old are you now, Tiny? Seventy-two?" Ha ha ha. The next thing we knew, Tiny's turn was finally up.

"Give 'em your best shot, Tiny," I coached from the sidelines. "I'm really proud of you, pal!"

I will never know exactly what happened over the next fifteen minutes. You know what it's like watching a car wreck — you can't remember exactly what happened or when and what color the lights were at the time. All you take away from the crash site is a dizzy feeling in your head, the realization that something really bad just happened and you're going to be messed up over it for awhile, and the feeling that you need to lie down.

I don't remember exactly what was said, but it was something to the effect of, "Okay, Tiny Tim, give us the straight story. The weird clothes, the crazy hair, the high voice. It can't be for real. Is it all an act? Who are you kidding, anyway?" He immediately put Tiny on the defensive. It was like he was an investigative journalist trying to expose some crooked politician. What did he mean, was it all an act? Of course it was an act. Tiny Tim was a performer, for God's sake.

To say I was dumbfounded would be a huge understatement. I had brought my best friend here for this?

Larry King might as well have said, "So, Tiny Tim, tell the jury, just how long have you been a freak? And exactly how long do you expect people to buy your horseshit? That's it! We've had enough of you. We sentence you to public ridicule and twenty-five years of community service, during which time you will dress up like the clown you are and let us throw tomatoes at you…"

Everything about King's body language and voice inflections telegraphed the message, "Why am I even speaking to this weirdo loser?"

I've got to hand it to Tiny. He held his own. I could see that he was boiling mad, and he came up with the best retorts he could…

"Why, what do you mean? I am sure you understand the ins and outs of show business, Mr. King… I am afraid I do not understand the tone of your questions. What are you getting at, anyway?"

As if King's obvious disdain for Tiny Tim wasn't enough fun, King totally ignored him during commercial breaks. I was seeing red. You can't make a fan out of someone if they're not, and clearly Larry King was not a fan.

I felt like a total jerk for bringing Tiny all that way just to be tarred and feathered. If Tiny felt like Charles Manson in the guest chair, all the other guests got the royal treatment. Larry King was pleasant and decent to them all. During commercial breaks, they would bullshit and laugh, and people would fuss over them and make sure they were comfortable.

During Tiny's commercial breaks, King actually swiveled his chair all the way around so his back was to Tiny. I wanted to grab Tiny and run for the nearest exit. The poor guy just sat there, looking at King's back, feeling like an unwelcome, unwanted intruder. Nice.

I wanted to help Larry King overcome whatever roadblock he'd hit inside his head. I wanted to dump ice over his head and towel him down, like the guy in the corner of the ring at a boxing match, spouting encouraging words.

"Come on, Larry!" I wanted to shout. "You can do it! Find one single nice thing to say about this guy. Just one f—ing thing! After all, he worships you and he came all this way just to talk to you. I know you have it in you, Larry. You're the best. Just one nice thing. One single compliment. Any kind word to acknowledge that even if he doesn't ring your bell, the guy is a bona fide entertainer."

Nope. It wasn't going to happen. The great host of the evening couldn't do it. He was on a crusade to divest the poor misguided American people of their notion that Tiny Tim could be a lot of fun and put on a hell of a show.

"Is it just me, or does it seem to you like Larry King hates Tiny Tim's guts?" I asked the nearest luminary.

He just shrugged and shook his head, baffled. "You're right on, Steve. I don't know what to make of it, but Larry definitely seems to be gunning for Tiny." It was as plain as the nose on Tiny's face.

"Why? What was Larry King trying to prove with this dirty trick?" Tiny asked me afterwards. "I have always liked him and admired him so much." Tiny was crushed.

"Why, Mister Plym?" Tiny continued. "Why would someone intentionally, maliciously, go after me like that?"

I couldn't think of a single comforting word to say, so I said, "Hey, Tiny, f— him." And with that brilliant intellectual reply, I turned on the car and we silently drove back to our hotel.

♦ ♦ ♦

Weeks later, Tiny got philosophical and tried to see it from Larry King's point of view.

"I suppose…" Tiny mused, "Mr. King simply could not help

himself. He could not tolerate the thought of himself in any way being aligned with my type of image. I imagine it completely goes against his traditional mainstream thinking…. He seemed actually embarrassed that I was there, didn't he?"

I nodded.

"He was. He was actually embarrassed by me. There he was with all these political types and perhaps he felt he would lose face or stature if he looked cozy with such a weird controversial oddball as myself… You know, Mister Plym, I do forgive Mr. King, but there is one thing I cannot understand."

"What's that, Tiny?" I gulped, knowing where he was going with this line of reasoning and still not wanting to state the obvious — that Larry King would never in a million years have invited Tiny, and I had bullied my way into a show we should have avoided like the plague.

"I will always wonder why he went to all the trouble of inviting me in the first place, paying our expenses, our hotel, our plane tickets. It is very strange," Tiny concluded.

"Yeah, Tiny," I shrugged my shoulders and made a face. "It's pretty f—ing weird, all right."

What was I going to say?

Under Where?

Tiny Tidbit: Tiny Tim liked to say,
"Ah, romance... a wonderful thing
that is spoiled by bad breath and body odors."

One day Tiny and I had gotten to my offices early and we were strategizing before the suits showed up for a meeting.

Determined to put some investors in the mood to bankroll a couple of projects we had in mind, I said, "Now, Tiny, baby, listen to me. Remember that when these guys show up, the point is to get them to give us their money. So, that means you better promise me you're not going to do or say anything to piss them off or alienate them, got it? I'm begging you, man, please don't blow it."

"Why, Mister Plym, are you suggesting that perhaps there have been times in the past where I have put my foot in my mouth?" Tiny pretended to be insulted and shocked.

"Not just the foot, Tiny, the whole shoe. A fillet of sole sandwich, so to speak." We laughed.

"I was thinking it might be effective to dwell on my glory days..." Tiny suggested.

"You're damn straight, man! Yeah, in fact, that's a great idea. Lay it on thick. The more we can get them remembering the days when dollar signs were floating in your cereal bowl, the better the odds that they will be willing to cough up the dough."

Tiny slumped down in a luxurious leather swivel chair and stared out the window.

◆ ◆ ◆

"Mister Plym, I must say, remembering when we were at the World Wrestling Federation show truly brought me back to the good old days when I was at my box office peak," Tiny reminisced.

"Those days were really something, weren't they, man?" I was trying to turn the key in his back to wind him up and get him talking.

"I lived in a perpetual whirlwind of fame. It was a never-ending stream of studios, autographs, airports…" he began.

"Not to mention the chicks, right, Tiny?" That ought to get him going. Plus, it cracked me up to watch him blush.

Tiny pulled his head down a bit like a turtle about to go into his shell and looked up at me with his cheeks turning red. He leaned back in his chair, with one leg stretched out in front of him, and with the other, he started tapping his foot and fidgeting. He was rubbing his hands together, saying, "Ah, the women, the women and the girls. I was so very sinful. Sinful and weak. All of them wanting to touch me, grabbing at my clothes, trying to get a lock of my hair. The temptations were so great…"

"Oh, sure, I can totally relate. The chicks are always begging to have sex with me. I have to fight them off with a stick. Happens all the time," I said sarcastically.

"I only hope the Lord will forgive me for all my sins," Tiny said. "Wait..." His face brightened. "I just remembered something I have not thought of in years... that beautiful girl in the shower... on this one particular evening, I was playing at Caesars Palace and it was past my bedtime. So I went to my hotel suite and lay down on the bed."

"Yeah? Then what happened? Then what happened?" He had me eating out of the palm of his hand.

"Well," Tiny spoke in a voice rich with suspense, like he was telling a child a ghost story, "I heard a strange noise that seemed to be coming from the bathroom. I must admit I was a little frightened. I was always hearing stories of people stalking celebrities and I was shaking, thinking, oh Lord, what if they have a gun? So, very carefully, and as quietly as I could, I tiptoed into the bathroom, looked in the shower, and what do you suppose I found?"

"The chick was hiding in the shower? F—ing A, man."

"Yes, she was. This incredible vision, standing completely naked like a sculpture. She was so curvaceous, so incredibly captivating. She did not look used up, like so many women do. She was still the picture of purity and innocence, like a painting by Raphael..."

I didn't have the faintest idea who Raphael was — must be some Puerto Rican guy from his neighborhood in New York — but I got the point.

"...And there was no question what she wanted. She wanted me!" He shook his head, still having a hard time believing all the love — not to mention all the action — that came his way.

"So what happened, man? Did you nail her?"

"No, no, no. That time I did not break. It was a miracle. She went on and on about how wonderful I was and how much she wanted me to make love to her. And she was very persistent, if you know what I mean. Yet, somehow, I managed to stay strong." He paused and then added with a shy smile, "I decided I would compromise with her."

"Compromise? How in the hell did you do that? How do you compromise in a situation like that?"

"Well, let us say I bent but I did not break."

I couldn't wait to hear this one.

"She had gone to quite a bit of trouble to slip into my room and it was clear she really wanted to spend some time with me. I felt badly for her, and I did not wish to be cruel and throw her out. So, I found a way to fulfill her fantasy and take care of her needs…while not giving in to the sin of fornication. I went into my bathroom and got four or five of my favorite lotions and a couple of big fluffy white towels. Then I had her wrap herself up in the towels and lie face down on the bed…."

"Yeah? Then what? Then what?" Tiny loved to really get me sitting on the edge of my seat, like I was now.

"Then I rubbed the lotion on my hands and took her gorgeous body in my hands and…" He stopped and grinned at me.

"Come on, man! Don't stop now!"

"…and I massaged her whole body for hours and hours."

Tiny stopped.

"Yeah? Then what? Then you nailed her, right?" I asked.

"That was it. I gave her a massage. Nothing more."

"You've gotta be kidding me, man!"

"I did not touch her in any …any sexual way. I simply rubbed her gently as we talked for hours and hours. She wanted to know everything about me, so I answered all of her questions for her — questions about money, music, stardom…"

"The funniest thing happened," Tiny finished his story with a laugh. "When she was finally ready to leave, I decided I had better telephone the security guard to walk her downstairs to her car. When the guard arrived, I said goodbye to her and sent them off together, saying to her, 'Remember to be careful. Las Vegas can be a dangerous place for a young girl by herself late at night, you know.'

"Well, as I was closing the door to the hotel room, the security guard saw me hand her a fifty-dollar bill to pay for her cab. And with a wink and a smile, he told me not to worry, that as far as he was concerned, he heard nothing and saw nothing, because us famous guys deserve our privacy, too. You know what he thought!"

"Sure, I know what he was thinking. And you know what I'm thinking right now? What a f—ing original you are!" We spent the next ten minutes laughing.

♦ ♦ ♦

Once we had both calmed down, I said, "So, anyway, Tiny, back to the meeting strategy…" but even as I said it, I saw that he was still far away, and judging by the weird look on his face, I figured wherever he had gone must be a pretty bad neighborhood.

"What's up, Tiny?"

"Mister Plym, something is bothering me. We both know what that guard was thinking, but what if he had known what really happened? What if he had known the truth? Would he have thought what so many people think about me? I mean if he had known that I had a beautiful naked girl on my bed but I didn't take advantage of her…" Tiny was clearly upset.

"You mean, would he have thought you were a fag?" I know, I know, I'm not exactly the picture of sensitivity.

"Oh, Mister Plym, Mister Plym, you do not believe this means I am a … homosexual, do you?"

"What? Tiny, get outta here! What the f— are you talkin' about, man? No, of course not. I've never seen anyone who loves the chicks more than you do."

"Even though that one time…? Oh, Mister Plym…there was one time years ago when I was young…with another boy…"

I had been pacing around the office, waiting for the money people to show up and now I suddenly felt like maybe I'd better sit down.

I slipped into a chair and leaned forward with my eyebrows knitted together and my eyes bugged out. "Tiny, what??? Are you saying what I think you're saying?"

"I wish I had told you years ago… but I suppose when Howard Stern coaxed it out of me on the radio, I was just so humiliated… I hoped I would never even have to think about it again."

"Look, Tiny, baby. Listen to me. How long have we known each other? Even if you told me you'd had sex with a …" Seeing the nervous look on his face I decided not to come up with an example. "Anyway, there's nothing you could tell me that would change the fact that we're friends for life. You and me, all the way, got it? Now, what the hell happened?"

"When I was a very young boy, I had a friend in Brooklyn…We were just good pals…" Tiny began, his face scrunched up in a miserable expression.

Tiny told me that he and the boy were best buddies, the way you can only be when you're kids. They went everywhere and did everything together. So, Tiny trusted him completely, and didn't blink when one day the boy offered Tiny a back rub.

"A back rub! Wow, I had never had a back rub before. Naturally, I jumped at the chance," Tiny explained.

"Nothing wrong with that, Tiny." I didn't want him to feel like a freak, and definitely did want him to feel comfortable enough to keep going until he got to the punchline.

"Anyway, it felt wonderful, Mister Plym. So relaxing and calming. Then my friend said it was his turn and asked me to give him a back rub. Well, that seemed only fair so I agreed…"

Apparently as Tiny was obliging his friend with an innocent back rub, just trying to reciprocate and return the favor, the boy took off his shirt.

"Then he said, 'Lower, please rub lower.' Oh, Mister Plym,

Mister Plym…" Tiny had been slouched over in his chair but now he stood up and started pacing around, wringing his hands. "Suddenly, he took off his pants, too, and asked me if I would please massage his buttocks and legs."

Tiny said that at that point, his head started to swim and he got nervous and shaky and just generally disoriented. Like the feeling that the world is suddenly underwater. Everything was surreal to him and he didn't know what to do with himself.

"I was saying to myself, relax, relax, I know this fella. He is my good friend. He is okay. How silly for me to worry about anything. Then he rolled over on his back and to my horror and shock, I could plainly see that he was aroused!"

When Tiny saw the kid with a hard-on, his brain just melted. He didn't know what to say or do and he became a walking anxiety attack.

"Shit, man! What happened next?" I couldn't believe my ears.

Tiny rolled his eyes and stepped up the hand-wringing to a faster pace as he said, "Oh, Lord, how did I let it happen? He… he took my hand and placed it where it did not belong."

"What the f—? Tiny, what do you mean? You mean on his penis? You put your hand on the guy's cock, Tiny? Are you serious?" So much for not making him feel like a total freak. What can I say? I've never been very good at playing it cool.

I had gone too far. I had totally embarrassed Tiny and he wanted to put the whole horrifying subject to bed. Sorry. Bad choice of words.

"That is it. No more! No more! I am sorry, Mister Plym, but I cannot discuss this anymore. It is all simply too awful and I must ask you not to ask me another question. This conversation is over."

Tiny buried his face in his hands and started praying. I felt like a total jerk for being so blunt about a subject that was so painful for Tiny. I had just taken a baseball bat to a beehive and my friend was the one who was getting stung, not me.

"Hey, look, Tiny, you can tell me anything." I was desperate to calm him down and make him feel better. "I don't give a shit what you did when you were a kid. It's not going to change how I feel about my best pal, I swear. Nothing is going to be any different with us, just finish the damn story!"

After crossing my heart, hoping to die, and swearing on my mother's life and the Bible that I would never repeat what he was divulging to me, he went on. The ironic thing was he had already told this story to millions of listeners on Howard Stern's show.

"All right, if you promise… My friend pulled his pants down very slowly. I became almost hypnotized. It was like I was in a horrible dream and could not wake up. Nothing seemed real. Anyway, as I said, he took my hand and put it on his penis…" Tiny was whispering. "Then my friend said, now rub this for me, nice and gentle."

I couldn't hide the disgust on my face as I asked Tiny, "What the f— did you do, man?"

"Mister Plym, I honestly do not know what came over me. I

believe I must have been in shock. I just did as I was asked. Before I could think of how I could get myself out of the situation, I was massaging him heavily," Tiny went on with a look of disbelief in his eyes. "We were both so young and I had never in my life seen or touched anyone who was naked before. It really was like I was in a strange dream and could not wake up. The whole experience had such an unreal quality."

Tiny was so worked up, so agitated telling me this, and now I was the one who felt like I was in a dream or a strange movie. And I was speechless. I sat there on the edge of my seat, silent and breathlessly waiting to see how the movie would end.

Tiny said he was unable to stop what was happening, and opened his mouth for the kid. "Just for a second. I kissed it lightly, just barely, and let it enter my mouth a tiny bit. Then it was as if reality broke through the experience with a jolt and I snapped back to life. I pulled my head back, got up, and told my friend he had better get dressed and leave."

Tiny was totally flushed and out of breath. He had completely and utterly freaked himself out by telling me this story and, frankly, he wasn't the only one who was freaked. "I swear," Tiny pleaded, "you've got to believe me. Nothing else happened. Not then or any other time in my life."

The poor bastard. Tiny went on and on explaining himself, guaranteeing me that he was not gay, had never found himself naked or half naked or with his mouth open or his hands on any other guys. I didn't for one second think Tiny Tim was gay. I had seen him, firsthand, up close and personal, with too many babes. On the other hand, I did feel really strange about him now. I didn't want to feel strange but I did.

Just in the nick of time, they arrived. The cavalry from hell. Five ultra-conservative money people. The last thing on earth we needed at that particularly awkward moment — and just what the doctor ordered. As weird as it was having them show up right then, it was a Godsend. An armadillo would have been welcome. Or a scorpion or a herd of elephants. Anything.

I asked our guests to give us just a moment, seated them in the lobby, and realized I'd better think fast if I wanted to normalize our now sweaty, flushed, out of breath, traumatized star so he could appear to be remotely like the kind of guy that investors would want to shower with gold coins. I gave them my version of a smile, left them absent-mindedly flipping through old magazines in the lobby, and slipped back into the conference room.

I had to find something to say. "You know, Tiny," I started, having no idea where I was going with this. "Here's my theory on how one single homosexual experience could happen to someone. Anyone, for that matter…" Yeah, that's it. "It could have happened to anyone. You were young. You were shocked at seeing your first naked ass, and even more importantly than that…" Yeah? What? Where the hell was I going? "Even more importantly than that," I bluffed, making it up as I went along, "I think the real point was that…" I was just buying time.

Suddenly, it hit me. "Look, you were the weird kid in school, in your neighborhood, right?"

"Right, right…" He was willing to grab hold of any explanation I could pull out of thin air.

"Well, here was a guy who was — in a very strange way, admittedly — but still here was a guy who was making you feel special."

"Why Mister Plym, I believe you may be on to something." Tiny was perking up, the color in his cheeks returning to normal.

"That explains everything. The guy was giving you his brand of attention, affection and love, and you've always been a love junkie. You couldn't resist. Even if was coming from a dude."

Tiny smiled at me and said, "Mister Plym, you are wonderful, simply wonderful." He was so grateful that I'd let him off the hook and I was grateful that I'd found an explanation I could hang onto during those long sleepless nights ahead when I would wake myself up from the nightmare of remembering Tiny with some guy's tool in his mouth.

"So you don't think any less of me for this?" As he asked me the question, he put his hand on my knee for emphasis.

I slowly looked down at his hand and joked, "No, man, no way. It was just one of those things that happen. God, your hand feels good on my knee." I have never in my life seen anyone fly so fast or scream so loud.

"Tiny, calm down, man. It was a joke." We burst into the kind of laughter that builds up under the kind of pressure we'd just been under, the kind of laughter that tickles your bladder.

"Will you ever be able to forget this conversation took place?" Tiny needed reassurance.

"Conversation?"

"You are the best, the best, Mister Plym."

As we walked out into the lobby, our guests looked at us with horrified, questioning looks on their faces that told me they had heard his blood-curdling scream.

"Mice," I said and smiled — or tried to, anyway.

♦ ♦ ♦

Tiny-ism: "No washing can ever rid the cloth

of those awful germs.

Underwear worn once are soiled forever."

♦ ♦ ♦

Before I tell you what happened next, you might want to sit back and let me give you a guided tour through the loose screws and other weird mechanical workings of Tiny's brain. Picture a funhouse, a real bizarre place full of shadowy corridors and trick mirrors that could talk and did, distorting the truth and telling him all sorts of strange things that he had no choice but to act upon.

It didn't take much to flip that switch inside of him — some strange random thought flying around would get lodged in there. Once the guilt and shame were awake, they would quickly wake up Mr. Obsession and Mr. Compulsion and that's when the fun would really begin.

Little did I know that as we started the meeting, his usual mental gymnastics had grown into full-blown Olympic games.

It would have been really handy if Tiny had a red warning light that would go on in the middle of his forehead when he was off kilter. Then I could have seen it and found a way to get him away from people. I could have looked right at our guests and said something like, "You know that mice problem I mentioned? Well, it's worse than we thought. Behind that conference room door, they're everywhere. Millions of them. They're climbing the walls, swinging from the light fixtures, having babies in the curtains. But, hey, I hate to cancel, unless for some reason, all of *you* might feel more comfortable rescheduling?"

◆ ◆ ◆

The meeting started out promising enough. According to the game plan, I was going to be the opening act, the very businesslike and official numbers man, the guy who appealed to their logic. Then I was going to use all my enthusiasm to play cheerleader. By then, hopefully, they would be all warmed up for Tiny to launch right into endless recollections of his glory days.

I got the ball rolling, demonstrating for them how the only sensible use of their millions of dollars was to put them behind our latest project. Then I cued Tiny to take over. I passed him the ball and let him start running with it while it still had some good spin on it.

Tiny smiled at them, psyched himself up into one-hundred-watt star mode, closed his eyes for just a second, and started recounting some of the more impressive details of his glory days.

"I will never forget the time," he recalled, summoning all of his charm, "I was having lunch at a very classy restaurant in Los Angeles. I cannot recall the name right now, but it was one of L.A.'s very chic watering holes where everyone who is anyone eats lunch and hangs around making the scene and being seen…"

I sat back, buttoned my lip, and let Tiny do his thing. He seemed to be doing just great. Damn, I was proud of him. They had loosened up a little bit and were getting carried away by his story.

"… In any event, the place was quite elegant, a real who's who of show business. I let my gaze wander around the beautiful, star-studded room. It was so very posh. Anyway, a couple of tables away from mine, my eye was caught by a very sophisticated lady who was openly staring at me."

The investors giggled and smiled and made cooing noises, enjoying the story.

"She was an older lady, but was still very beautiful and refined. You could tell she had taken excellent care of herself… I can always tell these things."

Tiny went on to tell them that while he was trying to eat his lunch, the woman's eyes were stuck to him like two spotlights. Tiny started out finding it flattering but it got uncomfortable pretty quickly as his every bite of food was being watched.

Mentally, they were already at the bank, drawing out the money we needed.

Tiny went on to say that, as he left his table, he noticed the woman ease out of her booth and slowly and stealthily make her way over to where he had been seated, like a wildcat tracking his scent. At this point, the starched investors all leaned in closer to Tiny, their eyebrows raised and their eyes wide.

"I simply could not believe what happened next," Tiny went on, baiting them. "After slyly looking around the room to assure herself that no one was watching her, she snatched my lunch plate and shoved it into her huge purse! The plate was a complete mess with my leftovers, but all of it went right into her elegant handbag. I honestly could not believe my eyes."

As Tiny watched, the woman also grabbed his napkin, planted a big wet kiss on it, and then plop! She stashed it in her purse.

Our guests were appropriately shocked and wowed.

"The woman simply had to have my plate and napkin. I think that was the very first time I realized I had become the 'f' word…"

Everyone gasped. Oh, no, Tiny, don't blow it now. I was holding my breath. Then he delivered his punchline like a pro.

"You know, the 'f' word — famous." Everyone let out a relieved sigh and chuckled. That starstruck fan may have gotten Tiny's plate with the leftovers, but Tiny had these people eating right out of the palm of his hand.

◆ ◆ ◆

I should have leapt to my feet right then, thrown them a pen so they could write us a check, patted them on the back, thanked them for coming, and made sure the door didn't hit them in the rear on the way out. I should have had the sense to quit while we were ahead.

For Tiny, it was like the encore at a performance. The performance had gone over big, they gave him a standing ovation, and of course, he was anxious to come back out on stage for another tune or two.

So he got revved up again and he talked. He talked about Vegas and a Sammy Davis, Jr. look-alike who followed him around all night. He talked about the twins from *Hee-Haw* and getting his picture taken with Buddy Ebsen from the *The Beverly Hillbillies*.

"How did I first get noticed?" Tiny fielded one of their questions. "It was at a tiny club in New York called the Scene. Mo Ostin, the head of Warner Reprise Records, happened in that night and…"

Tiny remembered that night in early 1968 when his ship came in, and how it felt to put out his initial album, *God Bless Tiny Tim.*

Okay, perfect. Great history lesson. Now, say goodbye, Tiny. Please.

The investors were hypnotized, mesmerized, and ready to whip out their checkbooks.

Tiny couldn't shut up. *Life, Time, Newsweek, Look, Playboy, The New York Times* and even *Sports Illustrated.* Tiny had been featured in every rag and mag from the west coast to the east.

They were sold. I wanted to finish with a flourish, so I started quoting an article I'd read that said that the pit bosses in Vegas called Tiny Tim the only celebrity they had ever seen who could bring the dice, the wheels, and the cards to a complete standstill just by walking through the casino. And then it happened. That spring in Tiny's brain that had been wound too tightly finally sprang loose.

The meeting should have been over. Everyone stood and prepared to go. Not Tiny. He got a very serious look on his face.

"Before you leave, I must speak to all of you about something very important," Tiny announced.

The investors looked at each other like, I don't know what's going on but — uh, okay, I guess. They sat back down.

"What I want to ask you is this. Can you please tell me what kind of underwear each of you is wearing?"

The question hit them hard, throwing them all backwards in their chairs. It was like someone had dropped a stink bomb in the room. They started coughing and choking and laughing.

"I know many of you may never have considered this before, but I have given it a great deal of thought. Cloth underwear is a hotbed for dangerous organisms. I never, ever wear real underwear. At this very moment, I, myself, am wearing adult diapers. Depends, to be more specific."

They all started staring at his crotch, trying to detect the outline of his diaper. Then they caught themselves staring. This embarrassed them even further, and soon they were squirming and fidgeting like there really were mice running up their pants legs.

Tiny was not deterred. He was going to deliver his lecture and save those people from the evil germs in their underwear whether they wanted to sit still for it or not.

"Don't be shy. Won't you share with me what kind of underwear you are wearing today?" Tiny asked gently.

Everyone was giggling hysterically, but, needless to say, nobody answered the question.

"Well," he continued, "let me assure you that if your underpants are made of any kind of cloth, they are crawling with germs. The microscopic bacterial organisms on the penis and vagina simply cannot be eradicated in a washing machine."

The words penis and vagina being tossed about in open company was too much for them.

"Really, it was so nice meeting you both." They tried to leave.

Yeah, right. I'm sure it was the highlight of their lives.

"I simply cannot stress to you the importance of wearing disposable diapers," Tiny said with a perfectly straight face. "I would like you all to make a commitment before leaving here today that when we meet again next time, you will all be wearing Depends. Okay?"

As they were scrambling and pushing each other out of the way to get out the door, Tiny called after them, "Remember to change your diapers often. Personally, I go through several changes daily. You cannot be too vigilant. Remember…" he yelled as they were climbing into their cars and screeching away. "This must be treated as a war. The war on germs!"

"So, Mister Plym, do you suppose they will take my advice and return for our meeting next week wearing disposable diapers? It would make me so happy to see I had been able to help them in such an important way."

This guy is too much, I thought. He is totally oblivious to

the damage he has done. I just shook my head and replied, "Absolutely, Tiny. No doubt about it. Just as soon as they eat the bars of soap they have in their pockets and fly home on the backs of their winged pigs, they will probably run right over to the local drugstore and buy out the supply of throwaway diapers for grown-ups. Then they will run as fast as they can to get back over here for our next meeting."

After I spent five minutes with my hands around his throat pretending to throttle him, and I had called him every bad word I could think of, we laughed so hard that I wished I'd been wearing a disposable diaper.

The Destroyer

"If I had to label myself,
I'd say I was the Master of Confusion.
Nobody knows. Nobody knows me."
--*Tiny Tim talking to an interviewer*

"Mr. Plym, did I ever tell you about the time I was in the heart of the South, right smack in the middle of the Bible belt? It was a very lovely, elegant supper club," Tiny began. "Opening night turned out to be more than any of us bargained for. An evening to remember, shall we say. As the guests filed into the club, dressed to the nines, none of us had any idea the kind of mischief that was afoot..."

So there he was on a lovely Southern evening, the air thick and sultry, the humidity suffocatingly oppressive, making the audience's clothes stick to their bodies, June bugs popping people in the forehead. That's if it was the summer. Or, if it was winter, picture people wrapped in scarves, cranky and soggy from the icy air wrinkling their evening clothes. He didn't happen to mention the year or the season, but he sure was having fun telling this story.

♦ ♦ ♦

"So, there I am in this ritzy dinner club. The musicians are doing a sound check and I am back in my dressing room trying to put myself into the right frame of mind and psyche myself up," explains Tiny. "Someone who works at the club slips into the dressing room and quietly closes the door behind him.

"'Ahem,' says the man, clearing his throat, 'Mr. Khaury, or, um, Tiny. May I call you Tiny? As the entertainment director... Oh, by the way, I am a huge fan of yours. Vincetti's my name...'

"He thrusts his young hand into mine and looks up at me, adoringly, and says, 'Anyway, as I was saying, I am such a fan of yours and it is so important to me to make you happy tonight. I mean, we are so honored to have you here.'

"Yes, Mr. Vincetti? I egg him on, noticing as we talk that he is terribly young, and does not seem very savvy or hip about the business. We talk about everything under the sun and then eventually he works his way around to more delicate matters."

"Out of nowhere, he says, 'What I am trying to say, Tiny, is, well, if it's not too personal, how do you feel about the ladies?'"

"The ladies? Why, I love the ladies, Mr. Vincetti. So then he asks me, 'Which ones in particular? You know, tall, short, skinny, voluptuous, blonde, brunette...?' Well, I love them all, I tell him. I consider them to be God's finest creations."

"Needless to say, Mr. Plym, once he starts talking about sex, he has my undivided attention. The next thing I know, we are sitting down in front of the dressing room mirror and sharing sexual secrets and preferences like two young men in a college locker room. I had never seen him before in my life, but he was so guileless and genuinely interested and eager to please, well, I was completely at ease. He seemed to find the subject of my personal sex life to be fascinating. He was like a wide-eyed student sitting at my knee, harmless and innocent. Of course, I answered all of his questions."

"'Tiny Tim,' Mr. Vincetti continues, 'have you ever had two

women at the same time?'"

"Let me tell you, it was like someone had removed all the air from the room. I reeled, and felt like I was going to faint. My heart started to race, my mind started to race, and oh, Lord, I cannot even begin to tell you the improper thoughts I was having. This fellow was entering dangerous territory. Why, just the mere mention of a ménàge a trois was so titillating, I couldn't help myself. The vision of two goddesses lying in my arms filled my head and the next thing I knew, the blood was pounding through my body with the force of Niagara Falls. I was ready to go in seconds..."

"I was thinking, Heavens above, I must change the subject immediately. This man was leading me through a mine field. Mr. Plym, Mr. Vincetti did not have the faintest idea how weak I am in this area."

Now, a normal guy in Tiny's position might think he had won the lottery, that by some stroke of luck his wife was in another galaxy and some stranger he had never met before had somehow managed to arrange for two beautiful women to show up in his hotel bed in a town far, far away, in another solar system. That's two women. At the same time. Not that the married guy thinking like that wouldn't be a jerk. Of course he would. But he'd also be your average run-of-the-mill guy thinking regular guy thoughts. Not Tiny.

Run. Fast. Escape. Pray for discipline and strength. These were the thoughts running through Tiny's head. When I say his thoughts were running, you have to understand, his thoughts never ran in a straight line, but in a very crooked, detour-and-go-over-the-bridge, under-the-overpass, past-the-gas-station, left-at-the-second-stop-sign-and-down-the-hill kind of running through his mind.

"So then I said, 'No, Mr. Vincetti,'" Tiny continued, "'I have never made love to two women at the same time, and if you will excuse me, I am afraid I really must, um, return to my hotel. Yes, that is what I must do. Return to my hotel. You know, I need to rest and prepare my mind and body for the show.' And then under my breath, I said to myself, not to mention my soul. I must protect my soul."

Mr. Vincetti's halo was starting to tarnish a bit, shall we say, as he closed Tiny's dressing room door. Tiny, meanwhile, collapsed into a chair, throwing his legs out in front of him and his arms at his sides. Letting his head roll to the side, he breathed a huge, very premature sigh of relief. He was thinking, "Thank God, I am safe." But he was not out of the woods yet. Not by a longshot.

Once he got himself standing right side up again, he started stuffing his belongings into his bag at record speed and eyeing the exit. He nearly made it out of the club, but just when he was about to make a break for it, Vincetti reappeared. Like a mind-numbing oasis appearing to a parched man crawling through the Sahara. Like a lousy practical joke, a feast prepared for the man who has just begun his diet.

"Oh, Tiny Tim! If you could just wait for one moment before heading back to the hotel, there is someone I'd like you to meet," called the entertainment director, walking in with a girl on each arm.

"They were two of the most beautiful young ladies I have ever seen in my life," Tiny gushed. "They looked so identical, I thought my eyes were playing tricks on me. Then I realized that they were twins. TWINS. Oh my God, twin beauties. And not a day over twenty-one or twenty-two. I was absolutely sunk. Identical, golden-haired angels fallen right out of the clouds. They looked like Playboy bunnies."

♦ ♦ ♦

Vincetti, who at the beginning had seemed like such an aw-shucks-golly-I-think-you're-swell kind of guy, introduced the girls to Tiny with the finesse of someone in white patent leather shoes who spent his days selling used cars.

"In that moment, I understood where the phrase blonde bombshell came from," continued Tiny. "When those two visions materialized in front of me, my head almost exploded. It was too much for me to take. The odd thing was that as Mr. Vincetti spoke, his sheep's clothing began to fall off and I could see the wolf underneath."

"'Tiny,' Vincetti says to me, 'the girls were so anxious to meet you. You are, after all, the one and only Tiny Tim. They made me promise I would arrange for them to meet you and say hello. They would have killed me if I had let you slip away. Girls? This is Tiny Tim. Tiny? Meet the girls. They work here at the club as waitresses, or hostesses as we like to call them.'"

Sidling over to Tiny, Vincetti lowered his head so the girls couldn't hear — like a hey, buddy, wanna-buy-a-watch character opening his suit jacket to display the merchandise.

"Tiny, baby," continued the so-called entertainment director in a greasy voice, "these two dolls are yours after the gig tonight. Tiny, sweetheart, listen to me, you're in for the time of your f—ing life. Hope you took your vitamins, baby."

Grinning, sauntering, posing like a cartoon gangster, the lounge lizard slipped an arm around the waists of the after-gig darlings, smacked them both on the behind, and whispered good-byes into their ears. The twosome had an extra special good-bye reserved for Tiny.

"Before they leave," Tiny remembers, "they come over to me, one at a time, slip a pretty hand behind my head, and with my knees knocking and my heart in my throat, each one gives me the longest, most mouth-watering kiss I have ever had in my life. Their tongues are deep inside my mouth and they are exploring me like we had been lovers our whole lives. I was seconds from soiling myself as they left. To say I was shocked, Mr. Plym, to say I felt like I was in a dream, would be a gross understatement. I nearly fell over flat on my face."

A dream? A science fiction movie is more like it. What do the women see in him? Anyway, the lucky sap. Not that I would want such an improper, erotic overture made to me by two drop-dead gorgeous women miles and miles away from my wife who would never know any better. Absolutely not for a minute.

"Dazed and bedazzled," Tiny slumped into a chair, again trying to recover his composure and his normal pulse rate.

"Now, check this out, Tiny Tim," Vincetti goes on, knowing that Tiny is foaming at the mouth. "These two broads are yours, man! Both of them. At the same time. Can you dig that, baby? I always take care of my entertainers here, Tiny. I know what you f—ing guys are into... These chicks can suck the holes off a bowling ball..."

"All I can say is that I was absolutely stunned," reported Tiny. "I wanted not to listen to him anymore, to stick my fingers in my ears. But by then, it was too late. I had definitely heard every word he said, and the images were torture. Pure — or, rather impure — delicious torture."

Staring into his lighted mirror, he saw Vincetti's reflection as he reached for the door. The guy winked a couple of times and exited, yelling, "You're in for the f—ing treat of your life. You'll always hit the jackpot when you're with me, pal."

♦ ♦ ♦

Tiny sat there, trying to get his head to stop spinning and his heart to slow down. It was like the devil himself had shown up, handed Tiny a pen, and asked him to sign on the dotted line. All it would cost was his soul — a small price to pay for the one thing he craved more than anything in the world. S-E-X. Adoration, attention, affection, love, and sex. For Tiny, it was all rolled up together into one big sticky pink mess of cotton candy.

"The prospect of going to bed with those two beauties was a temptation I cannot even put into words. It was beyond overwhelming," Tiny told me. "I did not have the faintest idea what to do. I mean, of course, I know what I wanted to do, what my weak flesh was aching to do, what I was about to do if I wasn't careful — but the sin. The sin! How could I live with myself if I went through with it? On the other hand, oh, what regret I would live with if I refused."

Pacing around his dressing room, the two sides of Tiny Tim fought it out. The mortal man in him was prancing around the room, delirious, jumping up and down, screaming, yelling, hooting, clapping his hands and celebrating the fact that miraculously, out of nowhere, a genie had appeared and granted his heart's desire. The God-fearing side of himself, on the other hand, was climbing the walls, wringing his hands and trying to obliterate from his mind the picture of those twins hanging from the chandeliers wearing nothing but the lather of bubble bath. Just when he felt like he had an unsolvable problem, Satan — er, I mean, Vincetti, returned to the room, and showed him the perfect way to spring the trap he had set for him.

"Uh, by the way, Tiny, you better listen up," ordered Vincetti. "I forgot to ask you something important. You saw how petite those girls were, right? I've gotta warn you up front, man. I hope you're not hung like a horse because I know these chicks. They are not into big dicks. So, if God gave you a little something extra, you're really going to scare the hell out of them. You would tear them up. Just wanted to give you a heads up, man."

At this point, Tiny had heard everything. He was beyond speechless. All he could do was smile weakly and nod at the guy. With those words, the great Vincetti — the one who forever changed the meaning of the phrase "entertainment director" — left.

All Tiny wanted to do was go lie down and pray. Pray really long and hard. "Lead us not into temptation but deliver us from evil..."

◆ ◆ ◆

Tiny knew what was on the agenda, or should I say, the menu, and he knew what he had to do. The only question was, where was he going to find the courage, strength and conviction to do it?

"I had to resist the devil's power and influence. I had to find a way to defeat temptation," he explains. "So I sat down and with all my heart I prayed. 'I know, Father, my flesh is weak and I must seek your power to crush my evil, sinful desires.' Then, a thought would come to me of one of the girls wearing next to nothing. Ping! It would distract me, like a raindrop falling on my head. 'Forgive me, Father, for I have already sinned in my heart,' I would continue. Then, ping! Another image of the girls undressing me. It was becoming unbearable. It was like sitting in the rain and trying to pray. How do you pray when it is raining all over your head?"

"To be honest," he confessed, "I wanted to resist, but all I could focus on was that my orgy fantasies were about to come true. The truth was, I wanted this to happen. Those girls were so young, beautiful, and delicious looking. What a sinful man I am."

Wrestling with himself, Tiny vowed to put up a good fight, but he was having a hard time putting his hand on a defense more powerful than the thought of those two girls putting their hands all over him. He resigned himself to the fact that he would probably, like Adam, fall for the apple when Eve showed up wearing nothing but a fig leaf.

"Too big?" Tiny was thinking to himself.

Then, like Moses descending from the mountains with the tablets under his arm, Tiny's deliverance came. Like a lightning bolt or a burning bush. Like a terribly upset stomach saving you from eating the Thanksgiving feast.

"Wait a minute! I thought to myself. Too big! Too big! Mr. Plym, I was on to something," Tiny screamed at me. "Mr. Vincetti had unknowingly shown me a way out of the torture chamber I found myself in. If they were afraid of well-endowed men, I would become their worst nightmare! It was my only hope, Mr. Plym. Oh, how I loved this idea," recalled Tiny, practically jumping up and down. "I knew how I could make the girls run for cover."

He raced back to the hotel and into his drummer's room. He had a strategy and it couldn't fail. When Cookie and Candy, or whatever their names were, got a load of the new improved version of Tiny carrying a load onstage, he knew they would head for the hills.

"My drummer used to tell me about his box of tricks. When I lifted the lid, I could not believe my eyes. Inside were dozens of sex toys of every description. Of course, I picked out the largest dildo that was in the box," Tiny gleamed. "Of all things, it was called The Destroyer. I couldn't believe it — it was perfect. The Destroyer, indeed! It was about to destroy the most incredible, incomparable fantasy of my life, and I was not sure whether to be grateful or to kick myself."

Tiny checked out the fake and determined that the ten-inch-long, very thick imitation looked like the real McCoy. He was certain that The Destroyer would have frightened even a lady elephant away.

♦ ♦ ♦

Remember, Tiny Tim did not wear actual underwear. Ever. The fact that Tiny had been wearing adult disposable diapers, was about to come in very handy. By the way, Tiny's disposable underwear reasoning — that you wear them, then you throw them away, and voila!, no more germs following you around the house — was the same kind of super-duper-problem-solving logic that was about to be at work, or at play, in this situation.

Here's what Tiny did. He placed the base of the dildo in his diaper and draped it down his leg. Then he wrapped the tape around and around his leg until he was sure it was nice and secure.

"Let's see... I know. White trousers!" he mused. "Bright stage lights illuminating the outline of the Destroyer in these white pants. That should do it..." he thought, pleased with his plan. "This will definitely stand out boldly. They should be able to see this thing from a mile away."

Then he heard, "Ladies and gentlemen, let's give a warm Southern welcome to the inimitable Tiny Tim! Please give him a hand!"

The audience politely put their hands together for a demure

round of applause, picked up their cocktails, and sat back, ready for their usual evening of entertainment. Tiny followed his band on stage, accompanied by his new friend who was anything but tiny and was, at that very moment, hiding in his pants.

◆ ◆ ◆

Boom! The keyboard player hit the piano keys in a fierce tribute to Jerry Lee Lewis, as Tiny Tim belted out the Lewis signature tune, "You shake my nerves and you rattle my brain. Too much love drives a man insane..."

"I do not have to tell you the crowd went wild," Tiny recalls. "Within seconds, everyone was pointing to my crotch and laughing. While I was singing, I was watching their faces. Their eyes were bugged out, some were horrified, some were laughing raucously, and everyone was shocked. Everyone was pointing below my belt and going, 'Ooh, ahh....'"

"When I sang the line 'great balls of fire,' people couldn't believe it. The play on words was just too much. People were laughing so hard, clutching their sides and their stomachs. They were unable to stop laughing."

"Bringing the band's volume down, I vamped a bit, saying, 'I want you to know how pleased I am to be with you in your fair city. Tonight's show is dedicated to the lovely twins that are serving your tables.'"

The girls, flattered, looked up at the stage and one of them saw the snake that was slithering down Tiny's leg. She dropped her serving tray.

As Tiny ranted and raved about great balls of fire, he watched the twins go pale. They were spilling drinks, the customers were screaming at them, and Tiny knew he was in the clear.

"Mission accomplished. The Destroyer had lived up to its name. I had destroyed them, all right, along with any chance I had of living a fantasy that night."

The story wasn't over. As he finished the song, the dildo began to slip out of his diaper. I guess the adhesive had come loose. It had come to life and was creeping its way toward his ankles. The Destroyer had a mind of its own.

"As I'm singing, I'm trying to nonchalantly rearrange and retrieve the Destroyer that was about to make an appearance out of the bottom of my pants leg. I figured, the show must go on, so I just kept singing. Suddenly, plop! Out it went, front and center stage in full view of everyone in attendance. People were howling, and no one in the band could keep a straight face, either.

"I figured, well, I better finish the song, so I did. 'Come on baby, drive me crazy, goodness, gracious, great balls of fire!'"

What a way to open — and in this case, close — a show.

His brilliant maneuver did indeed scare the lovely twins away, he did not give in to temptation, but needless to say, the club owner was less than thrilled.

"He didn't understand what had happened at all," Tiny remembered, pouting. "He fired me, saying I had turned his beautiful dinner theater into a cheap porn show! As if I would do such a thing on purpose."

Wacko in Waco

Tiny-ism: "I have a much higher source to answer to."

Most of the time, Tiny Tim had no use for newspapers or television. Face lotions, body creams, cologne, music, and good food — those were definitely indispensable. But the news? It just didn't seem relevant to him. He lived in his own world, and it's not that he didn't care what the rest of us mortals happened to be doing, he just had his hands full keeping up with all the current events, real and imagined, that were going inside his brain.

That is, until he found himself hooked by the guy who had barricaded himself behind a fortress in Waco, Texas. Suddenly, I couldn't pry Tiny away from the news with a crowbar. He was mesmerized by what he heard on the tube, just like everyone else, hanging on David Koresh's words as if they were coming from God himself.

One day during that period of time, Tiny and I were having lunch in one of our favorite haunts.

"I have the answer! I have the answer!" Tiny screamed at me between bites of a sandwich, his eyes glued to the restaurant television set that was tuned to CNN, broadcasting the unfolding drama in Waco.

"I know exactly what I have to do!" he continued, very

excited and hyped. "I have a great vision here!"

"Tiny, whoa, settle down. Put your seat belt on, man. Everybody in the whole place is listening to you." I was picking at a plate of fries and all eyes were on us. "Calm down for a second and talk to me. What's up?"

Snapping back to reality, Tiny realized that his outburst had drawn the attention of everyone in the place. Sliding down in his seat, he started to whisper to me, cupping his mouth with his hands so no one could hear him.

"Mister Plym, I am going to offer my services," he whispered, dramatically. "I will go to Waco, Texas, and negotiate for the release of those poor people Mr. Koresh is holding hostage."

"What??? Are you out of your f—ing mind? What's wrong with you?" I don't know why it always surprised me that he always surprised me.

Completely ignoring my reaction, Tiny reached into his ever-present oversized shopping bag and pulled out his address book. It was crammed full of scraps of paper, notes, and business cards, and they started falling out on the table and floor.

"I am going to call one of my friends at the *National Enquirer*," he explained. He was possessed. "He can help me. I happen to know that Mr. Koresh is into music, and although he is grossly misguided, he is a minister, after all, and seems deeply spiritual. We do have something in common…"

Ahh, of course. Naturally, Tiny Tim would feel an affinity for a fellow religious extremist.

"…Due to my name and my notoriety, and thanks to the fact that my religious convictions are widely known, I believe Mr. Koresh would agree to meet with me." Tiny had it all figured out.

"Oh, sure he would, Tiny," I said sarcastically. "He's obviously a guy with a good head on his shoulders who's anxious to listen to reason. Are you shitting me? He's so far gone at this point, he doesn't listen to anyone except the voices in his head."

My words were having absolutely no effect on him. He was dead set on a mission and he was totally stonewalling me. Tiny refused to listen to reason.

"I can save many lives here," Tiny concluded. "I must go. The Lord is calling me."

Now, I've got to say that as always, his heart was in the right place. He honestly saw himself as a one-man cavalry, the only guy who might be able to understand the fanatical lunatic mind. He did have a point there.

◆ ◆ ◆

He planted himself at the restaurant pay phone and dialed. "Here is what I would like you to do," he explained to his contact at the *Enquirer*.

"If you will print a story detailing my offer to go to Waco and meet with Mr. Koresh…" I loved this. Even David Koresh was a mister in Tiny's mind. He afforded everyone the same courtesy and respect.

"…Be sure to include my reasons for why I believe I can successfully negotiate with him," Tiny continued. "I believe the law enforcement agencies will see the story and follow up on it immediately."

I was thinking to myself, oh absolutely. Right away. No doubt about it. The FBI is likely to happen upon the story one day while flipping through the magazines at their local 7-Eleven where they have stopped in for a pack of breath mints and mini doughnuts. They will see Tiny's offer and think, my God, of course! Surely Tiny Tim alone can do what we, the Federal Bureau of Investigation working with the Central Intelligence Agency and law enforcement agencies, could never do.

I knew Tiny was coming from a good place and I didn't want to blow him out of the water. I wanted to be supportive. "So, Tiny, let me get this straight," I said to him after he hung up the phone. "You believe the FBI will see the story, contact you, and send you out to Waco…"

"Yes, Mister Plym, yes! Would that not be wonderful? I am actually in a position to save the lives of all of those innocent men, women and children," he explained, downright giddy from the excitement over his plan.

"Tell me, how did this go over with the reporter at the *Enquirer*?" I wondered.

Tiny wasn't listening. He ran back over to the phone, dialed directory assistance, and asked for the phone number of the FBI. Then he handed the phone to me.

I looked at him like he was off his rocker. "Why the hell are you giving me the phone?"

"Mr. Plym," he pleaded, "as my manager, I need you to call the FBI and let them know that I am volunteering for duty in this crisis. You must convince them. Please."

"Tiny," I said, "They'll send out the guys in the white coats! You don't want to spend the rest of your life in Bellevue, do you?"

He didn't respond, so I said, more gently, "Look, Tiny, listen to me, man. Leave it alone. I know you're just trying to help, but trust me, they're not going to take you up on your offer. Not until hell freezes over."

He was dead serious and not about to back off. He stood his ground, looking at me with a pleading expression.

"Okay, fine. Fine." I pretended to surrender. "If it means that much to you, pal, I'll call them and offer your services. Why not? It's a great idea, and I'm sure they'll jump at the chance to have your help." I tried to sound hopeful.

Then I did what anyone in my place would have done, what any friend would do for a buddy who had lost his mind and was about to throw himself under a train. I faked the call. Just to put his mind at ease.

Speaking to a very loud, irritating beeping sound, I pretended to have a very serious telephone conversation with an imaginary official on the other end of the line. I pulled it off without a hitch. Tiny didn't have a clue.

♦ ♦ ♦

"So, Tiny, I was thinking," I teased, "imagine the FBI does call you and they put you up in a hotel room in Texas. I was just trying to imagine their reactions when they got a load of your room…"

Tiny started to giggle. He knew what I was talking about, and loved to laugh at himself.

"Why, my friend, I am highly offended." He pretended to sulk.

"Yeah, man, can't you just picture it?"

"Suddenly, there would be a knock at the door," Tiny played

along, "but I would be napping and would not hear them. So they would use their secret door-jimmying equipment and slip into the room undetected…" He was speaking in a very suspenseful voice.

"Right, right!" I laughed. "'What is this?' They would say, stumbling over the walnut shells all over the floor. 'What the hell is this? What luck! Just look at all the evidence we have right here… right here in the hotel room of Tiny Tim. I knew he was strange, but I never would have figured him as the notorious cleaning solvents bandit…!'"

I had Tiny in hysterics. As you know by now, he absolutely loved hotels. Bellhops, maid service, room service. Service, service, service. What was not to like? He had people willing to run at his beck and call at any hour of the day or night. This was his comfort zone, his version of home.

Haunted as the poor guy was over germs, the second he set up camp in a hotel room, he had to germ-proof the joint. That meant turning all the pillowcases inside out. After all, other people's skin, faces, hair had at one time touched the outside of the pillowcases. Wait a minute. Weren't the pillowcases clean? What kind of hotels was he staying in, anyway? Of course they were, but as you know, this was a guy who wouldn't even wear real underwear or use a towel because laundry can never really eradicate germs.

Once a proper room scrubbing and bedding inspection had occurred, Tiny would lie down on top of the covers like a corpse, on his back, wearing his suit and tie, and wait. Wait for the phone to ring, for the call of duty, for whatever.

Tiny and I started laughing, imaging that he was hiding out in some hotel room, courtesy of the feds.

"So the moment finally comes for your big powwow with Koresh," I imagined. "But you don't know they're watching you, Tiny," I was ad-libbing, "just to make sure you're on the up and up. After all, they can't be too careful. They've got to check you out before they send you in for a heart-to-heart with their most wanted man. So, they've got your room wired, and they're watching you on video from outside in a van…"

"Yes, yes!" he jumped into the game, "What a sight they would see!"

"No, shit, Tiny. They'd get an eyeful. A fully dressed guy in a tie, sleeping on top of the covers with every light on in the room…"

"To keep away the mice and the spiders, Mister Plym. Remember…"

We were slapping each other on the back and clutching our stomachs from laughter.

"Hey, Tiny, remember that time I was in your room going over those photos with you, and we'd had a few beers? And I rushed in to use your bathroom before you could stop me? What if that was one of the feds instead of me?"

Tiny had stood outside the bathroom door during the entire time I was taking a whiz, shouting instructions in a very distressed, pleading voice.

"Please, Mr. Plym, please, I beg of you. Just sit down. Do not stand up because the urine splashes!"

Then he spent the next hour dousing the bathroom with every toxic chemical known to man and rubbing until his skin was raw, all the while muttering his aggravation under his breath.

"I'm trying to picture the look on their faces, pal, when you open the door and say, 'If you do not mind, kindly leave and go use the toilet in the lobby before coming into my hotel room.' Then you could give them your lecture on dangerous germs and the many reasons you forbid anyone to use your toilet. What do you think, Tiny? Do you think they'd go for that?" I slapped him on the back.

"I never mean any offense, you know. But germs are very clever little creatures and we do have to stay one step ahead of them all the time…," He said, half laughing and half serious.

Oh yeah, the FBI would love him. Even their best men, the ones who had spent an entire lifetime following the world's craftiest criminals, shadiest shysters, and most twisted minds, would have a hell of a time figuring out Tiny Tim…. And speaking of figuring out Tiny Tim, before I finish with the story about the wacko in Waco and the FBI, I've got to take a little detour to tell you about the time that an entire organization made it their mission to figure out my pal, Tiny….

◆ ◆ ◆

Tiny-ism: "Absolutely nothing gets by you!"

◆ ◆ ◆

"Hello?" I answered the phone.

"Yes, is this Stephen Plym? The manager for Mr. Tiny Tim?" A very formal voice was on the other end. This guy was a far cry from the street-talking one-syllable types that usually rang my phone.

"Yep, you got me, Iowa's big city big-shot, I hook 'em and book 'em, I'm the best of the Midwest, the hand-holding, baby-sitting, manager to the stars…," I said. "What's on your mind?" I lit a new cigarette off the butt burning down in my mouth.

He told me his name and said he was telephoning on behalf

of Mensa. Oh, of course. Mensa was calling me. It made perfect sense. No doubt, they had heard about my superior intellect. Anyone who's fool enough to manage the amazing Tiny Tim has gotta be a real brain. They probably wanted to recruit me.

Obviously this was some kind of a joke. Wait! I thought. Maybe it's Tiny, disguising his voice. This guy had those same formal speech patterns that Tiny loved so much. I listened closely for a hint of the person's real identity.

"You are familiar with our organization, are you not?" the voice asked.

"Sure, everyone's heard of you guys," I played along, still trying to see if I could recognize the person's voice on the other end and bust them on their joke. "You're those high I.Q. guys, right? The genius fraternity?"

I half expected the person on the other end to start cracking up, and admit to making a prank phone call. "Shit, man, it's me! Curly! I was just pullin' your leg, Plym…"

"Yes," he said, sounding very amused, "I suppose you could say that…although most fraternities do not admit women into their membership, so it wouldn't be a completely accurate characterization."

I laughed, still waiting for someone to pop out of the closet and tell me I was on some kind of *Candid Camera*-type show.

"In any event," the voice continued, "we are in the process of organizing a rather large conference that will take place over three days and we were wondering if Tiny Tim might be available. Naturally, price is no object."

What? I pulled the phone away from my ear and shook it.

Now I knew this prankster was yanking my chain.

"Excuse me, but we must have a bad connection. What did you just say?"

"As I said, price is no object," the man patiently repeated. "We are quite interested in Tiny Tim's appearance and would, of course, make it worth his while."

I'd always wondered how I would feel if life was ever kind enough to let me hear those four magic words. I asked the guy to hold on for a second, covered the phone with my hand, jumped up and down, and screamed. Then I reached into my pocket, whipped out my needle and thread, and tried to get that deal sewn up before the guy could change his mind.

Mensa's mission statement boils down to three things. First is to identify and foster human intelligence for the benefit of humanity. Hmmm. What could they want with Tiny, exactly? I mean, sure, there were plenty of times when I wanted to pull out my own Swiss army knife, cut a perfect circle around Tiny's skull, and peek in at that marvel he called a brain, but what did Mensa have in mind? I mean, I know what they have *in* their minds — major horsepower engines — but what did they want with Tiny Tim?

The second thing they're known for is encouraging research into the nature, characteristics, and uses of intelligence. Ahh, maybe that was it. Research into the nature and characteristics of intelligence — they could have a lot of fun with Tiny. As to uses for his intelligence? Hell, if they could find some way to take Tiny's boomeranging, obsessive-compulsive, ricocheting pinball thoughts that bounced around in his brain and put them to good use, I'd sell the tickets myself and maybe we'd finally get rich after all.

Third on their purpose statement is the promotion of stimulating intellectual and social opportunities for its members. Wait a minute! I thought, that couldn't be it, could it? What were they going to do? Sit Tiny down in the middle of a room, pass around the refreshment plate, and amuse themselves with Tiny's own peculiar brand of stimulating intellectual and social entertainment? Sit him in the middle of the conference and just let him talk? Why were they calling, exactly?

I put the guy on hold, ran into the bathroom, sloshed some cold water onto my face, and tried to steady myself. That price-is-no-object comment had my brain swirling. Naturally, they were calling for the same reason anyone ever called. They wanted to see Tiny perform. Period. Come on, Plym! I said to myself. Snap out of it. You're complicating things. All they want is to see him do his thing. Go on! Ask him the usual questions.

"I've gotta say, this is really great. Tiny Tim performing for Mensa, the great brain trust. That's really cool," I said, thinking, somehow it just didn't compute. Of course, I didn't say any of that.

All I said was, "So, how many shows will you require and what is the size of your stage? How about your p.a. system, and what about the lighting?" I was laughing at myself for thinking all those other crazy things.

There was absolutely no sound on the other end of the phone. Uh-oh, I thought. This guy finally snapped to, realized he had meant to call Timothy Leary, not Tiny Tim, and fainted from the shock of realizing he'd just made a deal with the wrong guy.

"Hello? Hello? Are you still there?" I said into the phone.

"Oh, no, no, no, no!" The spokesperson apologized.

Here it comes, I thought. I knew it was all a big mistake.

"…I am terribly sorry. I should have explained myself more clearly," he went on. "We do not want Tiny Tim to perform at all. We simply want him to attend our convention, share some meals with us, and converse with our members."

"Huh? No performance at all?" I didn't get it. I was completely stunned. "What is it you want him to do? I guess I'm not following you."

Damned if I wasn't right! When I was imagining that they wanted to sit Tiny Tim in the middle of a room and amuse themselves by listening to him talk, I wasn't far from the truth. The guy gently explained to me that the reason Mensa was inviting Tiny to the conference was that they wanted a chance to study him. Study him! Like a bug. Like a germ under a microscope. Like a rare jungle cat seen through the binocular lens of some guy wearing short pants fatigues and a combat hat, hiding behind a tree. Only no trees and no one was planning on hiding. They had no shame. They wanted to put Tiny under a microscope right out in the open, and they didn't care who knew. No voyeuristic intentions there. They wanted his full cooperation.

"…You see, our organization considers Tiny Tim to be one of the most interesting individuals we have ever observed and we would truly savor the opportunity to be able to converse with him, ask him questions…"

"So, you're inviting him down there to find out what makes him tick?" I laughed out loud. "Sooner or later, everyone tries to figure him out. I've known him forever and I still don't have a clue. If you guys can do it, my hat's off to you! Good luck. I will look for the contract in the mail, and thank you…"

All I could think of after I had hung up with the guy was that Tiny was never going to believe this. We'd had some unusual requests but this was the topper. The big brain big boys actually believed that if they could just get their hands on Tiny, they could really understand him, get into his mind and psyche, and solve the mystery that was Tiny. I laughed all the way over to Tiny's hotel, talking to myself in the car.

"Well, Mensa, all I can say is, even with all your brain power together, you've definitely got your work cut out for you!"

◆ ◆ ◆

"Hey, Tiny, you'd better sit down for this one, pal." I sat across from him and watched the excited anticipation in his face.

"Would you believe," I taunted him, watching his eyes get as big as silver dollars, "that the prestigious Mensa society wants you for a personal appearance. You, pal! Can you believe it?"

"Those people are the biggest minds in the world!" Tiny exclaimed, rolling his big brown eyes. "My goodness, they want me?"

I had to drop the big bomb.

"Uh, Tiny, pal, hold on to your horses for a second. This gig's got a little different twist to it…" I looked him in the eye and explained very slowly, "They don't want any show at all. No singing, no stage performance."

Tiny was looking at me blankly, uncomprehending.

"…No stress, pal. A total cakewalk. The most easygoing appearance you've ever made. You're not even going to believe this scene, Tiny."

"No show?" Tiny asked, totally baffled.

"Yep. You've got the picture," I gleamed. "No show, and double your usual price. What do you think of that, my man?" I was hoping he wouldn't be hurt over the fact that they didn't want him to sing.

"Mr. Plym," Tiny said hesitantly, "am I understanding this correctly? No show. Big money. These fine folks are not exactly living up to their reputation, are they? This isn't too bright!" Tiny started to laugh.

Then he said facetiously, "All right, Mr. Plym, what are they planning to pay me for? Dinner and a movie?"

Now we were both cracking up. "God, you're close, Tiny! You're really close! They simply want to meet you. Talk to you. Have a couple of luncheons and dinners. You'll sign some autographs and just shoot the shit with these I.Q. superstars. Can you even believe it? All they want to do is have the one and only Tiny Tim at their convention and they're willing to pay through the nose to get you.

"I say, take the money and run, pal! This will be easier than robbing a blind lady on crutches."

Tiny and I were crying, holding our stomachs and stumbling around his room, laughing. I hoped the fact that we were having so much fun might distract Tiny from the other fact — that Mensa didn't care to hear him sing.

Tiny's brain started to churn and turn and sputter and he opened his mouth to talk, paused, and thought again for a few minutes. Then, he got right in my face, and said, "I know exactly what is happening here, Mr. Plym. There is no point in sugar-coating the truth…" He was pointing his finger a few inches from my nose.

"…They want to examine me, do they not? Just like an insect. Wait, do not tell me, I am to be some sort of a guinea pig, right? An experiment, yes? Some sort of a special project? What other reason could there be…?" He had it all figured out.

I was scared he was going to be totally insulted by the outlandish, unbelievable, incredible assumptions he was making — all of them true. I knew how quirky Tiny Tim could be and I was racking my brain trying to think of something clever and comforting enough to calm him down when he exploded. Where were those Mensa geniuses when you really needed them, anyway? Sure, they wanted to study Tiny, and they were willing to pay for the privilege. Great. What about telling me how to explain it to Tiny Tim? That would have been helpful.

Just as I was about to open my mouth, Tiny grabbed his head with both hands and started laughing hysterically.

"They think I am insane!" He pranced around the room, yelling and bellowing, laughter bouncing off the walls. "They simply wish to prove to the world what the world already believes to be true…that I am completely mad!"

I couldn't believe it. He wasn't pissed off at all. He actually thought it was funny!

"Oh, oh, oh, Mr. Plym, this is wonderful!" he exclaimed. "Simply wonderful! When these people are finished with me, I will not only be labeled the weird, outlandish, and nutty performer I already am, but they will validate my ticket. I will officially be certified as insane! This is marvelous. Marvelous!"

This whole idea tickled Tiny's funny bone big time. In no time flat, he had convinced himself that the whole gig was some sort of elaborate conspiracy to prove that he was, in fact, crazy. Stark, raving, finger-sucking crazy. A real bona fide lunatic. Leave it to Tiny. He loved it. He never ceased to amaze me.

♦ ♦ ♦

On the day of the gig, Tiny said goodbye to me, with a big grin. "If they can figure me out, more power to them," he stated. "I have been trying to do so for many years, to no avail. God bless them for trying."

What a good sport he was.

Then he turned to me as he was getting into the limousine and added, "I am certain this will make CNN!"

Off he went. The willing specimen climbing into the Petri dish and staring back at the scientists through the Cyclops eye of the microscope. I paced and bit my nails and waited and waited for the conference to end.

Finally, he returned.

"So? How did it go?" I asked him anxiously.

"Well, they were very nice to me," Tiny explained cryptically, with a sly smile. "And the meals were delicious."

"What? That's it??? They were nice and you liked the food? Shit, man, what went on there?" I wanted the dirt.

"Everyone was so friendly and kind. We just talked about many subjects, you know. Life in general. There was absolutely nothing to it. Very delightful, really, but very ordinary everyday conversation."

"Tiny, man, what did they conclude? What was the outcome of the whole thing?" I was dying to know.

All Tiny would say was, "I am truly amazed that I got paid

so much money for simply being myself."

Of course, I couldn't drop it. I had to call. They couldn't take Tiny onto their spaceship and return him to earth without telling me what they had done to his brain. Or what his brain had done to them.

I had to know.

"So, what did you find out about Tiny Tim?" I asked.

In his super-high-octane-twenty-syllable-razzmatazz way, the guy confirmed what I, and everyone close to Tiny, already believed to be true. Tiny Tim was an idiot savant, a genius who had a hard time functioning in the everyday world.

Yeah, like I always said. Tiny Tim was a star man, out of this world.

◆ ◆ ◆

Anyway, back to Waco and the FBI....

"After dealing with you, Tiny, they'd all need a vacation. Can't you just see the headline? 'FBI Agents Survive Waco, But Buckle Under Pressure of Dealing with Tiny Tim. All Retire to Deserted Island For Mental Health Break. Last Seen Wearing Beanies with Propellers on Top and Engaged in Top Secret Basket-Weaving Exercises.'"

◆ ◆ ◆

Tiny waited anxiously for the *National Enquirer* to come out, pacing around, and endlessly watching the horrors unfold in Waco. He grabbed the paper the second it hit the stands, but what do you know? There was no story. Imagine that.

"Why, Mister Plym? Why did they not print the story? He promised me." Tiny had naively taken the man at his word.

"I don't know, man. Maybe they didn't have the room...?"

He set up vigil next to the phone. Even if the *Enquirer* hadn't run the story, maybe the FBI would look him up anyway. After all, I had called them directly, hadn't I? Hadn't I?

Tiny looked like a guy camped out next to the hospital bed of a loved one. I could hardly get him to leave the house. When the FBI called, he definitely didn't want to miss them.

The days stretched on. Tiny agonized, paced around, slept fitfully. He couldn't understand why the FBI was taking so long to contact him, or when the *Enquirer* wasn't planning on running the story. What in the hell was the matter with everyone? Couldn't they see how serious this situation was? Didn't they know it was a matter of life and death?

Along with the rest of the country, Tiny and I anxiously watched David Koresh as he stayed holed up in that desolate spot with all those hostages. Like everyone else, we held our breath and prayed. Then, the situation erupted and the boulder that had been perched at the top of the hill started to roll downhill. Fast. The government meant business and finally they went in, guns blasting. That was it. Total disaster. I could hardly stand to look at Tiny's face as he watched the entire place explode in flames.

"Mr. Plym, Mr. Plym, I do not understand how they could have let this happen!" He was weeping. "How could they? All of those poor innocent people dead! I could have helped, I could have helped to save them. Oh, if only they had let me."

Tiny was inconsolable for a couple of days. Then one night, I got a call that let me know I'd made the right decision by faking the call to the FBI.

"Hello?" It was three in the morning.

Tiny sounded frantic. "I have been thinking and even though I was distraught that I was not allowed to help, it just hit me…"

"What, Tiny?" It was awfully late, but I knew he needed to talk.

"Well, I was thinking about what happened in Waco, and all I can say is thank God I never got the chance to go. I might have been burned to a crisp! Oh, oh, oh, I could have been killed…"

"I know, pal, I know. That's what I was trying to tell you all along. Just imagine if the FBI really had called you," I offered.

"I would be a goner, Mr. Plym. A goner!" He sounded so relieved, I decided to level with him.

"Hey, Tiny, you know what? Now that it's over, I can tell you the truth. I never really called the FBI. I faked the whole thing." I held my breath.

"Oh, Mr. Plym," Tiny gushed, "you are wonderful! Simply wonderful! You saved my life by not calling. I just know the FBI would have jumped at the chance to send me to Waco and I would have died in that fire."

Sure, Tiny. He got to hang on to his delusion that the only thing that stood between him and heroism was me, his good old pal, trying to save his life.

"Somehow you must have known, Mr. Plym. You must have had a vision," Tiny went on. "You really saved my life."

Oh, yeah, I saw the whole thing in advance. In some mysterious psychic premonition, it was revealed to me that they were definitely going to send Tiny Tim in to meet with Koresh… the second the Seven Dwarfs came to life, took over the White House, and invited

Snow White over for high tea.

From that day forward, nearly every time Tiny and I ever saw each other, he thanked me for saving his life. Fearing everyone would think he was a coward for being so thrilled he had not rushed to his death, he never told a soul about his great plan to free the hostages from David Koresh.

Whenever I think back on that strange time, all I can think of is what the papers would have said.

"Just imagine, Tiny," I would joke, "the press would have had a field day with that situation. Your obituary would have read, 'Tiny Tim Dies Trying to Save Wacko in Waco.'"

"All I can say, Mr. Plym, is how much I will always appreciate you for saving my life. You are my hero." Tiny smiled shyly.

"Tiny, listen, man. You're the hero. You were actually ready to put yourself in harm's way to help those people."

Yep, that was us, all right. A couple of real life heroes. Tiny Tim and his cynical, sarcastic sidekick. The Dynamic Duo of Des Moines. In times of crisis, the world could definitely count on us. For laughs, anyway.

Guess Who?

Tiny tidbit: Tiny used to say,
"I know my fascination with young girls is wrong
but I can't help myself. It is a curse, a real curse."

One day I called up my old pal, Walt Reno (God rest his soul). It had been a couple of years since we had spoken and he had no idea that I was now Tiny Tim's manager. I smiled to myself, anticipating his reaction.

"Walt Reno!" I yelled into the phone. "Who's your f—ing tailor?" This was an inside joke just between us, so he knew it was me.

"Well if it isn't Stephen F—ing Plym. Someone break your index finger, buddy? It's about time you picked up the God-damned phone! How the f— are you?"

After a few minutes of agreeing how long it had been and how good it was to hear each other's voice again, I said, "Listen, Walt, can you do me a favor? I manage Tiny Tim, and..."

Before I could finish my sentence, he shouted, "Tiny F—ing Tim? Are you out of your f—ing mind?" He let out a huge roar of laughter.

"I know, Walter, I know it's hard to believe," I replied, laughing too. "But I swear, it's for real. In fact, that's why I'm calling.

I'd love for you to meet Tiny. He's in town playing at Bally's and I was hoping we could all have dinner. What do you say? I know you're going to love the guy."

"Tiny F—ing Tim? Oh God, yes, you know I've got to meet him!" Walt yelled. "That f—ing flake!"

I could hear him still muttering "Tiny F—ing Tim" to himself, over and over, and then exclaiming "Oh my God!" before he clicked off the line.

On the outside, Walt looked like a distinguished, classy, conservative, sharp-dressed, great-looking, silver-haired businessman. Send him into any truck stop and everyone would turn around and stare at him because he looked so out of place — until he opened his mouth.

Underneath it all, he just happened to be a street talking, savvy, Las Vegas mover and shaker with a mean golf swing, who could keep up with any trucker in any truck stop anywhere. In short, he was a TV and radio censor's worst nightmare. My kind of guy, and a man after my own heart.

Between his friendships with Jerry Lewis and Shecky Green and his radio show and car commercials, he was a big name around the Las Vegas strip. And like another icon who drops the ball in Times Square every New Year's Eve, Reno seemed to have discovered the fountain of youth, earning himself the nickname "The Dick Clark of Las Vegas."

Considering that Tiny Tim was appearing at Bally's Hotel, calling Walt had been at the top of my to-do list. For one thing, he was just the connection I needed to get some radio publicity to help promote Tiny's show. Secondly, he was a one-man laugh riot and a great friend, and half an hour with Walt beats the hell out of a day at the spa. He makes you feel good all over.

◆ ◆ ◆

We met on the strip and had dinner at one of the wonderful hotel restaurants.

"Tiny F—ing Tim! God, glad to meet you, man!" Walt exclaimed, shaking Tiny's hand. If you took the "f" word out of Walt's vocabulary, he couldn't speak.

Tiny and my old buddy Walt hit it off beautifully. Well enough, in fact, that after a lot of laughs and plenty of drinks, Walt decided he wanted to put Tiny on his morning radio show. That's what I was waiting to hear. It was perfect, exactly the kind of publicity we needed.

When we arrived at the radio station the following morning, Walt explained the setup to Tiny and me. We were going to do a "Guess Who This Star Is" routine — live. Tiny was supposed to disguise his voice and give clues about who he was, and callers would call in after each clue and try to guess his identity. The caller who guessed correctly would win some kind of prize.

Walt emphasized to Tiny, "Now don't make the f—ing clues too obvious, Tiny. Make them difficult because we're going to do the show for two f—ing hours. Tiny, baby, are you listening to me? This is important. The show has to last two hours. You got that? I don't have any other guests scheduled, so we have to drag it out. You're really going to have to stump them with your clues. Got it?"

Tiny nodded and smiled and seemed to be one hundred percent with the program. No confusion at all.

Somehow Walt wasn't convinced that Tiny really understood

the importance of stumping the audience. He looked Tiny dead in the eye and said one last time, "And Tiny, for God's sake, whatever the f— you do, do not accidentally tell them who you are. They can't know until the very f—ing end, okay? Or else, I'm f—ed."

More nodding and smiling from Tiny and then it was show time. Walt did his introduction and set up the game for the audience.

In a really weird voice, Tiny gave the first clue. Immediately, the phone lines lit up.

As for me, I was sitting there thinking, "Two hours of this shit and I'll definitely be ready for a double Bloody Mary."

The first caller listened to Tiny's clue and made a wrong guess. "Are you so'n'so?" the caller asked.

Now, what do you suppose Tiny did? Follow up with another hard-to-figure-out clue? Stretch out the minutes in Radioland? Make my old pal Walt happy he had us on the show? Of course not.

"Oh, no, I'm Tiny Tim!" Tiny immediately blurted out. Then he realized what he had said and his hands flew up to his face to cover his mouth. "Oh dear, oh my, ooh, ooh…"

Unbelievable! I was mortified, not to mention embarrassed as hell in front of Walt. And needless to say, Walt came unglued. He couldn't believe it. With his face on fire, he immediately segued into music, and turned to Tiny.

"The very first f—ing caller!!! What the f— is the matter with you? Didn't I just f—-ing tell you I had two f—ing hours to fill? Two f—ing hours! To fill with what? You were the only one scheduled! What the f— were you thinking?" Walt just went off on Tiny, and who could blame him?

"Are you f—ing nuts, man? You are! You're a f—ing nut

case!" Poor Walt. Tiny had totally blown it, totally let him down.

"Now what am I going to do for the next two hours?" Walt was busy panicking, and all I could think to do was stare at Tiny Tim with my chin to the floor, my mouth open, and my head wagging back and forth in disbelief.

"Mr. Reno, I am so sorry!" Tiny said, his face screwed up into an expression that said, oops, I really blew it. "I am truly sorry. I do not know how that happened. When the caller asked who I was, it just popped out. Ooh, ooh, I am so sorry."

Suddenly, the sheer, crazy absurdity of the situation hit me and I started laughing so hard I actually fell off my stool onto the floor, and, thank God, that cracked Walt up and brought some levity to the situation. It wasn't long before we were all hysterical.

Walt regained his composure and called the comedian Marty Allen, who happened to be in town, and, luckily, Marty wasn't busy and came right down to the station. He saved the day. And frankly, he saved Tiny's ass and mine, too. Walt had every right to be pissed and, after that stunt, I wouldn't have been surprised if he'd never spoken to me again. Thank God for Marty Allen, who was able to take a little bit of the sting out of that fiasco.

As we walked out of the studio, Tiny was still apologizing profusely to Walt. We said our goodbyes, and Walt just shook his head and said, "Tiny F—ing Tim... Look, next time you're in town, don't call me, I'll call you. Okay, man?"

"Come on, Tiny." I grabbed his arm. "I could really use that Bloody Mary now."

Tiny turned to me and said, "Mr. Plym, I can use a f—ing drink, too. Yes, I f—ing can!"

In the entire twenty-five years we knew each other, I could count on one hand the number of times I ever heard my good friend, Tiny, say a swear word, and that was one of them.

♦ ♦ ♦

While we were sitting in the bar area of a nearby hotel trying to calm down, a young, hot little doll walking from the restaurant started giving Tiny the eye. Now, keeping Tiny away from underage girls was always a trick, but considering how shaken up he was after the radio debacle, he was especially ripe for the picking. Nothing like the allure of a fresh little flower to take Tiny's mind off his troubles. As I said before, fifteen-, sixteen-, seventeen-year-old girls — there was something about that adolescent combination of openness and shyness, innocence and willingness, that just totally flipped Tiny's switch.

At least when we were in the nightclub circuit, the age limit kept Tiny Tim from his worst impulses. It was like an enforced chastity belt for him — the only girls they let in the doors were at least of legal age. Out on the street, the very girls he needed to stay away from him were drawn to him like kitties to catnip. He must have sent out some pheromone vibes that only underage chicks could smell. Young girls followed him down the street, curious to get closer to the strange guy they had seen on television. Even at that age, girls could feel his desire for them, and girls of all ages love to be loved.

♦ ♦ ♦

Being with Tiny when a teenage girl would start flirting with him was like walking your dog on his leash. There you were, minding your own business, lost in your thoughts, letting the dog roam around on the end of the leash, letting him sniff and snoop to his heart's content. Then, suddenly, you feel that sharp tug on the leash that lets you know another dog is nearby, and you have to hold on with all your might so the dog doesn't go flying down the street with you flying behind him.

Watching this particular schoolgirl eyeing Tiny, and watching him watching her, made me remember one of Tiny's more dangerous trespasses into the garden of underage love.

"Hey, Tiny, baby, I have an idea. I'll bet this will cheer us both up." I sipped my drink and grinned at my pal.

"Yes, Mr. Plym? I certainly could use some cheering up. I really do feel terrible about what happened," Tiny said.

"Let's play our own little game of guess who, okay? Right now, I am remembering someone from your past. I'm not going to tell you who it is. Just like with Walt, I'm going to give you some clues as to who I'm thinking about, and you see if you can guess who is it is, okay?"

"Oh, yes, Mr. Plym! Yes! You are wonderful, simply wonderful! Anything to take my mind off poor Mr. Reno. I am so, so sorry, Mr. Plym…."

"Yeah, Tiny, I know you are, pal, I know you are…"

What was I going to do? Stay mad at him? That wasn't the first time that exactly the wrong words had come flying out of Tiny's mouth and ruined the day, and I was sure it wouldn't be the last. The fact is that he couldn't help himself. I took my mind off the radio station and tuned in to one of Tiny's more memorable moments.

"Okay, are you ready? Here goes. First clue: Jail," I said.

"Jail!" Tiny jumped. "When have I ever been to jail, Mr. Plym?"

Good. It was working. He had already forgotten about the radio station. "I'm thinking about a close call, Tiny. Too close. Okay, here's another clue: Los Angeles."

"Los Angeles? Hmmm…" Tiny's mind was searching the file drawers full of memories.

"Remember, I said 'close call.'"

"Okay," he pondered this, "so it was someone I met in Los Angeles where the meeting nearly resulted in a night in jail? Is that what you are saying? I do not recall meeting anyone and getting into any sort of skirmish…"

"No, no, no, pal. You're on the wrong track. It wasn't a confrontation, exactly. More like a close encounter." I was totally giving it away now.

Tiny's whole face turned red. "Wait! Oh, dear, are you remembering that lovely young girl?"

"That's the one, pal, that's the one," I laughed. "How old was she again? Fourteen?" I teased him. "Not even old enough to drive a car, Tiny. You ought to be ashamed of yourself."

"I know, Mr. Plym, I know. I have prayed and prayed…" He wrung his hands and shook his head.

♦ ♦ ♦

Here's what happened, or what I can remember through the haze of too many years and the fact that when it happened, I'd been enjoying too many drinks in the hot West Coast sun.

I know for sure we were in Los Angeles. And I know Tiny was playing a gig at a very plush hotel. That's all I remember. I couldn't tell you where the hotel was or any of the details of the gig, but damn, they sure know how to pour a drink in L.A. Anyway, it was in broad daylight, maybe the day of the gig, maybe the day after, who knows, but in any case, Tiny went wandering the streets like he loved to do and ran smack into some hot little California number barely out of pigtails and braces.

So, he got her phone number, closed his eyes, held his breath, and started walking that tightrope between right and wrong, between salvation and destruction. Or, should I say between salivation and destruction. Afraid that God would strike him dead if he actually ate a piece of the cake, he just stood outside the fridge and licked off all the icing with his finger.

"You swear you never had sex with her, Tiny? I know that's what you told me back then, but come on, man, tell me straight. I won't hold it against you," I was trying to get a confession out of him.

"No, Mr. Plym, no, no, no. I did not violate her. All I did was speak to her on the telephone, and… well, we did become very close and very friendly, but I never touched her," he insisted. "I promise."

Apparently, while Tiny was tiptoeing around the obvious with her on the phone, asking her suggestive questions, using a seductive tone of voice and telling himself that what they were doing did not actually qualify as phone sex, she had the tape recorder going. After all, she was being romanced by a real live celebrity and the girl wanted something for posterity. She was going to make absolutely sure she could prove to her friends that she'd been talking to a real s-t-a-r.

Needless to say, any girl young enough to have to ask for a ride to the mall is fair game for parental room invasions. and it wasn't long before her daddy found the tapes.

"She may have been hot, Tiny, but her daddy was hotter — in fact he was smoking, wasn't he?" I was cracking up, remembering it all. "He was so mad, there was steam comin' out of his ears! Didn't he threaten to kill you, man?"

"He certainly did." The memory made Tiny sweat.

"Man, you were scared shitless, weren't you, pal?" I laughed.

"I was. I was, indeed," Tiny admitted. "Do you remember how I hid inside my room for days, afraid to come out?"

"Yeah, then you call me up, begging for me to get you out of it, as usual," I teased. "'Oh, Mr. Plym, Mr. Plym,'" I mimicked him. "'What in the world am I going to do? I am in over my head this time! Please help me. Please!'"

We were both laughing at the memory.

◆ ◆ ◆

The day he called me to tell me what had happened, I spent the first hour or so yelling at him, and when I finally calmed down, I tried to figure out what the hell we were going to do. I drove right over to his hotel.

"Tiny, you've gotta level with me, man. Is this motherf—— really violent? Do you think he might try to press charges? Or go to the press?" I was totally freaked out. "How bad is this?"

I couldn't believe it. All of our careful strategizing — the move to Iowa, getting him back in the limelight again, getting some decent publicity after so many years of Tiny scrounging around in the trashcans for leftovers — all shot to hell over some pubescent girl.

"Damn, Tiny, I can't believe you! You're willing to risk everything we've worked so hard for just to get some adolescent piece of ass?" I was pissed. "The last thing we need is a scandal. If this gets out, you'll be totally finished."

"I know, Mr. Plym, I know. You have every right to be angry, but I suppose I thought that if I did not actually have sex with her, it would be all right. I was very careful not to cross the line," he said, his head hung.

"Careful not to cross the line? Are you out of your f—ing mind?" I yelled. "Just taking the phone number of a fourteen-year-old girl and then calling her at two or three o'clock in the morning is crossing the line, man. Who do you think you are, Jerry Lee Lewis? Fourteen years old, man! Unbelievable…Look, Tiny, this isn't getting us anywhere. We've really got to put our heads together and think of some way to get you out of this f—ing disaster."

"All I ever did was talk to her on the phone, Mr. Plym. I honestly cannot understand why her father is so upset," Tiny agonized. "It was only conversation."

"Only conversation, Tiny? Really? Okay, let's think about this. Why the hell is her father so upset, exactly? What the hell did you talk about with this girl?" I asked.

"Just typical ordinary conversation. Everyday, normal topics," he insisted.

"Well, you know what, pal? No offense, but your definition of normal, everyday conversation is usually pretty out there," I pointed out. "For this guy to be threatening to kill you, he must have some pretty heavy-duty ammo up his sleeve. Think, Tiny, think. What does he have on you? Give me an example of the kinds of things you talked about. Be specific. I know you're embarrassed but this is serious. I have to know what we're up against."

"Well," Tiny said innocently, staring up at the ceiling, "sometimes we talked about her clothes."

"Her clothes? Come on, man, cut the shit!" I yelled. "Do you want my f—ing help or not?" I could match Walt Reno curse word for curse word any day of the week. "What could be on those f—ing tapes that you would not want anyone else to hear? Tell me right now, or you are on your own, man. Give it up. No bullshit!"

Tiny started shaking and sputtering sentences like a machine gun.

"We did talk about her underwear. I told her what kind I liked," he admitted.

"Depends, Tiny? You gave her the germ speech? You told her she ought to wear diapers like you? Are you kidding me?" That was the last straw.

"No, no, Mr. Plym," Tiny shrieked. "Lingerie. We talked about her panties, what style she wore, what colors she liked. And she told me that sometimes she does not wear any at all. Oh, oh, oh, oh, I know I am in trouble here, Mr. Plym."

"You're damn straight, Tiny. You're damn straight you're in trouble." I said.

"…Truly, it was all innocent, believe me. Nothing but talk, but yes, yes, yes, just repeating it here now, to you… I can just imagine what it would sound like to someone else! Especially a father."

"Never again!" he declared. "Never, ever again!"

Tiny knew he was in it up to his knees and he was really starting to come unglued. Having me pissed at him on top of being terrified of the girl's father was just too much for him to take. Time to slow it down a little.

"Look, Tiny," I said, "I think we should call it a night. I'm going to bed. I'll be able to think much more clearly after a good night's sleep. Try to get some sleep, and after we're rested we'll decide what to do."

I patted him on the back and left. He'd had enough for one night.

♦ ♦ ♦

The next morning I knew what I had to do. I had to march right out and meet the dragon head on.

I picked up the phone. "Tiny? Listen, it's me. I'm calling her father. I'm gonna get the facts and find out what the sonofabitch is planning."

Tiny gave me the phone number and I got her dad on the phone. I could tell he wasn't exactly a Boy Scout, himself.

"I'm thinking about killing that f—ing fag, Tiny Tim," the guy announced.

Then he proceeded to tell me in vivid detail how he'd like to take Tiny apart piece by piece like a roasted chicken.

"Mr. Blankety-blank, I can assure you that Tiny Tim is very sorry for talking to your daughter, and he promises he will never do it again," I offered. "I know this has been a big pain in the butt for you, and Tiny wants to make it up to you. Immediately!"

He didn't seem to be objecting to the fact that I was blatantly trying to bribe him, so I went on.

"What kind of alcohol do you drink? What's your favorite brew?" I asked, crossing my fingers.

"What the f— difference does it make?" The guy shot back.

"Well, Tiny wanted to send you over a few cases to show you how sorry he is, but if you would rather he didn't…" A lot of guys would have been totally insulted by the fact that I was trying to buy him off.

"Budweiser!" he yelled. "Send Budweiser!"

"Great. We'll get a few cases right over to you, sir." Whew. I breathed a sigh of relief.

"Hold it, now, just hold it." he said. "Is that f—ing queer, Tiny Tim, still performing at that fancy hotel there?"

"Well, yeah," I admitted. "But why?"

"Personally, I can't stand the long-haired asshole but I wouldn't mind being at that fancy joint with my girlfriend, if you know what I mean…," he said.

I said, "Oh, of course," thinking, this guy is too much!

"… I mean it would be nice to see how the other half lives, have a few drinks and supper and watch that Tim guy singing his weirdo songs. How about it?" he asked gruffly.

It took everything in me not to laugh.

"No problem. We will be happy to take care of you," I assured him. "Just show up. Everything will be taken care of, compliments of Tiny Tim. And it's our pleasure."

"Okay, that'll work fine…" the guy said.

I was just about to hang up when he added a little postscript to our conversation.

"Do you remember what he did then, Tiny? After he'd gotten us to comp him for the show, the meals, the drinks, and the beer?" I laughed and shook my head.

"I certainly do, Mr. Plym. How could I forget? I believe he

also requested a hotel room for him and his lady friend, did he not?"
Tiny was giggling.

"You've got it, pal. The sonofabitch says to me, 'Look,
buddy, don't forget the room. You see, I'm plannin' on getting pretty
drunk and I ain't driving home loaded.' Then he hung up on me!"

"Even though I did not meet the girl's father that night, I
certainly was nervous just knowing he was in the audience," Tiny
remembered.

"Hey, you know what would have been hilarious?" I had a
brainstorm. "I should have said to her father, 'Oh, absolutely. We
will arrange for you to have an adjoining room with Tiny. He will be
staying at the hotel with your daughter after the show!'"

We had a chuckle over that and finished our drinks.

"All I can say, old pal," I said, draining my glass, "is one of
these days, your mouth is going to get us both killed. Lucky for us,
Walt Reno is an old friend of mine, and as for that young chick's dad
— thank God he didn't push the issue. You just better pray that
angel on your shoulder never falls off..."

"Mr. Plym, from this moment on, I shall take an official
vow of silence. I will never speak again," Tiny joked. "Especially
over the phone."

"Perfect, Tiny," I joked back. "That's just great. From now
on, whenever you have something to say, just blow a little horn.
Then the papers will claim that Tiny Tim has lost his mind and thinks
he's Harpo Marx."

"Silence worked for Charlie Chaplin... There is only one
problem, Mr. Plym. How will I make a living if I become mute?"
Tiny wondered.

"Don't worry about it," I said sarcastically. "I bet there's a whole world of people out there who would pay big money just for you to keep your mouth shut. Finally, we'll be millionaires. Wow! I don't know why we didn't think of it before."

Birthday Doll

Tiny Fact: Tiny Tim's one true, consistent,
passionate love was New York City.
"I will always be in love with the
good ol' Manhattan Isle," he would say.
"She is the only woman who has never hurt me."

Tiny Tim waited for the moment when my second wife asked him what he wanted for his birthday meal and then he rattled off the menu on cue, like an awards acceptance speech he'd been memorizing for weeks: eight baked potatoes, twelve ears of corn, a pound of pasta with meat sauce, salad for twelve, and a loaf of Italian bread... and, of course, two large glasses of tomato juice with Tabasco sauce and a six-pack of Busch beer.

She was planning to do all the cooking and Tiny was planning to do all the eating by himself. What? You're saying it's impossible for one human to eat that much food? You are, of course, absolutely right, but I had witnessed Tiny perform this particular feat often enough to know that he would pull it off like a professional bottomless pit. The question was, where did the food go? He ate like a sumo wrestler but he was built like your average bear. Weird.

A birthday party, or any party in his honor, was Nirvana for

Tiny — absolute, unadulterated Heaven. One person fawning over him was incredible, but an entire house full of people whose sole agenda was to make him feel loved and special for the evening? For Tiny Tim, the ultimate attention junkie, and for most people in fact, life just didn't get any better than that.

The big bash took place on Tiny's birthday, April 12th, 1993. Just the right combination of adoring friends and fans showed up at my humble house but they could have been ascending the steps of the castle to see the crowned prince, himself — throwing their arms around him, hugging him, kissing his cheeks, smiling and squeezing and telling him how young he looked. It was music to his years. His favorite line was, "Oh, Tiny, you look so young; it doesn't seem that you've aged a bit since the Miss Vicki days!"

He received them with grace, intense appreciation, and a desperate kind of gratitude. He was as thrilled to see them as a man who had been locked up and living a life of solitary confinement for years; as thrilled as a delirious man hanging onto a piece of driftwood might be to see a life preserver floating by. That's what Tiny's audiences always meant to Tiny — absolutely everything. Not even the feast Tiny had devoured all by himself before the guests arrived could compare to the deep satiation he felt when he looked out into an audience and saw affection in their eyes. And it didn't make one bit of difference to Tiny whether the audience was filling chairs in a big auditorium or sitting around my living room. He needed them. More than they ever knew, more than he could ever explain or admit.

Tiny Tim had a hole in his soul. He never talked about his

childhood enough for me to know what had put it there, but he carried an endless emptiness inside. And right up until the very day he died, the only thing that could fill him up to where he was completely content was the love of an audience. And on that birthday night, a few years before his death, all the planets aligned just so. The stars lit up and twinkled and everything in the world conspired to set his universe right by giving him all the love he could handle.

He told jokes. Everyone laughed at just the right moments and stayed laughing just long enough. He told show business stories, and his friends and fans sat wide-eyed on the edges of their seats and oohed and aahed. And for every story, they asked for another. Watching his face that night, I wanted to cry. He was like a kid who wanted to crawl up into your lap, lay his head down, hold on tightly, and fall asleep.

People shouted out requests, and he happily complied, singing every song they asked for at least once or twice. In between singing and regaling them with reminiscences of the glory days, he managed to down four pieces of his birthday cake and a whopping thirty-two bottles of beer. Wait a minute! You know how I just said that Tiny seemed to have a hole in his soul? Well, maybe the hole was actually in his stomach, just like one of those porcelain dolls where you feed them through the mouth and the food falls right out of a giant opening at the bottom. The ones your mother used to use to trick you into eating that awful oatmeal — "Okay, Junior, one spoonful for the ducky and one for you. Come on, now…"

Even without a single present, the buckets and baskets of

love and adoration everyone brought would have been enough for Tiny. He did also get lots of nice gifts. He opened them very carefully and slowly, preserving ribbons and bows and throwing kisses. Watching him open his gifts, I was smiling because I had a little surprise up my sleeve.

◆ ◆ ◆

After he had finished opening everyone else's gifts, I presented him with mine, careful not to let on that it was a gag. When Tiny opened the package, he found my note, which read, "A female companion for the road. Hope you're never lonely again." I had gotten him a large, plastic blow-up doll.

Tiny looked at it for a long minute. A really long, slow-motion, dragging-out-every-one-of-the-sixty-seconds-contained-in-it kind of minute. Then he got a shy, embarrassed look on his face and started laughing along with everyone else.

"Come on, Tiny! Blow her up! Let's see you put some life into your new date!" People were shouting. Tiny wasn't the only one who'd been hitting the brews and everyone was having a great time with the joke. The usual jokes and comments and asides flew around the room and Tiny seemed to thoroughly appreciate the gag along with everyone else.

"I will make sure I pack this little dolly in my luggage on my next trip," he announced with a grin. "I think she is going to be just the ticket. Perhaps she will keep me out of trouble. One thing for certain… no matter what I do, I know she will never give me any lip!"

Everybody laughed and drank some more and Tiny sang some more songs and eventually his birthday party burned itself out and we all called it a night. Tiny went to bed as happy as a man could be, and I felt so glad that we had been able to put that smile on his face.

◆ ◆ ◆

About two weeks later, around four o'clock in the morning, my phone rang. I mumbled a feeble "Hello?"

"Mr. Plym, how are you?" Of course, it was Tiny. Who else would call me at that ungodly hour?

"Yeah, hi, Tiny," I groaned. "What can I do for you as I lie here in my bed? I'm trying to sleep." I figured he was on one of his telephone marathons again, calling people all over the world. That was one of his favorite pastimes, a game he could play by himself, in the comfort of his own room, at any hour of the day or night.

"Mr. Plym, Mr. Plym, I am so very, very sorry to awaken you, but this can not wait! It is urgent!" He pleaded with me not to hang up.

"Okay, pal. Get to the punch line," I said, yawning.

"Do you remember that urethane doll that you gave me for my birthday?" he asked me, somewhat breathless.

"Yeah, Tiny? What about it?"

"Well, I must tell you, the doll was absolutely fantastic! Unbelievable! Ooh, ooh, ahh… the thrill of it!" he exclaimed.

I looked at the phone like it was broken. Damn, I thought, I must be more out of it than I thought. I tried to wake up and follow his rap. "What in the hell are you talking about, Tiny?"

"Mr. Plym, do you not see?" he said, excitedly. "I have been with the wonderful urethane doll all night! It has been so exciting!"

Where were my cigarettes, anyway? I downed whatever was in the glass on the nightstand and lit a smoke.

"…She is so sensual! I have made passionate love to the doll in every orifice…" Tiny said.

I started choking on cigarette smoke.

"…I held it, I kissed it, I caressed and fondled it… and when I lay on top of it in just the right manner, the arms and legs came up around my body and enveloped me." Tiny paused for effect, and then he said, "Mr. Plym, she actually clung to my body!"

"Tiny, is this a joke?"

"Do you not see what I am saying? This urethane doll loves me!"

"Tiny, pal, this is a joke, right?" I was hoping like hell. "You're not really, not actually… I mean you wouldn't really fuck a toy doll, would you? I mean, did you?"

"Yes, yes, I did!" Tiny announced, very proud of himself. "But listen, please," he pleaded. "After giving this a great deal of thought… what I am trying to tell you is that I am now very sorry for the terrible things I did to this urethane doll." Tiny was agonizing over having had sex with the doll, not for the obvious reasons. Not because it was warped to be making love to plastic, but because he felt just like he felt whenever he had sex with a live human being. Ashamed and guilty as hell.

"It was just like taking advantage of a young, innocent girl! It was a sin! A sin!" he yelled. "So I took the scissors… I stabbed it and stabbed it many times. I had to, Mr. Plym. I had to kill the temptation…"

I felt like I had awakened in the middle of some weird comic horror flick.

"…Then I cut it up into a million little pieces and threw them out my hotel window. It was wrong, wrong, wrong, Mr. Plym."

"I know, Tiny, I know," I said, trying to sound comforting, realizing that I just needed to let him get this out of his system.

"I must now go pray for forgiveness. Anyway, Mr. Plym, I had to call you and tell you how sorry I am. Although I truly loved your gift, it had to be destroyed. I hope you will understand. I had to kill the wonderful doll. Such pleasure, but… Out! Out! Out the window. No more sin… I just had to let you know." Click. He hung up.

I let the phone fall out of my hand as I fell straight back onto my pillow. Needless to say, my wife was awake and giving me very strange looks, having heard only my side of the most bizarre conversation in the history of the world.

After Tiny had hung up, that was it. We never discussed it again. Unless you count the fact that I would, from time to time, bring up the subject whenever I needed to shut Tiny's mouth. From that day on, all I had to do was turn to Tiny and say, "Urethane, baby! Takes you anywhere you want to go. Right, Tiny?" That would always do the trick. It would shut Tiny up in a New York second.

After that phrase, it would get so silent, you could hear an ant piss on a rock. I used it freely and often.

♦ ♦ ♦

Lying on the pillow staring at the ceiling while my wife, propped up on one elbow, stared down at me, I started laughing. Laughing until I cried. Then I shared the whole thing with her, and we both cracked up.

"Hey, remember that anniversary dinner? For some reason this reminded me of that night…," I said to my wife.

It was a year or two before that birthday party, and it was my wedding anniversary. Racing out the door to the restaurant, I had stupidly stopped to answer the phone.

"Yeah, what is it? I'm really running late," I said into the phone, not knowing who was on the other end.

It was Tiny Tim. "Mr. Plym, what are you doing tonight? Are you busy? How is the family?" Tiny asked, oblivious to the fact that I was trying to get out of the house.

"Tiny, baby, listen to me. I'm out the door, it's my anniversary, got to go to dinner. Can I get back with you?" I was fidgeting, dying to hang up.

There was dead silence on the other end. "Hello???" I barked. "What's up? Tiny, talk to me, man. What do you need?"

"Mr. Plym, I am so sorry I forgot it was your anniversary. Oh, oh, God, Mr. Plym. Please forgive me." On and on he went. I couldn't hang up on him but I was like the cartoon Roadrunner, my feet spinning and my eyes fixed on the door.

Tiny finally started to speed up his rap. "I can tell you are in a hurry. I do not mean to intrude or be rude, but I simply must talk to you. It is so, so, so important, a new discovery… Is there any way I could join you and your wife for dinner?"

Oh, absolutely. Just come on over. Take your time. No problem. I couldn't believe he was really going to try to make the evening into a threesome.

"…Believe me, dinner is on me," Tiny raced on. "I would really love to be with you two on your anniversary, all those wonderful memories…. Me singing to her as you proposed marriage…."

It was true, he had. And now he was going to make damned sure I didn't forget it.

"…and of course, being best man at your wedding…." He had a mouth full of honey and he was laying it on thick. "Although I did not actually realize that today was the day, I do feel that I am destined to be with you. Destined," he repeated for emphasis, with his typical over-the-top dramatics.

I knew Tiny Tim, I knew he wouldn't drop it, and I knew when I was licked. "Listen, Tiny, I'll pick you up in ten minutes. Got it? Ten minutes. Not eleven minutes, not twelve. Ten minutes. Okay? That means if you've got to do your makeup, shower, shave, or meditate, I'm going to have to pass. I hope you understand, man. We've got dinner reservations and it's our anniversary, for God's sakes!"

"Oh, no, Mr. Plym, I am ready!" Tiny was jumping up and

down with happiness. "Honestly! Thank you, thank you, you are wonderful, simply wonderful. I will be in the hotel lobby. Thank you sooo much. You are the best, Mr. Plym."

Okay, great. So then I had to break the news to my wife that her wonderful husband had invited a friend along to their anniversary dinner.

I told her straight, "Look, honey, believe it or not, we've got a guest, it's Tiny Tim, yes I know it's our anniversary, I'm sorry but it couldn't be helped," and so on and so on.

The wife was cool, gave me just enough grief to look legitimate, and off I went to Tiny's hotel.

I got to the lobby and, what a surprise! Tiny wasn't anywhere to be seen. I waited a few minutes and he was still missing in action. Was I pissed? Oh, no, not at all. Tiny had only invited himself to my damned anniversary dinner, got me to agree that he could come along, swore he'd be waiting for me outside the hotel, and now failed to even show up. Steaming mad, I pounded on the elevator button and took it up to the fourth floor to Tiny's room.

Banging on the door, I started yelling, "Tiny, it's Steve! Come on, man, I'm f—ing late! You said you'd be in the lobby!"

"Oh, Mr. Plym! Thank God, it is you!" Tiny yelled through the door. "I am locked in my room! I cannot get out! Someone locked me in! Thank God you have arrived to save me!"

I stood there listening to his crap. Someone was out to get him? Tonight? Tonight??? My f—ing anniversary night?

"What now, Tiny? What the f— do you mean?" I said,

230

showing great sensitivity for the situation. "Open the damned door!" I demanded.

"But Mr. Plym, I cannot seem to figure out these locks…" The simple mechanics of three inside door locks had poor Tiny so confused and frustrated he was a prisoner in his own hotel room. That was Tiny Tim. The King of Common Sense.

Even with me talking him through opening the locks, it was over his head, so I had to enlist the maintenance people to help. As if the room was on fire, they rose to the challenge and … promptly took the door off its hinges.

Happy anniversary to me!

All the way to the restaurant, Tiny apologized, and when we got there, my wife helped to calm me down. Then, just for good measure, I downed three Stoli martinis and smoked half a pack of cigarettes.

Okay, I thought, the veins in my neck seem to be bulging a little bit less, my blood pressure is returning to normal. I'm just going to enjoy the evening, live for the moment, get in the mood.

So there we were. Just the three of us.

Dinner arrived looking scrumptious and as my wife took her first bite of lobster, Tiny began some scintillating dinner table conversation.

"Mr. Plym, I have found the ultimate way to masturbate. It is beyond anything I have ever experienced," he announced.

As my wife was busy choking on her lobster, I started spitting my martini onto the table. "What did you say, man?" I asked him, incredulous.

Tiny looked directly at my wife and said, "I have discovered the most satisfying way to masturbate. It is painful, but definitely completely worth it. It is so, so, so, unbelievably wonderful! So much ecstasy…"

Just in case, we hadn't gotten the gist of what he was saying, Tiny went on to elaborate, explaining that he had, like a great explorer, ascended the heights of the big sex mountain — and conquered. He had planted his flag proudly and announced that he, the great Tiny Tim, had discovered the quintessential orgasm.

"Do you not see?" he asked, downright giddy. "Do you not see what this means? I will not have to sin any longer! No more women! No more sin! I must tell you all about it! It is so wonderful…"

Well, what a f—ing anniversary dinner this is, I'm thinking. My wife and I looked at each other, our expressions saying, boy, great romantic mood, huh?

Like a trooper, she took the lead. "Tiny, sweetheart, what are you trying to say exactly?"

That did it. The door flung wide open and Tiny went flying on through. "You both know how terrible I am with women. The worst lover ever, right? Well, I have been experimenting with my masturbation techniques, trying to find the answer to a consistent orgasm…"

A bite of food, a sip of a drink, a little more talk about another man's dick. Perfect.

"…the kind of orgasm that will allow me to avoid women and sin…" he went on like a public speaker, addressing the room on proper technique. "At last, I have found the answer. My penis has spoken to me! It was as if I heard a real voice. Ooh, ooh, ooh, unbelievable! So wonderful! I must tell you both and get your input!"

Definitely. There was nothing my wife and I wanted more than to spend our anniversary talking about Tiny's cock.

Deadly calm, I sipped my fifth martini, and looked at Tiny and said, "Yeah, sure, Tiny. Lay it on us, man!" Then I exploded, screaming, "Are you out of your f—ing mind here?"

My outburst had no effect on Tiny, whatsoever. Seeing he was totally undaunted and determined to proceed no matter what, I decided to relax and go with the flow.

"Sure, Tiny, we're all yours, man, let us have it." Just think of it as dinner and a show, I told myself.

"So, I stroke myself gently with a wonderfully delicate lotion until I become totally aroused…" he explained.

"You mean you had a roaring hard-on, right pal? Harder than Chinese arithmetic?" That was one of Tiny's lines. At that point, I had thrown any ideas of a wonderful evening out the window, so why not?

Laughing heartily, Tiny told me I had a way with words, then guzzled an entire beer in one gulp.

"Then what I do is lie on my back, take my index finger, put it directly on the top of my penis and press down, slowly and very gently. Using constant pressure, I keep pressing straight down until my entire penis disappears up inside me and it looks like I have a vagina." Tiny beamed.

Wonderful. Just absolutely wonderful.

"Then, all I have to do is hold it inside and wiggle my index finger on top of the penis back and forth as fast as I can," Tiny continued. "Now, in the beginning, the feeling is one of severe pain…"

Just like I was feeling at that moment, I thought.

"… but within a minute or two, the pain is transcended and it becomes pure pleasure, absolute ecstasy. Can you believe it, Mr. Plym? The hottest sexual feeling I have ever felt and I do not even need a woman!" he said, triumphantly.

Over dessert, he declared that having discovered this great sexual secret, he would never again find himself in carnal sin with a woman.

"I have banished temptation for all time! Satan can go back to hell! I have finally won this battle!"

He may have won that battle, but he never won the war. Sex or God? God or Sex? The ultimate moral dilemma was his for life. And he was mine for life. My very own wind-up doll, ready to amuse and entertain at any hour of the day or night.

'Til Death Did They Part, Take Three... Or Is That Four? Miss Sue and the Unknown Wife

"Every day above ground is a good one."

--Tiny Tim

As Tiny Tim's number came up and the universe got ready to call him back home, God sent him a very unlikely angel to ease him down the last little side streets of his life. Now, I've got to say, looking at the situation through my hard-boiled perspective, I didn't exactly spot her as an angel right off the bat, but as their relationship unfolded, I began to see that the woman Tiny Tim called Miss Sue had come along at the perfect time, and was bringing Tiny the one thing he desperately needed — security. Two things, actually. Rest and security. Okay, so I can't count. It was three things — absolute undying devotion, rest, and security.

But before I get to Miss Sue, the girl who will go down in the history books as Tiny's last and final wife, and his angel of mercy, I have to tell you about a little tiny skeleton Tiny kept in the closet and in the deepest recesses of his heart.

Now, let's see, Miss Vicki was Wife Number One, Miss Jan was Wife Number Two, so it doesn't take an astral physicist to figure out that Miss Sue would be Wife Number Three, right? Well, not exactly. In between Wives Two and Three was the Unknown Wife.

What??? How could there have been an extra wife thrown into the strange mix that was Tiny's life? Well, Tiny Tim, with his particular way of bending things to fit his rules and his conscience, found a way to have a "spiritual marriage" while he was already married to Wife Number Two, Miss Jan. He convinced himself it wasn't anything to worry about — or get arrested over — and even Miss Jan couldn't stop him.

Her name was Miss Stephanie Bond. Notice how I did not say "Miss Stephanie"? Yep, Tiny considered her so unique, so special, so otherworldly, that he actually broke his own steadfast, lifelong rule of always addressing a woman as "Miss," followed by her first name — just her first name. He never used last names for females.

First and last name for this girl. This was heavy stuff for Tiny Tim. He was madly in love.

Now, I'd seen Tiny twisted up and torn up and torn down and messed up over many a woman, but this was the one time I knew he was out of his mind, over the moon in love.

"She is the most beautiful woman in this universe!" Tiny would exclaim. "She is truly like an angel. No words can adequately describe her, try, try as I may."

I'd never seen him so absolutely one hundred percent absorbed in a woman, and I mean unrelenting passion and fire when he spoke of her. To Tiny, Stephanie Bond was perfect, and he worshipped her with the fervor he usually saved for the good Lord, Jesus.

Having only seen a photo of her, I never got the full effect of her halo and wings, but from her photo it was easy to see she was very blonde, very pretty, and surprise, surprise, very young.

As you know by now, after his usual bout with trying to fend off the fear of fire and brimstone raining down upon his mortal soul, Tiny would often find himself in bed with a woman (or girl), even if it did mean a week of penance after the dirty deed. But with Miss Stephanie Bond, it was different.

"I would never, ever, ever have sex with her!" Tiny would moan. "I could not even consider it. I am beyond sex with her, for I truly love her with all my being... all my soul... I know that God has sent her to me. This is my one true spiritual love."

His one true spiritual love. There you have it. That's how Tiny would always refer to his relationship with her. Tiny believed that when he died one day, he would be joined in Heaven by Miss Stephanie Bond.

"Not on earth, only in Heaven," Tiny would say with absolute certainty. "God made this one perfect woman for me alone, and I believe it is God's will and plan that she and I are joined together in the only perfect place — Heaven!"

"But Tiny, man, what about your current wife? Miss Jan? Remember her? The one in New York? What about Jan, baby?"

"It does not matter," Tiny would explain. "Miss Jan and I are husband and wife on this earth only and even if I feel it was a mistake, I must live with it and honor my commitment to her in this life. But in Heaven..."

Sure, he was married. On earth. Heaven was a different story.

Tiny went on to explain to me that his first obligation was to God and that anything related to the flesh, earthly desires, or earthly vows for that matter, was going to have to take a back seat to what had been ordained from above.

"… In fact," Tiny continued, pacing the room and gesturing towards Heaven, "I have prayed for direction and His wisdom and I've already told Miss Jan of my intentions."

Tiny folded his hands prayerfully and closed his eyes.

I wasn't sure I was getting his drift, exactly.

"What intentions, Tiny? You've lost me here…"

"I intend to marry Miss Stephanie Bond. I have made up my mind and explained it to my wife and I am going to have a spiritual wedding with Miss Stephanie Bond. Oh, ooh, I cannot wait!"

Tiny truly is nuts, I thought to myself.

"This wedding will not be dictated or controlled by those here on earth. It will not even be a legally binding ceremony…"

Whew. Thank God, he could save on attorney's fees for the bigamy arrest.

"…It will be a spiritual wedding to symbolize our true destiny and what God has in store for us when we both reach Heaven. This will be our spiritual vow — to be married one day in Heaven and spend the rest of eternity in love and peace together!"

As I watched Tiny making wedding plans, while the current Mrs. Khaury went about being his missus, I couldn't believe it.

"Tiny, this is illegal! You can't be married by a minister!"

"No marriage license! No legal papers! This is a spiritual marriage so we can be together as man and wife when we die!" Tiny was screaming at me, unable to understand how I could not comprehend something so simple.

He did it.

Marathon phone sessions — and matching phone bills, his and hers love letters and cards.

"My dahling husband, the dear sweet thing," Miss Jan said, gritting her lovely teeth, "has temporarily lost his f—ing mind!"

Unbelievable! He would go on and on and on about Miss Stephanie Bond in the presence of the actual Mrs. Khaury.

"But I do still love him. Right, dahlink?"

Even when the courts had torn asunder what God had joined together between Tiny and Miss Jan, he stayed true to his vows with his spiritual wife, and informed the new about-to-be-legal wife about the already existing spiritual bond. His spiritual Stephanie Bond, that is.

Needless to say, Miss Sue was not exactly thrilled over the prospect of marrying a man who was already — in his heart and spirit anyway — betrothed to another.

"Do not ever try to change me!" He would yell through the phone at her. "I will be with you and love you here on earth but when I go to Heaven, I will be forever with one woman only throughout eternity. My darling Miss Stephanie Bond!"

I had to hand it to Miss Sue. She must have really loved Tiny. Who else would put up with that spiritual marriage crap? Can you imagine trying to compete with the one perfect woman sent directly from Heaven?

♦ ♦ ♦

When he met his final wife, the year was 1995, and Tiny Tim was not well. Both his health and his strength were on the downhill slide. He was a diabetic, but he ignored his dietary restrictions and ate whatever the hell he wanted. Not only that, he ate such huge quantities of whatever the hell he wanted that he was seriously overweight. He was getting up there in age, and quickly running out of gas. He didn't have it in him anymore to perform very much.

On top of all that, he was absolutely flat broke. What a surprise. He had never been able to save a nickel for ten minutes, and now, when he needed a retirement fund, he was lucky to have enough dough to cover his monthly nut — or his monthly nut supply for that matter. Forget a savings or even a checking account, whatever he carried in his wallet on any given day amounted to his life savings. And considering that he could piss away a week's pay within seventy-two hours, he didn't have much to show for himself.

At the time he met Miss Sue, Tiny was doing a couple of engagements in Minnesota, and I was back home in Iowa throwing a special party for him at my home. In the middle of running around like a chicken with my head cut off trying to get the preparations together for the big bash that night, I answered the phone.

"Mr. Plym? Are we still having the party?" Tiny asked.

"Sure, Tiny," I assured him. "In fact, at this very moment, I am back here in Iowa, working my ass off to get everything ready for tonight. What's up on your end?"

"Uh… how is your lovely wife? How are the kids?" Oh, no, I thought, here we go. Tiny was doing his small talk routine, which he would launch into whenever he was trying to buy some time to find the courage to bring up a sticky subject.

"Okay, Tiny, what's going on?" I asked. "Is there a problem? You are going to be here, right? Don't even tell me you're going to miss the party after all this…"

"Oh, yes, yes, Mr. Plym. I will be there. I wouldn't miss it for the world. But..." He was beating around the bush and I was running out of time.

"What is it, Tiny? Spit it out, pal! I've got a lot to get ready here. What's up?" I said impatiently.

"Well, I have met this extraordinary girl here at one of my shows. She is absolutely wonderful and ... quite different. I was wondering if it would be okay with you if I invited her to the party," he asked nervously.

That's what all the fuss was about? Bringing a chick with him?

"Tiny, if she's eighteen, bring her," I shot back. "If she's under eighteen, you'd better ask her parents, okay?"

Tiny said nothing. I knew he was still there because I could hear him breathing.

"Just messing with you, pal," I laughed. "Bring her, man! Who is she, anyway? What's she like? Give me the lowdown."

There was a long, long pause before he started whispering to me in a confidential voice.

"... She is a little different," Tiny confided. "Her family is very wealthy..." He went on extolling the attractive features of her bank account, the lovely curves of the cars they drove, the gorgeous, sensual carpets and sofas in her home. Just like any guy in love.

I replied, "Tiny, way to go, baby! Found a pot of gold, did you? By all means, bring the broad along to the party!" I was half teasing, but only half.

"No, no, it is not like that, Mr. Plym, but I cannot talk now. Thank you so much for inviting her. We will see you tonight and we

241

can talk more then. By the way, her name is Miss Sue." Tiny hung up.

At that point, I didn't know that this chick had loved him her whole life, cutting out press clippings and saving pictures of him ever since she was a little girl. All I knew was that she had money — and Tiny had very little of anything. Very little money, even less energy. The stamina that had carried him all over the country for all of his adult life and allowed him to get up on stage and sing for endless hours at a time had simply petered out. The landscape of his life was beginning to shift, and as it did, his priorities were changing.

The guy who had spent a lifetime wanting nothing more than a good audience and a decent p.a. system was plain old tuckered out now. He had struggled all his life and the fight was draining out of him. Somewhere inside of his soul, I think he knew that he couldn't go on performing forever, felt his life winding down, and heard the footsteps of the grim reaper approaching. His days were numbered.

So, when he found himself one more time playing in a nightclub, like he had so many thousands of times before, and this adoring fan came along to rescue him, I think he knew it was more than a coincidence. She was the answer to his prayers. "Dear Lord, if you can hear me, please, give me a break..."

◆ ◆ ◆

Everyone who was invited showed up at Tiny Tim's party. Everyone except Tiny Tim. A half hour went by, then an hour, and at that point, I didn't know whether to be furious or worried. Where the hell was he? I tried to keep from worrying by reminding myself that Tiny was notorious for being late. Sure enough, he did eventually come waltzing in — about two hours after he said he'd be there.

"Where the f— have you been?" I shouted at him as I opened the door.

Grimacing and gesturing at me not to swear, Tiny stepped aside and said, coyly, "Mr. Plym, I'd like you to meet ... the lovely Miss Sue!"

I thought to myself, oh, shit! I forgot he was bringing the girl.

Looking at Miss Sue, I have to say I didn't get it. On the outside, she was nothing like the girls that usually flipped Tiny's switch. She was plain looking, frighteningly thin, and she didn't wear a drop of makeup. She reminded me of the earth mother-type girls I knew in the sixties.

They came inside, and Tiny introduced her around and all I kept thinking was ...her? Her? Why her? What did he see in her? Could it really be all about dollar signs, as I suspected? Actually they were quite a pair — Tiny with his obsessions about germs and Miss Sue, who seemed to be plagued by every allergy and physical nuisance known to man, or woman, and didn't mind sharing her annoying ailments with the party guests.

I managed to corner Tiny without anyone noticing and asked him, "So what's the dirt on Miss Sue? What's really going on here, pal?"

We locked ourselves in the bathroom like any two junior high school boys — or girls, actually — would, and tried to keep our voices down.

"She is a big fan of mine, and she has been since she was twelve years old. You should see all the newspaper clippings and photographs she has of me! Mr. Plym, she has never been married..."

Tiny whispered, his huge frame crouching down in the tiny bathroom.

"…and she's loaded." I pointed out.

"She is infatuated with me," Tiny pointed out. "Her father is a very prominent, very wealthy businessman. She wants to settle down and they have plenty of money. More than they know what to do with. You never know what could happen here."

It wasn't hard to jump to conclusions, and I got a shit-eating grin on my face as I said, "Why, Tiny Tim! You devil! Do you have larceny in that heart of yours?"

Gasping and shaking his head and gesturing with his hands, he swore, "No, no, no! You have it all wrong. I think she is a wonderful girl."

I could see he was blushing so I kept razzing him. "Are you hooking up with her because you dig her or are you trying to set up a line of credit here? Level with me, pal."

"Honestly," he said, giggling, "I believe she is a wonderful girl. She just needs some guidance and direction. She is very nice to me…"

I was having too much fun teasing Tiny and assuming the worst about his relationship with Miss Sue to see what was right in front of my face. Sure, she was offering financial security, and that was something Tiny sorely needed, but this girl had also arrived in Tiny's life carrying a big fat bag stuffed full of things that were even more irresistible to him, things Tiny Tim really couldn't afford to do without any longer — adoration, love, devotion, kindness, caring, someone to take care of him.

Money flew in and out of Tiny's life like flies through an open window. He was used to that. He'd been without money before, and always survived. But this particular brand of love she was offering was something he couldn't turn his back on. The fact that he could relax about money and not have to worry about a rat race he was too weak to run anymore was gravy. And the combination was irresistible.

"I would like her even if she were penniless," he said. "I like her as a person, not because she is rich, although I must admit, it is nice to know she is independent and will not be looking to me for money I don't have...like all the other women."

"Look, Tiny," I chimed in, "tell this bullshit to women and small children. You've finally found a chick who can take care of you for a change and I think it's great!"

Then I did the old can-you-look-me-straight-in-the-eye-and-swear-it's-not-about- money challenge and of course he was giggling and squirming too hard to pass the test. So I said, yeah, sure you love looking into Miss Sue's eyes, where you see an intoxicating IRA account and a seductively easy retirement.

Of course, all he could do was laugh.

Herbs, cleansing enemas, vitamins, what to eat, and what to avoid for optimum health — Tiny had found himself a nurse and an amateur pharmacologist and none of us had any idea at that point how much he needed exactly what she brought to the party. Not really realizing what bad shape he was in physically, I just found her annoying.

As for Tiny, I think in his quiet moments, he realized that the Man Upstairs, who he'd tried so hard to please all his life, had taken mercy on him and sent him someone to look after him — whether he wanted it or not. Most of the time he wasn't seeing her as a Godsend, but was yelling at her on the phone, saying loving little nothings like, "Don't you ever order me around! How dare you? If you want to be with me, you had better learn your place, woman!"

I had to hand it to Miss Sue. She really knew how to get Tiny's blood boiling.

Around and around we would go... me pointing out that she was pushy and annoying and drove him nuts half the time and him reminding me that he loved the vulnerable, little girl side of her and the mothering caretaker underneath her apron strings.

It had to be serendipity. Just when he couldn't go on anymore running around the same old maze, he found a girl who unquestionably loved him and had loved him her whole life — and who just happened to have the resources to keep him sheltered and safe for the rest of his days. At the bottom of his soul, he knew that he couldn't refuse. He believed she was the best thing that could have happened to him.

◆ ◆ ◆

Of course, any time Tiny started contemplating marriage, there was the whole problem of the marriage bed to contend with, and that meant his age-old problem of s-e-x. Funny enough, his delicate flower was very bold about what she wanted from him between the sheets — or in Tiny's case, on top of a fully made bed where he slept with all his clothes on and a tie, too.

"I love the way she woos me into sexual fantasy," he would say to me. "She talks to me in very explicit details, telling me what she would like to do to me. She has a very unique and special gift, an ability to paint a wonderful sexual experience in the mind."

"Why, Tiny, you're not actually thinking of committing fornication, are you? Having s-e-x before marriage? I'm shocked!" I joked.

"Oh, no, no. Only talking, kissing, and hugging. And a little petting," Tiny said shyly.

"And when are you going to drop the bomb about wanting separate bedrooms?" I asked. "Or have you already done it?"

Tiny screwed up his face into an expression that said, well, she wasn't exactly thrilled.

"Didn't go over too well, did it, pal?" I laughed. "Wives are funny like that. They like to feel your arms around them at night. Go figure."

Marriage or no marriage, Tiny had to have his privacy. Period. Tiny and Miss Sue got out the boxing gloves over that subject but he wouldn't budge. Then of course, there was the matter of how to satisfy his new wife-to-be, no matter whose bed they found themselves lying in — or on top of. It was the same old story, played out over and over again throughout his life, only this time it was with a different girl. The last girl.

And this time, Tiny was even more freaked out by his performance anxiety than usual. Just like a chick, he would worry himself sick, thinking, wait a minute, if Miss Sue is going to be supporting me out of the goodness of her heart, I am going to have to do everything in my power to make sure there is goodness in her heart when she thinks of me. Not sexual frustration.

"What if she cannot cope with the sexual frustration? Out I will go into the street! Homeless!" He would say, nervously wringing his hands. "Homeless, Mr. Plym. At my age..."

◆ ◆ ◆

One night, I was driving Tiny to his hotel and he had me pull over and park the car. He wanted to have one of his talks.

"At last, I have found the answer to my problem, Mr. Plym," he whispered to me even though the car was soundproof and we were parked on a street with no one around.

"Tiny," I laughed, "why are you whispering, man? No one is listening."

"I am serious. This is the answer, at last. It came to me in a dream and it really works. It is going to change my life. I cannot believe I never thought of it before!" Tiny was leaning in close to me, beaming.

"Tiny, pal, listen to me… do you know how many times you've said this?" I pointed out to my favorite drama queen how often he'd been hit with incredible solutions to the great sex problem, only to be disappointed time and time again.

"I promise! At last, I will be able to have sex like every other man!" He was fidgeting in his seat, flailing his hands. Watching his eyes pop and his hair flop around his face, I had to laugh. He was pure theater.

"I am not kidding. It is a miracle!" Tiny was breathing like a marathon runner and his makeup was smearing all over his face.

"Tiny, you've got to calm down," I said. "You're going to have a heart attack. Let's go to the bar and get you a double something. You can finish your story there." That was my motto back then — when in doubt, stress, or trouble, have a drink.

I slammed a double Stoli while Tiny signed some autographs. Then he slipped something into my palm.

"Look at it! Look at it!" He shouted, removing his hands from my eyes. "In your hands you happen to be holding the miracle that is going to change my sex life forever! This little tube will give me the lasting power I need. From now on, I am going to be a new man. I will never let another woman ... er, I mean, Miss Sue down. I will never let Miss Sue down. My penis is reborn! My penis is reborn, I am telling you!"

He was screaming, and like a scene from a movie, the place went completely dead. Every person in the bar put down their drink and slowly turned around to look at Tiny Tim.

Then they all looked at each other, broke into grins, put their hands together and started to applaud. "Oh yeah, Tiny? You've got a new dick? Way to go! Enjoy that new reborn penis of yours!" They were howling.

We, on the other hand, were dying.

"Come on. Let's get the f— out of here!" I grabbed Tiny and we ran back to the car. Panting and out of breath, we slipped into the car seats. Suddenly I realized I had forgotten to look at Tiny's super-duper-once-in-a-lifetime-available-for-a-limited-time-only-solid-gold miracle cure. I opened my palm and ...it was called ... Orajel!

"Tiny, Orajel? Orajel? This is the miracle cure?" I couldn't believe it.

"Yes! Is it not wonderful? I am going to make Miss Sue so happy..." he exclaimed.

Apparently, it had all started when he'd gotten a toothache and someone recommended he pick up some Orajel.

"You see," he explained, "they told me it would completely numb the area, so I would have no sensation at all. And I started thinking, hmmm… numb… no sensation. I figured, well, if it works on my tooth — which it did beautifully — why not…?"

"Why not try it on your dick? Are you kidding me, man? I can think of a million reasons why not!"

"I have done several tests on it, very scientific, and it did not let me down… No pun intended." Tiny laughed. "Anyway, here is what happened… I lay down on my bed, removed my pants and, of course, my Depends…"

Of course.

"…Then I stroked myself," he continued, "until I was aroused. Then I squeezed out all of the wonderful Orajel ointment, spread it all over my penis, and massaged it into the skin. What a rush I got!"

Sitting in the car with him that evening as he described for me in excruciating detail his unbelievably absurd numb penis test, I had one of those moments where you step outside yourself and think, wow, what a strange life this is.

"…the Orajel is cold at first, but after a few minutes, I lost all feeling in my penis, and wasn't that a miracle? For once, I didn't feel like he was about to burst, so I was able to go on like that for a full ten minutes, which," he pointed out, "would be plenty of time for Miss Sue to have an orgasm. I have hundreds of tubes in this bag…."

"…I was hoping that tomorrow, I could bring my largest suitcase and you could drive me around to other stores…"

Sure, Tiny. First thing in the morning. We'll get right to it. Right after I fly us to the moon so we can have a nice green cheese omelet for breakfast.

♦ ♦ ♦

I have to say that while the allure of Miss Sue was somewhat over my head, the one time I really needed her, she knocked my socks off. She came through for me, loyal and generous like only family would be, like only your best friend in the whole world might be if you were really lucky and he was having a really generous day.

Here's what happened. I found myself in a financial pickle where the only way to save my business from its dying breath was to pull ten thousand big ones out of thin air. The first person who came to my mind was Miss Sue, so I called her up, held my breath, and told her I needed to borrow ten grand for thirty days.

I immediately started apologizing for imposing on her and she cut me off, the picture of graciousness and class, and said, "Steve, of course I'll loan you the money. No problem. You've been great to Tiny and you've helped him so many times... In fact, if you'll give me your bank account number, I'll transfer $20,000 because if you're asking for ten, you can probably use twenty. That way, you won't be short."

She absolutely bowled me over with her generosity. I was totally shocked, and humbled and pleasantly surprised. I had sold her short, but she hadn't held it against me. She showed me what a giving person she could be.

Strangely enough, this was also the one and only fight I ever had with Tiny. He got wind of the loan and blew his top. He spoke to me in a tone of voice he usually reserved for other people, telling me he would not stand by and allow me to take advantage of Miss Sue.

"Because she is planning to marry me, I do not want her to feel obligated to loan money to a friend of mine in order to avoid offending me. I do not want her to feel like I am using her in any way to help my friends."

No matter how I tried to reassure and soothe Tiny, he was pissed off and he was having no part of it. Tiny Tim had spoken and there was no arguing with him. He nixed the deal, put the kibosh on it, and left me in the cold. Man, was I pissed!

I'll never understand why he did that — it was a thirty-day loan plus interest. Nothing sinister. I knew Tiny lived by his own set of rules and there was no point in us mere mortals trying to figure them out. According to the Herbert Khaury Law Book — I've never actually seen it because there was only one copy in the world and he kept it hidden in his head — I was in the wrong. Period. Amen.

Miss Sue called me and told me how sorry she was, how shocked, how she didn't understand, either, why Tiny would object. Of course, she wasn't about to go through with the transaction knowing how Tiny felt about it. I told her I understood completely, thanked her, and got even more hot under the collar at Tiny. I was burning mad, and didn't talk to him for two whole weeks. Then one night, we trotted out the pizza and the beer, hugged and made up, and we were back to normal. Whatever that was.

◆ ◆ ◆

Tiny Tim had finally met his match in Miss Sue. While she couldn't by any means outdo him in the obsessive compulsive department, she ran a close second on phobias, and outdid him in the allergy department. Tiny and his cleaning products, paper towels, and Depends diapers was about to marry Miss Sue, who could often be seen wearing a surgical mask to ward off evil air particles.

One time Miss Sue tried to get Tiny to give up his beer

drinking and he almost blew a gasket. How dare she? And another thing, who the hell did she think she was to always ask him where he was going, when he would be back, and how she could reach him?

Prophetically, she would often warn him that if he didn't slow down, stop drinking, and get off the road, she would lose him.

"You are going to make yourself sick and die," she predicted. "I am only looking after your welfare. You don't need to work. I have money! By the way, when you are at these gigs, you are not cheating on me with other women, are you? Because I would absolutely die…"

Tiny Tim? Look at women? Where on earth would someone get that idea?

◆ ◆ ◆

I never knew what to do when Tiny agonized over entering into another legally binding, 'til-death-do-us-part contract.

"I think you should do it, Tiny. Looking at it from all sides, it seems like she will be good for you," I conceded.

"You know," he pointed out, "I am much older than she is and I am not exactly Clark Gable. Everyone is going to assume I married her for her money. I do hate that stigma being attached to me."

"F— 'em, Tiny. At your age, at this juncture in your career, you're going to worry about what 'they' think? You've never, ever cared what the public thought or said about you. Why start now? Like I said, f— 'em."

"What about her family? They must think it is all about money. I mean… look at me? I am old. I am broke. Every time I face her family, I can read their minds… they are thinking I am just a vulture, a gigolo who wants to live off their young daughter!"

"Tiny, balance it out in your mind. On the one hand, we have vulture and gigolo. On the other hand, peace, freedom, and a girl who is genuinely crazy about you. Sounds like a no-brainer to me. Freedom from anxiety, no more shit nightclubs, no more breaking your back to get to the airport on time, no more kissing the asses of sleazy agents and promoters who just want to use and abuse you… Serenity, Tiny! And you can have any f—ing thing your heart desires, anytime you want it! What picture of the future does this conjure up in your mind, Tiny?"

"Mr. Plym," Tiny said, smiling, "I see the picture of wedded bliss."

And it was. More or less.

No one knew on their wedding day just how short forever was going to turn out to be.

Tiny Tim - The Real Deal

And now it's time to go, no time for swinging vines.

No beating breast, no jungle call, no voyeuristic telephone lines,

Could possibly connect me now, to you — or you to winter, not this year,

The spider's web that was your breath can't hold you now, the spider's near.

And yes it's time to go, the pendulum has swung,

The sweetness of the life you leave has lost its flavor on your tongue,

No time to be forever young, no verses left of songs unsung.

--Vivien Kooper

Tiny Tim's marriage to Miss Sue put an end to his worrying days, an end to his hurrying days, and an end to his endless performing cycles. The helter-skelter non-stop hustle was history, at last. As I said, Miss Sue had a financial cushion the size of a whole sofa and the open-heartedness and generosity to make sure that Tiny was comfortable, too.

At the same time that marrying Miss Sue put Tiny into semi-retirement, it put me out of business as his manager, but how could I begrudge him? My dear pal, Tiny, finally had the one thing I couldn't give him — peace of mind. Sure, we'd had a hell of a time being in the trenches together, winning some battles and losing some, but only a big fat bank account — and a pair of loving arms other than mine — could put an end to the war.

Up until that point in his life, performing had been the one thing that kept the blood pumping through his veins. As long as he'd been able to summon up the strength to climb up on stage, he didn't care how decrepit the stage or how grimy and ramshackle the club, it made him feel alive. Somehow, he'd always risen to the challenge, finding a way to hold his broken-down body and spirit together with duct tape and string, like an old sound system that's on its last legs. When he got to the point that he could no longer even find the stage, much less climb onto it and sing, I think he started to lose his will to live.

♦ ♦ ♦

It was nearing the end of 1996 and while Tiny and Wife Number Three (three and a half, actually) were living in homegrown Minnesota, I was in the devil's armpit on the other side of the country.

Since Tiny had gotten hitched, we'd sort of naturally drifted apart a bit and every day, I'd say to myself, damn, I've gotta remember to pick up the phone and see how Tiny's doing. The days melted into weeks and months and before I knew it, an entire year had come and gone without speaking to the one guy who had for so many years been like my shadow.

It was the first day of December, and that winter blanket of bright white snowy lights covered the city of Las Vegas. The carolers sang — thousands of miles away in other cities where they really do have winter and carolers. Visions of sugar plum fairies carrying bottles of aspirin for my hangover danced in my head as I slept.

I was awakened by a very loud rapping on my door. Pulling the pillow up around my ears, I tried to ignore it, thinking, even Santa's elves aren't welcome at this hour.

"Who the hell is it?" I yelled. "Go away, whoever you are!" I couldn't think of a single thing important enough to get me out of bed.

Whoever it was, they were clearly on a mission — banging, screaming my name, banging some more.

I jumped out of bed, ready to take a swing at whatever lunatic I found standing in my doorway.

Flinging my door open, I was face to face with a friend of mine from my office. He was trembling all over and his horror-stricken face was covered in tears.

I remember the conversation like it was yesterday.

"Scottie, what's the matter, man? You look like your best friend just died!"

"No, Steve, yours did, man. Yours did… it's Tiny Tim. Turn on CNN," he said, sobbing.

The doorway started to sag over my head and the room got wavy and I suddenly felt like I was in one of those Charlie Brown shows where the adults are speaking but all the kids can hear is a sound that goes something like wah-wah-wah.

My eyes welled up with tears and my head got all scrambled up and then I felt like I'd taken a huge body blow. My entire being went numb. Even writing this now, the deep sadness and sorrow I felt over the loss of Tiny comes back to me in the form of stomach cramps and absolute devastation.

I was annihilated. Stomped into the ground and lain flat. I'd never felt that way in my entire life.

Staring at the television as, one after another, the news channels parroted each other, I couldn't believe my eyes. They were reporting the death of Tiny Tim and it was surreal. Picking up the newspapers and seeing it in print was absolutely unbelievable. Looking at his photo in the newspaper, I remember what Tiny used to say to me every day.

I'd come by his hotel to pick him up and we'd do our usual routine…

"Hey, Tiny Tim, how ya doin,' baby?" I'd yell out the window of my car.

And he would always answer, grinning, "Mr. Plym, every day above ground is a good one."

Every day above ground is a good one. And the day Tiny died — November 30th, 1996 — was the beginning of a string of very, very bad days for me.

I didn't go to the funeral.

I know, I know, it sounds heartless, but Tiny and I had a pact. Whichever one of us went first, we promised to remember the other one as he was — alive and vibrant. Not cold and stiff in a wooden box.

For about a New York minute, I wrestled with it… should I go anyway? Would it be disrespectful not to show up? Do I really stand by a pact I made with someone when death seemed very abstract and far away? Absolutely. That's the way he wanted it, and it was fine with me. The Tiny Tim I knew was alive and well in my heart and in my memory and this was the one last thing I could do for him and for our friendship — to remember him in all his eccentric, out-of-this-world glory.

Strangely enough, Tiny Tim died just as he had lived. Even if he'd been able to plan his own death, he couldn't have planned it better, and I'm sure he wouldn't have wanted it any other way. In fact, who knows? Tiny Tim did seem to have a direct Batphone connection that rang through to the Man Upstairs, and maybe they'd worked it out in advance. When it came to my pal Tiny, nothing would surprise me.

Here's how the song that was Tiny Tim's life ended…

Remember how I said Miss Sue had come from a prominent family? Well, her mother — Tiny's mother-in-law — had arranged for Tiny Tim to perform at a small, intimate gathering of some of her socialite friends. It makes me smile just thinking of it. Tiny Tim, the most unusual creature ever to hit earth, singing his heart out for a group of very well-dressed ladies of the upper crust and upper class. Perfect.

Anyway, he got up to sing, with all the ladies clapping politely, I'm sure. Then he opened his mouth and he belted out his signature tune.

"Tiptoe through the tulips… through the tulips…"

And then he fell down on the stage and died. That giant heart of his finally gave out. Heaven knows, he'd used it to the fullest, pouring more love on the world than anyone else I'd ever met.

As they say in music, *da capo al fine*, or in other words, play it once more through to the end. And that's exactly what he did.

He came here to cheer us up and entertain us, to get us to look at him, at each other, and at ourselves. He taught us to be more forgiving, more understanding, less judgmental, and more loving. And most of all, he came to remind us not to take ourselves, each other, or even life, too seriously.

He came and he went doing exactly what he came here to

do… he performed even when people had stopped listening, even when, after his heyday, sometimes all he could get for a song was a handful of walnuts to eat alone in his hotel room.

For me, I'll always believe he was sent to change my life, and change it he did.

♦ ♦ ♦

Whenever I hear *Tiptoe* on some radio station now, I always get goosebumps, a lump in my throat, and eventually, after my body systems return to normal, a smile on my face and in my heart. Because I remember the real guy. The real deal.

And that's what Tiny Tim was — the real deal.

So full of life and energy, he always had a smile and a kind word for everyone who crossed his path. He really and truly loved people.

Every day at some point, I look up towards the heavens and say out loud, "Hey, Tiny Tim, who loves ya, baby?"

And I hear him say, as he always did in life, "You do, Mr. Plym. You do."

Epilogue

In case you're saying to yourself as you close this book, so Tiny, God rest his soul, is in Heaven now, but what in the hell ever happened to Mr. Plym…?

Well, it is the end of 2003 and I am still alive and well and living, of all places, back in Iowa. But not for long. Within a year or two, I'll be back in Southern California, with my wonderful wife, Dawn, and our new baby daughter, our very own angel from Heaven, Cali Reno Plym. We named her after the great state of California and my dear pal, the late, great Walt Reno, whom you might remember from the "Guess Who?" chapter. My son, S.P., whom you'll also remember from the chapter where Tiny is playing baseball, is all grown up now and he turned into my best friend when I wasn't looking.

Along with Dawn came a wonderful couple of stepchildren, Joel and Jami. So when you do a head count and remember to include my precious daughters, Chyenne and Stefanie, we have a big brood and plenty of love to go around.

On those days when I'm missing my dear pal Tiny Tim, I need all the love I can get.

Tiny Tim changed me by touching my heart and bringing

out the best in me — just like he did with everyone. And believe me, anyone who could bring out the best in this fast-talking, hard-boiled talent manager from the Midwest had to be a genius, or an angel, or both.

Acknowledgments

First of all, Stephen Plym and Vivien Kooper would like to express our heartfelt thanks to Flo Selfman, our book shepherd, proofreader, and PR consultant extraordinaire, who carried the lamp and led the way down the path. Your energy and genuine enthusiasm for the project were indispensable. We would also like to thank James Kosnett, Esq., for knowing just what to say and how to say it. We really appreciate your invaluable input and good counsel.

Thank you to everyone who took the time and searched their hearts for the words to say about our story. We also want to thank all of Wayne Orkin's staff and colleagues who had a hand in the making of this book, and especially Sue Chidester Sealy and Patricia Siliga for all your hard work.

Special appreciation from Wayne, Stephen and Vivien to Brian Ahern. Without you, no one would be holding this book in their hands. You're a special person and you make special things happen.

And for his generosity, our gratitude to Ernie Clark, Tiny Tim historian and "keeper of the flame" via the official Tiny Tim Web site, www.TinyTim.org.

STEPHEN PLYM:

I am a procrastinator! I talked for several years about writing a book about Tiny Tim. It was my wife, Dawn, who finally kicked my butt and got me to work. Her motivation, enthusiasm, and faith in me went beyond the call of duty. Thanks, baby!

I want to thank my business partner, Wayne Orkin, for his investment of time, patience, and generosity that made the dream a reality.

Thank you, Mr. George Schlatter, for your kind words in the Foreword of this book. I know Tiny Tim would be so proud!

Kisses and hugs to my co-writer, Vivien Kooper! Your unique insight, vision, and spirit carried this project! Your ability to stay focused, your honesty and integrity, and your unbelievable positive mental attitude made it a pure joy to work with you. You have taught me a lot. Thank you.

A heartfelt thanks to my son and best friend, S.P., for your never-ending support...and thanks for making me laugh. I love you, pal!

VIVIEN KOOPER:

My first thanks have to be to Geri Novelli, who was in the right place at the right time to open her mouth and tell Wayne Orkin about me. And a big thank you to Wayne for believing in me — twice! — and for tossing me the ball and having enough faith to let me run with it before you were even sure I could run. You taught me a lot about life and business, and more often than not, you were a rock.

A big hug and a high five to Stephen Plym, my co-writer and pal, and a kiss on the cheek to dear Dawn. Thanks, Stevarino, for your incredible loyalty, friendship, and humor. And for believing in me, and entrusting your essence and the story of your best friend to me. I could always count on you to cheer me up.

My deep appreciation to George Schlatter for your wonderful Foreword and all your help, and a special thank you to Marta Lee.

I want to thank my ex-husband, Al Kooper, for showing me the inside of fame and the music business, and opening your heart and so many doors for me — in music and in life. Without my years with you, I could not have written this story. And I want to thank David Wolfson (and your folks) for your unbelievably positive outlook and belief in me, even in the face of adversity, and for reminding me that with God, everything truly is possible.

Thank you to Lydia, Jill, Karen, Paulette, Marc and Denise, Ray and Nicole, Dad, and Bob Lancer for listening, and for all your love, friendship and support during the writing and the tough times that went into this book. A special thanks to Paul Hayeland for knowing how to get a sinking ship sailing again!

And last, but not least, a big hug and kiss to my dear prince, David Nesheim, who always reminds me to give it to God. Thank you for all the ways you look after me and tickle me, for all your love, support, and massages, and for keeping my world right side up during phase two of this project. You make every day such a wonderful adventure!